CW00336419

John B. McMillan

THE VIRGIN BACKPACKER

The Ring of Fire

BrightSpark

www.brightsparkpublishing.co.uk

DEDICATION

For my sons,
Donald and Euan,
who are now 'older' than their father.

www.JohnBMcMillan.co.uk

This Book was published by BrightSpark Publishing, 2012.

First Edition.
© Copyright 2012.

ISBN: 978-1-908295-07-1

Designed, typeset, printed, and bound completely in-house
By BrightSpark Publishing.

www.brightsparkpublishing.co.uk
Office: 01343 208001
Editorial: 07967 178224

Introduction

To see an automatic washing machine bouncing around a bit when it starts the spin cycle, doing a bit of a boogie on the kitchen floor, is something we take for granted and hardly notice - or perhaps ignore completely. Because that is normal, what you have come to expect of it. But what if you saw the *fridge* deciding to boogie across the kitchen floor as well? And then the table and chairs join in the party? (Well, why should the washing machine have all the fun?)

Now that, I'm sure you will agree, is not normal!

But when all the beer bottles start chinking merrily against each other as they dance around inside the fridge, and you find that the bed you are (*were!*) sleeping on has joined the party and is jumping up and down as well, and you notice by looking at the clock (which you grab just as it was about to leap off the bedside cabinet to join the party with the rest) that all of this bizarre revelry has woken you up at 2.30am, then you quickly come to the conclusion that you are experiencing an event that is very *ab*normal, and can only be one thing: an earthquake.

If you are looking for a bit of excitement - I don't mean the artificially induced thrill that comes from roller-coaster rides, bungee jumping or white-water rafting, but the true excitement of experiencing at first hand some of the most awesome forces of nature (earthquakes, tsunamis, typhoons, floods, landslides, volcanic eruptions) - then the countries bordering the Pacific Ring of Fire, and in particular those in oceanic South East Asia, are where you can certainly find it.

The Ring of Fire is a fringe of volcanoes and earthquake-prone areas that border the Pacific Basin. Extending from Alaska down the coast of Canada, USA, Central and South America to Chile and Antarctica, then upwards from New Zealand, the Solomon Islands, Papau, Indonesia, the Philippines, Japan and Eastern Siberia, this ring of seismic activity is a result of the Earth's tectonic plates nudging against each other around the perimeter of the Pacific Ocean. This activity has thrust up mountain ranges such as the Andes, and creates earthquakes aplenty - upheavals which, if they occur under the sea, can result in a tsunami: like the massive one that devastated the coastal communities of Sumatra, Thailand and a few other areas on 26th Dec 2004.

In these geologically active areas, cataclysmic forces are forever altering the landscape with earthquakes and volcanic eruptions - and when you throw in a few typhoons as well, with attendant flooding and possible landslides - then you really have all the ingredients of a potentially exciting lifestyle.

To say the least!

It is a safe bet that there will be several earthquakes and volcanoes erupting somewhere around this ring every day. These are not always felt, or visible, for there are many active volcanoes erupting under the surface of the sea. Rising up from the ocean floor, these will eventually break the surface and become new islands. Most of the Pacific islands are volcanic in origin with some extremely active and still developing, such as Hawaii and the Galapagos Islands. Easter Island is a cluster of volcanic cones, extinct or at least dormant for many centuries, although in the early 20th century an emission of steam is reported to have been photographed coming from a fissure on Rano Kau, an impressive mile-wide volcanic crater at its south western corner. Many others like Tahiti and the Cook Islands are the remnants of extinct volcanoes.

For those of us who inhabit the more geologically stable parts of the world, it is easy to assume that living in these areas is dangerous, due to the risk of some natural catastrophe. However, statistically we live more dangerous lives every time we drive on our roads. It is not all bad news: the people who live on the slopes of a volcano take advantage of the mineral-rich, fertile soil that enables them to grow the most delicious fruits and vegetables. The volcano can be therefore be regarded as a benign influence in their lives, the source of their prosperity, rather than something malevolent. Many volcanoes lie dormant for hundreds, sometimes thousands, of years so there is actually minimal risk to life when living nearby.

However, there can be no disputing the fact that when major cataclysmic events do take place they can be absolutely devastating: such as the Japanese tsunami triggered by an earthquake in March 2011, or the great tsunami of Dec 2004 that took hundreds of thousands of lives along the coasts of Sumatra, Thailand, Sri Lanka and several other areas bordering the Indian Ocean. While earthquakes often occur without warning, volcanic eruptions are more predictable. The predictions of vulcanologists monitoring the activity of Mount Pinatubo in the Philippines resulted in the evacuation of people from the danger zone, saving tens of thousands of lives when it erupted in 1991 in what was the second largest terrestrial eruption of the 20th century.

While most travellers in these areas experience no cataclysmic events, for those who linger awhile there is a greater probability that they will have an earth-moving experience, either as a result of seismic activity or the effects of a typhoon, another of nature's forces that can literally move mountains - because the torrential rains that come with it often cause landslides. Extensive travel and observation in such areas reveals the impressive effects of nature's most powerful forces, even if the traveller passes on without disruption.

This sequel to *The Virgin Backpacker – You Are Never Too Old*, is a light-hearted account of my interactions with people and places and my personal involvement in a few earth-shaping events, on land and while diving underwater, around many of the Ring Of Fire hotspots and bordering areas during a series of six-month travel periods over a five-year span.

The motivation for this itinerary around parts of the Ring of Fire arose from the theft of my hand luggage at Buenos Aires Airport in 2005. In it was my laptop with all the photos taken on my first visit to Easter Island. I resolved then to return to that most remote human settlement and capture these images again and, en route from the UK, it seemed worth including some exploration and diving in the amazing Galapagos Islands. That trip took me the long way round, travelling from the Galapagos to Easter Island and on westwards via the Cook Islands, to South East Asia. This is an area which has much of the best diving in the world, a magnet which has since drawn me back again and again for more. It is also an area prone to some of the most extreme seismic events. So far I have been lucky, sometimes arriving in a disaster zone just after, or leaving just before, some significant natural catastrophe had struck, taking many lives. Occasionally I find myself drawn into the thick of the action. Most of the time, I just relax and enjoy life; exploring, diving, meeting indigenous people and other travellers, but always the thought lurks in the back of my mind that maybe one day…

But och, there is no point in worrying about something unpredictable that is very unlikely to happen anyway - and it's more fun than staying in Scotland for the winter!

Chapter 1

The Galapagos Islands

It was like standing on the moon: a dramatically barren landscape of volcanic ash and lava flows, pock-marked with a random scattering of spatter cones - the small craters dotted around the slopes of the volcanic cone on which I stood, where hot gases had forced their way out before the crust had cooled completely.

But although the vista was indeed lunar in aspect, this was not the moon. I have been about a bit, but I am not that far travelled – yet! This breathtaking view was of Bartholeme Island, one of the most spectacular and iconic of the Galapagos Islands.

Far below where I stood, our ship - Galapagos Adventurer II - lay at anchor in a bay that was once the caldera of an older volcano that had blown itself apart, leaving only one remnant still proud of the ocean: a sharp, conical lava pillar standing sentinel at one end of the elegant curve of a golden, sandy bay.

Without doubt one of the most remarkable places on Earth, the Galapagos Islands are located about 600 miles west of Ecuador, forming a group of 18 volcanic islands, only five of which are inhabited. They straddle the equator, yet have a temperate climate due to the cold water Humboldt Current which sweeps up the coast of South America from the Antarctic. This is moderated by the Panama current, bringing warm water from the north, while the Cromwell undercurrent from the west brings nutrient-rich water from the depths of the Pacific Ocean.

The result is a unique marine environment absolutely teeming with fish: whale sharks, hammerheads and several other several varieties of shark, manta rays, turtles galore, schools of devil rays flying past like squadrons of delta-winged aircraft, the biggest sting rays I have ever seen, spotted eagle rays, as well as a host of smaller fish. The density of the marine life is astonishing. The sea lions, abundant in such fish-filled waters, delight in joining divers and copying their actions, blowing bubbles in imitation of the discharge of air from the diver's regulator. They will come right up close and peer curiously through your masks, looking intently into your eyes. Playful as puppies, you easily could fall in love with these creatures.

On land you can walk among the hundreds of disinterested iguanas that litter the coastline as they bask in the sun to increase their body heat, motionless, statuesque relics from the dinosaur age. Further inland you can find the larger land iguanas lazing around, so well camouflaged that at first it is difficult to spot them.

Bird life is amazing too and, like the other creatures, they show absolutely no fear of man, allowing the visitor to wander among their nests. Here you can see the remarkable courtship displays of the frigate birds, the males puffing up the large, red, balloon-like sacks located under their beaks in order to attract the females. Waved albatrosses perform their mating dance, with a loud clacking of their beaks as they 'fence' with each other, followed by a vociferously joyous celebration as they recognize each other as mates. Blue-footed boobies and nazca boobies (birds of the gannet family - your minds, really!) are also found in abundance. Galapagos hawks will pose fearlessly on scrub vegetation, allowing the photographer to get to within a metre or so for close-up pictures of the fearsome looking beak and eagle eyes. Tidal lagoons are home to the islands' elegant pink flamingoes and other smaller waders that feed there. The lava flows are populated with brilliant red, orange, yellow and blue-coloured sally-lightfoot crabs which dance across the black surface of the lava, quite happy to investigate a bare foot if one stood still.

It is astonishing to find penguins this far north - literally on the equator. The Galapagos penguin is the only species of penguin to be found in the northern hemisphere, as the equator passes through Isabella island, one of their habitats, and they can be seen on both sides of the equator there. For anyone interested in observing wildlife, this is a naturalist's and photographer's dream.

The landscape too can be surreal. Some islands, like Bartholeme Island, are very young, mere infants in geological terms and are still growing with each successive volcanic eruption. On such arid landscapes, the earliest drought-resistant pioneer plants are only now beginning to take hold, and will add humus to the mineral rich soil as they drop leaves which will eventually compost to provide more moisture retentive soil that will allow other plants and trees to establish themselves. Some of the older islands (estimated at around a mere three million years) have desert-like vegetation along the generally arid low ground near the coast, but high up in the mountains there is lush vegetation due to the higher levels of precipitation. This is the home of the giant tortoises, from which the islands get their name, some weighing up to 250 lbs. They munch through the vegetation and have a liking for the succulent young opuntia (prickly pear) cactus.

Human habitation has a relatively brief history among the wonderland of wildlife of the Galapagos, hence their lack of fear of man. These islands were only discovered in 1535 by the Archbishop of Panama, whose ship was becalmed and drifted for several days until, almost out of water, he was saved from extinction when the Galapagos Islands appeared. It then became a pirates' lair, a source of food and fresh water, conveniently placed for plundering the Spanish galleons laden with riches from the west coast of Mexico. It proved a popular stop for whalers too as they could replenish food and water supplies. These temporary residents also laid waste to the wildlife: catching birds, tortoises and turtles for food was just too easy - hundreds of thousands were plundered.

In 1793 an enterprising British whaler, Captain James Colnett, allegedly established the 'Galapagos Post Office' - a wooden barrel, which exists to this day - in what has become known as Post Office Bay on Floreana Island. Outward bound whalers could then drop off mail and homeward bound ships could pick it up and deliver it to whatever country they were bound for. It is now used by tourists as a unique way to get postcards home without having to pay postage, although it may take rather a long time before someone from your particular locality, homeward bound, arrives on the scene to deliver it. Although a penal colony had been established in the late 19th century for a time, it was really only in the early years of the 20th century that real settlement began and the islands now (2010 Census) have a population of about 25,000 spread over five of the islands.

One name that will be forever linked with the Galapagos islands is Charles Darwin, the young English naturalist who arrived here in 1835 on the survey ship HMS Beagle. His observations and biological collections inspired much of the thinking that led to his theories of natural selection and evolution published in his Earth-stirring (and in the opinion of some, notorious) treatise *The Origin of Species*, which rocked the scientific and religious communities in the 19th century and still creates much controversy today as religious creationists and scientific thinkers present their arguments to the world.

My voyage of exploration in the Galapagos was arranged under the auspices of Gap Adventures, a Canadian based adventure travel company with whom I had enjoyed exploring the mountains of Patagonia and Antarctica nine months previously. Galapagos Adventurer II was a comfortable boat carrying 16 passengers, dropping us off at various locations for exploration of this unique environment under the care of an approved guide. Tourism is strictly controlled with just under 3% of the Galapagos area approved for human activity to minimize the harmful effects on the environment - so you won't find any large cruise liners here. Only small boats carrying small groups of tourists are allowed. My tour included the option of diving, as well as exploring on land. That is no longer allowed. You must now either dive, without any land-based exploration, or explore on land without any diving. If you want to do both you have to book two separate trips (which sounds more like a money-making decision to me, rather than a decision based on environmental considerations - or is that the canny Scot in me coming out?).

On the day Ecuador was playing Uruguay in a world cup qualifying match (football) we had a run ashore on Santa Cruz. The streets were almost deserted, but you could hear the sound of the match on TV from every shop and bar. Everyone was decked out in the bright yellow colours of Ecuador. When the final whistle blew, the result was in Ecuador's favour and the town went mad. Cars and motorbikes drove around the town in cavalcades, blowing horns and waving flags. Music and dancing took over all along the streets. Passing an open air café, I glanced towards a waitress who was dancing solo, her yellow shirt and blue jeans complimenting each other perfectly. As I gazed in admiration, her eyes met mine and her hands, in perfect time to the music, started to beckon me towards her.

Now, I really don't know how I get sucked into these things...

I wasn't wearing the kilt, so I don't know why she picked me out of all the crowds of passers by. Maybe I just looked irresistibly handsome, or perhaps she was attracted by my moderately proportioned but undeniably athletic physique, whose graceful movements exuded a powerful, pheromone-laden, animal magnetism – or maybe I am just a hopeless fantasist.

Whatever the reason, it would have been alien to my gentlemanly characteristics to refuse such an invitation and, well, her hips did move in the most delectable fashion. So I joined her, my hips swiveling in unison with hers.

I had just met a girl called Maria - honestly! And, proving that this real-life brief encounter was a combination of *South Pacific* and *West Side Story*, we danced like the star-crossed lovers. We improvised creatively, sometimes apart, sometimes holding each other close, gazing passionately into each other's eyes. At the end there were cheers of "Bravo" and "Encore" from the watching crowd, so we had to do it all again. I had absolutely no objection to that, and Maria was more than willing to get to grips with me again... so maybe that powerful, pheromone-laden animal magnetism was working after all!

Inevitably, several members of our ship's company were hovering around with video cameras. I therefore had an enhanced reputation by the time I got back to the boat - which did me no harm at all!

The Galapagos islands are unique, with such unforgettable wildlife and landscapes, truly a place with an enormous 'Wow' factor. It may not be the easiest place to get to, requiring flights to Ecuador and then onwards to the Galapagos, and it is not a cheap trip, but it is like nowhere else on earth. I would love to go back.

What a pity I didn't get Maria's phone number though!

Chapter 2

Return To Easter Island

It was one of those truly unforgettable moments; like a dream in which you are suddenly exposed, naked, in a crowded city street with everyone looking at you. The scene that unfolded was reminiscent of those old Hollywood western movies when the bad guy, or courageous hero, appears at the swing doors of the saloon. The honky-tonk piano stops playing, the card players all pause, smoke drifting lazily up from the thin cigars dangling motionless from their lips. Every eye is on him. No one moves as he paces slowly towards the bar.

Silence.

Except for the slow click... click... click of his spurs.

It was just like that when I walked into a bar on Easter Island. I was wearing my kilt.

I had been dragged out at mid-night (social life only starts at midnight there) to go dancing with Joanna, my host's daughter and her cousin, Oscar. This was an element of Easter Island social life I had missed on my previous visit. It was a must do, according to Joanna. They led me to a bar where the sound of a string band, six guitars and a drummer, drifted out into the warm night air. The door of the bar was just like the swing doors in those old westerns, and they pushed me forward to lead the way. On my right were several tables with people sitting at them. At the end of the room was a low platform on which the band played. A few couples danced. To the left of the band platform was the bar, crowded three or four deep with leathery-skinned macho men all swilling back their beer. Now, when you live in just about the most remote island community in the world and a kilted Scotsman walks through the door, sporran and kilt swinging, I suppose it does have an element of surprise.

It certainly threw the band. Hands froze: guitar strings twanged their last twang. The drum stopped beating. The dancers stopped dancing. The talkers stopped talking. The drinkers stopped drinking, glasses held half-way to their lips, mouths gaping open, eyes wide in astonishment. A tsunami of silence swept through the room, carrying away every decibel.

It was like looking at a photograph. Everyone froze. Except me.

I took a deep breath.

Brazen it out, I told myself, *set your shoulders and swing that kilt*.

I walked towards the bar; not quickly, but purposefully, with measured pace, one step per second (just like in the movies) click... click... click, as the steel-tipped heels of my sturdy brogues resounded on the wooden floor. It was just like being the head of a school again, walking with that undisputed air of authority into the assembly hall and the whole school goes quiet, waiting for words from the cousin of God. The set of the shoulders, the powerful, measured step, the swing of the kilt sent out a message: 'Nothing will stop me!'

The men were clustered deeply around the bar, but I was going to part them, like Moses raising his staff at the waters of the Red Sea, by the sheer power of my presence.

Oh, what a marvellous thing is faith! And would you believe it? It worked. I never faltered in my step and suddenly all those red-necks with their cowboy hats on (they do a lot of riding on horseback here – with the bad roads it is the most reliable form of transport), opened up and let me through. The last man, sitting on a bar stool, got off his seat hurriedly and, with a majestically flourishing sweep of his hand, ushered me on to his stool as though honoured by my presence. I felt like royalty. And not a word was spoken. I turned to see Joanna and Oscar a few steps behind me, beaming with delight.

"What are you drinking?" I asked them.

"No ningún, déjeme le consiguen una bebida!" exclaimed the man who had offered me his seat.

They speak Spanish here. But since I don't, I hadn't a clue what he had said. However, the barmaid immediately asked me, "Beer?" and indicated that he had offered to buy me a drink. She had one already in her hand, poured for another customer. Well, it never reached him - it found its way down my grateful gullet not long after she placed it in front of me. I had VIP status. Well, did you ever hear of a Scotsman who refused an offer of a drink? I raised the glass, looked around the silent gathering as still they gazed in a daze of still growing wonder, nodded and uttered, "Slainthe Mhath!", the traditional Scottish toast - "good health." They all smiled, raising glasses in acknowledgement. I looked at the band. They were all smiling at me too. I smiled back and nodded. They struck up again, a lively, celebratory tune, and the party took off once more.

Men crowded round to shake my hand and talk. Some had a few words of English. Behind them I could see a woman eyeing me up, a willowy, wild-looking creature with flashing eyes, part Chilean, part Polynesian, probably with a bit of Spanish from a few generations back. Must be an artist, I thought, by the look of her. I found her a lot more interesting to look at than the men and, as she was seemingly interested in looking at me, I smiled at her. It was all the encouragement she needed. She wriggled through the throng around me, pushing big, macho men aside. I held out my hand and she took it. Then she took both hands and held them widely apart. She looked me up and down, appraising me with her artist's eye for colour, shape and form. Her eyes flashed their appreciation.

"Oooooh..... you are so beeyoooootiful!"

"Och aye, I know," I muttered modestly and reciprocated the compliment: "You're no' bad lookin' yersel'." Well, when an attractive lady seems pleased to see me I just can't stop the intoxicating poetry that flows from my lips. There must be something incredibly powerful about the Scottish propensity for understatement when expressing compliments to a lady. It seemed to have a kind of Pheromone Effect, for she then dragged me out of the crowd and on to the dance floor where she held me tightly as our bodies swayed in harmony to the music. The band smiled their approval. The night had really begun to swing.

When the music stopped I got no more than two or three steps back towards the bar before another woman pounced on me and dragged me away from

Angela (we had formally introduced ourselves by this stage, whispering our names into each other's ears as we danced). She claimed possession of me for the next dance.

And that is how it went on all night, one woman after another. Wives abandoned husbands, girlfriends propped boyfriends up at the bar with a glass of beer to keep them amused while they had their way with me on the dance floor. I never had to make a move on any of them.

At 6.30am Joanna and Oscar hauled me away from the clutches of yet another another amorous woman. Her English was non-existent, but her body language was unambiguous. I think Joanna was becoming concerned that my austere Calvinistic sense of denial was about to crumble and yield to temptation after more than six hours of onslaught by the wild women of Rapa Nui, so she and Oscar dragged me home.

Spoilsports!

I recalled another of Joanna's cousins telling me on my previous visit, "You could get up to some mischief wearing that kilt at a dance here." She was right too. I could have - but for the attentions of my chaperones.

Easter Island, Rapa Nui in the local language, Isla de Pascua in Spanish, is a UNESCO world heritage site and ranks alongside the Galapagos Islands, Great Barrier Reef etc as one of the most treasured places on Earth. It is one of the most fascinating and atmospheric places I have visited. At the site of the quarry on the volcano Rano Raraku, where those massive stone figures, the Moai, were carved from a cliff face, I found myself among objects I had first encountered in books more than fifty years previously. It was a dream come true - an almost emotional experience.

In my previous book, *The Virgin Backpacker – You Are Never To Old*, I described in some detail the history of Easter Island and how it was settled by Polynesians, how they became consumed by the ideology of ancestor worship and became obsessed by carving these huge stone statues out of a cliffside on a dormant volcano. The more they erected, and the bigger they were, the greater power they felt it gave the tribe. But over about a thousand years they denuded the island of trees in order to achieve the engineering feat of transporting the moai several miles over the island. With all the trees gone they had no forests to provide food, no wood to build canoes or huts for shelter, or to fuel their cooking fires. The consequence was the complete breakdown of society: starvation, tribal wars, anarchy, cannibalism. The population was decimated in less than two hundred years and further depleted by slavery. In the mid 19th century an epidemic of smallpox left only 110 wretched people alive on the island. With the advent of air travel, it has now become accessible to adventurous tourists who come to marvel at the moai, which, ironically, are now the basis of the island's prosperity. However, being an awful long way from everywhere else in the world, you have to be really keen to get there.

Last time I had only stayed four days. It was not nearly enough to satisfy me. This time I stayed for ten. I had to recapture all the photographs that had been stolen with my laptop when I was in Buenos Aires, prior to my voyage to Antarctica. The quality of light in the mornings and evenings was ideal for photography when the low angle of the sun presented light and shade and a mellow colour. This meant rising early to get to the sites, or delaying till late afternoon.

Having more time allowed me to explore the strange stone houses at Orongo at the top of the volcanic crater Rano Kau near the one town on the island, Hanga Roa. It seems odd that people should want to build low stone dwellings high up on the edge of a volcanic crater where, on one side, the land fell off very steeply into the crater, now full of stinking, sulphurous water, while on the other side a fearsome cliff dropped vertically to the sea about 1000 feet below. But that is only one of many enigmatic things about Easter Island.

On many of the rocks here petroglyphs can be found, strange carvings related to the cult of the birdman. Each year the young men swam in competition to the small rocky island off the western tip of Easter Island where the Sooty Tern nested. Braving the strong currents that ran between it and the main island, the first man to return with an egg of the sooty tern became the birdman for the year. No one was allowed to touch him. Food was brought to him. He lived in isolation on the top of the crater rim and was regarded as a demi-God. It doesn't sound like much fun to me, but it was a prestigious role to play for a year it seems. I also had time to explore the many caves along the shoreline, also once the refuge of the inhabitants, some with paintings on the walls. Life for the inhabitants did not seem to be very comfortable back then.

Easter Island is a haunting sort of place and begs more questions than it answers, but perhaps it issues a very clear warning to us all regarding the over-exploitation of the environment. Here is a powerful message indeed, pointing to the devastation of a community as a result of blind adherence to a particular dogma. Whatever we do in this world we must be conscious of the effect of our actions, some of which may be virtually irreversible. We cannot rape our natural environment without serious consequences. Easter Island is a monument to man's folly in that respect.

I enjoyed a mostly energetic ten days with hikes up volcanoes or, to get to the more distant sites of interest, bouncing around in a jeep across the rough and dusty island roads. Did I say roads? One guidebook offered two classifications for the roads: the indescribable and the unspeakable.

One day at the airport I was taking photos of another aspect of Rapa Nui life, the arrival of the visitors when the thrice-weekly flights arrived from Santiago or Tahiti. This is always a cause for ceremony as visitors are welcomed to the island with garlands of flowers being draped over their shoulders, a typically Polynesian custom. Suddenly a lady appeared at my shoulder. It was Angela, the artistic lady who had been my first dancing partner on that first evening out. She seemed delighted to see me again. We agreed to meet for lunch to catch up with what I had been doing; an interesting event as we conversed in several different languages, improvising and switching from one to another to find the right words, with a bit of sign language thrown in. She spoke the native Rapa Nuian language, Spanish, French and German, but had only a little English. I spoke English with a little French and German, hardly any Spanish and a little Rapa Nuian, which is basically the same Polynesian language that is spoken with variations in Tahiti, Cook Islands and Hawaii. It is amazing how you can overcome the communication difficulties if you are creative.

Afterwards she took me to her cabano, a house she lets out to visitors. Of a unique design - she had designed and built it with her own hands - it was the kind of house that only an artist could have built. She asked me if I would take some photos of it to include in promotional brochures to be sent to prospective customers. I shot some pictures, processed them on the laptop and then we worked on a layout and got them printed. She then went off to chip away all night at a sculpture she was working on and I felt satisfied that I had done something which may have been of some economic benefit to this small remote community in the vastness of the Pacific Ocean.

Joanna, my host's daughter, also press-ganged me into helping out with her husband and cousin Oscar on her small farm. She sat on the horse driving it up and down the field while her husband walked behind, guiding the single-furrow plough. She grows pineapples, watermelons, peaches, taro and some other vegetables. I helped with the planting and hoeing the weeds around the peach trees. It was just like helping out on the croft back home, a communal effort to get the work done while the weather was suitable. That evening we dined by candlelight in the farm kitchen. It had no electricity or plumbed water, only rainwater, and that night there was plenty of it. We slept on a mattress on the floor while the rain drove down in a thunderous downpour, watering in the vegetables we had planted. The simple life, it was a delightful experience.

Easter Island is such a remote community, such a long way from everywhere else in the world that few visitors ever return. However, coming back to Easter Island was perhaps an even more enriching experience than the first visit. Walking along the road at any time, day or night, it was a common occurrence for taxis to stop, the driver calling out, "Hey Escosia! Weelliam Wallace!" Thanks to the film, Braveheart, everyone there knew about William Wallace, the 13th century Scottish patriot whose guerilla struggle against the imperialist ambitions of the English king have become the stuff of legend - and a blockbuster movie. They like the story of the underdog struggling against the oppressive colonial ambitions of the larger neighbour, something the people of Rapa Nui can identify with, having been annexed by Chile in 1888. Many of the drivers stopped to talk with me, and the passengers did not seem to mind in the slightest. Several local girls asked permission to have photographs taken with me, snuggling up close against me. I stoically endured it all without complaint.

A local girl I met at the airport astonished me when she told me she lived in Scotland with her fiancé. When I asked where, she replied, "Oh, it is only a small town. You have probably never heard of it."

"Try me."

"Kilwinning."

I laughed. "I was born only three miles from there, in Irvine." She was back on her home island for a few months, driving a taxi to earn some money and her fiancé was coming out for a month at Christmas.

So many people seemed to know me in such a short time there and the night before I left, while having dinner with Angela, I remarked on the friendliness shown to me everywhere I went. She nodded. "Si, everybody in Rapa Nui know you, John. Many people tell me about you."

"But why?"

"Mmmm…. you très sympaticos. Touristos come, look at Moai, go. But you make connection. You help Joanna with farm, help me, take photos for brochure. You work with us, dance with us, speak with us on the street."

I reflected on her words, especially on that important word: connection. Am I emitting some subliminal signal of need, subconsciously seeking to connect? I reflected on the question I have been asked many times, "Why are you travelling, John?" I don't know, but it is curious how I get drawn into things. How I seem to connect so often.

The mantle of tourist does not fit too comfortably. Tourist is too passive a description. When people ask if I am on holiday, I shake my head. I really don't see it as such. I regard it more as an itinerant lifestyle, wandering the world and learning from the people I meet, sometimes being able to offer something in return. Occasionally this may be fairly overt, like helping on the family farm or with Angela's brochure, but at other times it may not be a conscious act at all.

On the day I left, Joanna's mother, Theresa, who owned the guesthouse, surprised me by telling me my visit had helped her. Her husband had died shortly after I had left Easter Island on my previous visit. My return had meant much to her, she told me, knowing that I had also experienced the loss of my wife. "You help me so much, John," she told me. "Every morning you come for breakfast and you are always so cheerful. You talk with me. You make me laugh. This is good for me. I miss my husband so much, but you show me the way. I try to follow your example. Try to be positive. I never forget you, John."

It was comforting to know that simply through the example of lifestyle, a personal response to my own bereavement, and particularly in maintaining a positive outlook, I was unwittingly offering something significant to someone in need. We should never underestimate the importance of the apparently mundane things we do and how they may impinge on the lives of others. Our lives are shaped by a complex series of interactions. Somehow I felt I too had been granted something special from the Rapa Nui people. They made me laugh, made me feel cherished and respected, and thus fuelled any positive outlook that I managed to maintain, but it is not always easy. I still have my bad times when I can so easily plunge into grim moods.

On my arrival at the airport to check in my luggage, the three check-in clerks all stood up simultaneously, raised their fists in salute and cried out, "Weelliam Wallace." I burst out laughing. It was as though they had been rehearsing it for my arrival. I shook hands with them, said my goodbyes, then I waited for a while before going through security into the departure lounge because Angela had said she would see me at the airport before I left. As departure time approached, I finally gave up. Typical Polynesian, I thought, has no concept of time. I went through security and joined the crowd in the departure lounge. With only a few minutes left before boarding, I heard a cry: "John!" I turned round and there was Angela, rushing past the security guard to give me a final hug and say goodbye and thank me profusely for helping her with the brochure. She had even managed to talk her way through the security gates to get to me. Well, it is only a small island where everyone is known and rules are tolerated rather than slavishly obeyed, another aspect of island life that I liked.

But she wasn't the last to say goodbye. Walking out over the tarmac to the aircraft I heard a voice call out, "John!" One of the ground crew working under the wing was waving to me - everyone seemed to know me by now.

"You leaving now, John?"

I wondered what else I would be doing climbing the steps to enter a huge plane, but I just called back, "Yes." I gave him a wave, then climbed the steps to the aircraft door and took one final look back. With military precision, he stood smartly to attention and raised his arm in a crisp salute. I had to smile. My hand shot up equally smartly and I returned his salute. We held our salutes to each other for a couple of seconds. I lowered my hand and only then did he lower his.

His face cracked in a big grin and he called out, "Goodbye, John."

I turned into the aircraft and felt a wave of sadness on leaving this enigmatic island with its friendly people. Angela's words as she slipped into French in that last conversation echoed my sentiments exactly, "Quelle domage tu depart!": 'What a pity you are leaving!'

And it truly was.

Chapter 3

Surprises

The flight from Easter Island to Tahiti took about five hours. I arrived around 11pm, which wasn't too bad. However, that was followed by a five-hour wait at Tahiti to connect with the flight from Los Angeles to Rarotonga in the Cook Islands. We landed at Rarotonga around 6am. Adrienne, the manager of Tiare Village Hostel was at the airport to welcome me 'home' again. Two other customers from the same flight were already waiting beside her. She introduced us.

"Papajohn, this is Mike and Susan." As I shook hands with them both she told them, "If you need to know anything about Rarotonga, Papajohn is the man to ask."

"Papajohn!" exclaimed Mike. "You mean *the* Papajohn?"

"Yes, that's him," laughed Adrienne.

I looked bemused. "You've heard of me?"

"You're famous! I read about you on the Internet. Someone wrote about this Scottish guy called Papajohn who loves Rarotoga, comes every year, wears a kilt, guides them through the jungle, shows them where to snorkel and offers help and advice. Reading that persuaded me to come here."

Fame at last! It really is gratifying and humbling to know that I am contributing to the promotion of tourism in the Cook Islands.

Sharing the chalet with me this time was Christine, a Malaysian final year medical student who was a real bundle of energy and enthusiasm. I like energy and enthusiasm; when combined they can be a heady concoction. From the moment we met we got on very well. She was also a diver, so we formed a buddy team to explore the reefs around Raro and on her first few nights out she had been comfortable to have me accompany her as chaperone and guide. With just two of us in the chalet, we shared in the cooking, alternating duties night about so we could learn culinary arts from each other. She was good company and I have to tell you, for the first time in my life, I slept with a girl on the first day we met.

Now hold on!

Don't get carried away with images of torrid nights of passion under the tropical palms. My use of language is precise. I do not use the word 'slept' as a euphemism for procreative activities. The truth is, when we got back to Tiare Village after attending an Island Night show of traditional music and dance on her first night here, we couldn't open the door of the chalet. Christine had flicked the security catch on when she closed the door on the way out, so it could only be opened from the inside, and there was no one else inside to open it. It was almost 1am. We couldn't arouse Adrienne at that time. She doesn't live on site and it would have been extremely irritating to be wakened and have to come up to take things apart. There was a not too comfy settee in the lounge which could sleep one of us, but the other would have to lie on the floor. Christine was noble enough to suggest tossing a coin to decide who gets the settee. I was ready to rush in and say, "First come, first served." However, a better plan formed in my mind.

Luckily, another couple had come back with us; the others had all come home earlier - no stamina! They were the only occupants of a neighbouring chalet in which there were two free rooms. In these A-Frame chalets the rooms upstairs were only partitioned. If you are moderately agile with gymnastic tendencies you can, with the aid of a chair, haul yourself up and over the partition, drop down and then open the door from the inside. The single room downstairs was impossible as it was completely walled from floor to ceiling so the double room upstairs was the only option. I had done this several times before when I, or other people, had locked themselves out by mistake. The other couple allowed us to come into the chalet. I broke into the twin bedroom and Christine and I spent the night together there, but always in separate beds. Christine behaved with the utmost propriety at all times and never interfered with me at all.

I enjoyed telling Adrienne in the morning that I had broken into a bedroom and slept with one of her guests. She laughed, much to my relief. With the aid of a power drill she unscrewed the security guard from the window of Christine's bedroom, removed the slatted panes of glass and Christine then climbed in and opened the door from the inside.

That had been a night full of surprises. After the traditional dance show had finished a young man approached me and spoke in a Scottish accent.

"I didnae expect tae see a kilt in Rarotonga. Whit's the tartan?"

"McMillan."

"I'm a MacLean."

His accent intrigued me, so I asked, "Where are you from?"

"Kilmarnock."

"I thought your accent sounded familiar. I was born in Irvine." Irvine, a designated 'New Town' although its history dates back to 1140 (and I don't mean twenty to twelve!) is on the coast a mere seven miles from Kilmarnock.

"Oh, my father was born in Irvine."

I looked more closely at him. "Your father? That wouldn't be Donald MacLean, graduated BSc in mechanical engineering from Glasgow University in 1961?"

"Aye!" he gasped. "You know him?"

"Know him? We went to the same primary and secondary schools, the same church and Sunday school, we were in the Boys' Brigade together and we both went to Glasgow University. Not only that, we are related! Your great-great-grandmother was a sister of my great-grandfather so we have a common ancestor in my great-great-grandfather."

His jaw dropped. "Bloody Hell! You come half way round the world to a tiny island in the middle of the Pacific Ocean and you meet a distant relative and get half your family tree! I can't wait to tell my Dad this."

His wife brought out a camera. "We'll have to take a picture of you both and email it to him. This is almost beyond belief."

If I hadn't been wearing the kilt that family union would never have taken place. It never fails to attract people. A night or two later, after playing the spoons with the band at the Whatever Bar, several people came to talk to me. Waiting her turn was an attractive American woman.

She came over and told me: "John, I really enjoyed your playing. I have never seen anything like that before, but I also wanted to tell you how magnificent you look in your kilt. It is so beautiful and you look so... so ...oh, I am really struggling to find words to describe how you look." I was tempted to help her out by saying... "sexy?", but modesty restrained me - as usual.

"The colours are so wonderful. It is so unusual to see a man wearing bright colours unless he's gay." I nearly choked on my beer. "Oh, don't get me wrong. The kilt is not in any way effeminate, quite the reverse, it is so manly." My chest swelled an inch or two as I affected my most manly stance. "I was watching your body as you danced..."

Oh aye? This gets better all the time!

She carried on: "...You have such a natural sense of rhythm, and the way your kilt swings when you dance is just soooo... oh... I am really stuck for words.... I just think you are so.... handsome!"

Och, well, you don't want to argue with a lady, do you? Especially if they're telling the truth! But you know what Californians are like - they always go a bit over the top.

This was heady stuff indeed, so I thanked her for the compliment and, stepping back a pace and eyeing her up and down, I replied (with my usual rustic, highland charm),"Aye, and you're no' bad lookin' either." She almost swooned.

"Oh John... It's such a privilege to meet you!"

She beamed happily at me. I beamed happily back at her. Then we both stopped beaming at each other and she gave me a lingering hug to formalise our acquaintance. I could hear her muffled murmurings of delight in my ear and was just thinking about what the next move might be when she suddenly released me and turned to a big guy with shoulders as broad as a barn door who was standing behind her and said, "John, I'd like you to meet my husband, David." And that brought another promising looking story to a typically anti-climatic end.

The spoons were well used on this visit, especially following the arrival of Ronan Martin, my sailing friend from the Isle of Skye, Scotland, a very skilled fiddler and piper who was touring and playing in Australia and New Zealand. I suggested that he should come over to Rarotonga. We played several gigs on the island including the Clan Gathering of the South Pacific Cowans.

That same evening the fiddle and spoons were out again at the Whatever Bar. We joined the resident string band, with whom I had been playing every week, and played popular traditional Cook Island songs. Ronan is so skilled on the fiddle and he improvised, providing some beautifully crafted harmonies to accompany the guitars and ukuleles.

Then we played some Scottish jigs and reels that got the feet tapping and hands clapping and, with Ronan simply calling out the key changes, the guitar and ukulele players demonstrated their versatility by providing us with a powerful rhythm section. They liked this new sound and wanted us back to play with them again. Steve, aka Moko, the leader of the band, an old friend who plays with one of the professional dance team bands and is a former Cook Islands male dancer of the year winner, was keen to have us stick around for a while longer to work out some arrangements.

However, the heat and humidity seemed to affect the glue that held Ronan's fiddle together and it slowly came apart a few days before he had to fly back to New Zealand. That ruled him out of our eagerly awaited return performance at the Whatever Bar which was advertised in the Cook Island News with typical Cook Island tongue-in-cheek humour with the line, "resident band with guest stars, featuring some of the world's best musicians."

It was disappointing for the music lovers that Ronan was ruled out and I was the only guest artiste performing. Ronan makes beautiful music, I make a noise. That left us with a line up of three ukuleles, two guitars and spoons. Steve, the bandleader, gave me a worthy introduction as "our special guest star and spoon player, John, our cousin from Scotland. We claim John as our cousin because we have shared a common ancestor. His great-great-grandfather came to the Cook Islands in the 1820s - and we ate him! John has been playing with us for about two months now - and he is still single!" He shook his head pityingly. "So if any of you ladies are looking for a husband, he's available, and needs a good Cook Island woman to take care of him." Steve's outrageously cheeky humour always brought smiles.

"Oh, Papajohn!" I heard another female voice squeal with delight.

I turned and there was an attractive beauty therapist who worked in one of the big hotels, an English girl I had met a few nights previously.

"Och, it's yersel' Mandy." I effused.

She came over to give me yet another lingering hug, murmuring tenderly in my ear, "You are so sweet. You even remembered my name."

We talked for a while and she asked for my phone number. Now, don't get too carried away with all of this. I am merely a father figure, Papajohn. You don't believe me, do you? Come on, be realistic, how could a lovely girl in her mid-twenties be interested in me? You know that when she tells you she 'enjoyed the interesting conversation.' I'm simply a safe prospect. There may be just a wee bit of mild flirtation, but nothing ever happens. It is fun and amuses - and amazes - the other backpackers I go out with.

Like the young Scottish lad I had just been talking to. He looked on in amazement at this procession of admiring ladies, shook his head and muttered, "That kilt is a magnet for women! I'm kicking myself for not bringing mine with me." Aye. Look and learn, laddie.

In common with many other island communities across the world, here in the Cook Islands time is almost an irrelevance. Time was here before we arrived and time will be here long after we have gone, so there is no need to rush. Punctuality is a concept that few embrace.

The relaxed attitude of the Cook Islanders was typified by two stories in a local newspaper. As you may imagine, there is little serious crime here and with only a handful of prisoners, some of whom may be cousins or members of the same tribe as the guards, it is perhaps understandable that the prison regime may be a bit relaxed. So relaxed that the only prisoner in the female section, serving a life sentence for the attempted murder of her husband, had recently been found to be pregnant - for the second time in her five years behind bars! The father in both cases was a male prisoner.

Well, keeping the prisoners happy is good for morale.

However, while Cook Islanders may be pretty laid back, they are not without remarkable ingenuity. A series of recent burglaries had the police perplexed. The usual suspects were already locked up in prison and no leads were found to implicate anyone else. Eventually the burglars were caught on a surveillance camera and recognised. They were two inmates of the national prison! The enterprising pair had been breaking out of prison at night, breaking into shops and businesses and hiding the loot for disposal later. Then they broke back into prison before morning roll call. Brilliant! What better alibi than to be locked up in prison?

After informing the education department three months in advance that I planned to return and offer my services as a teacher on a voluntary basis again so that things could be arranged for me to start work as soon as I got there, no one bothered to do anything until I had actually arrived! However, after a short wait I was working again on a voluntary basis and enjoying it. In addition to my special needs work I had managed to fit in a range of teaching experiences in sport, craft and music. The boys, many of whom are keen traditional drummers, loved my playing of the spoons - "That's really cool" - so I was invited to join the percussion section of the school band for the concert at the end of term. I had also done talks based on my travels as well as covering for absent teachers, so I had worked with the entire age range in the school.

At an end of term social evening with barbecue arranged by the school board, to my surprise, the principal made a touching wee speech thanking me for my contribution to the school. She finished by saying, "You have been a gift from God, John. It was amazing how you arrived out of the blue, just when we needed you most."

I was then presented with a gift, a pendant made of carved mother of pearl with a variety of traditional carvings and the words Meitaki maata John (Thank you very much John) inscribed on it. The pendant is in the shape of a traditional Maori fish hook, a symbol of life and a safe journey over water. Carved patterns on the face of the hook include sea birds (manu tai) which symbolise good news to the fisherman, indicating fish to catch and to the sailor, an impending landfall. Tikitiki tangata, a pattern originating from the island of Mangaia, is symbolic of unity and strength. The wave pattern (ngaru) symbolises power and the weave pattern (raranga) represents the warp and weft of life. It all seemed so appropriate to my terrestrial nomadic and seafaring life-style.

However, I was in turmoil when the principal asked me to consider staying on, not on a voluntary basis, but with the offer of a full year's contract with salary. And just to pile on the agony, the mother of an autistic boy I had worked with offered me a two-bedroom bungalow rent-free if I would stay and continue to work with her son. With a salary plus free accommodation I could live off the salary and save most of my UK pension for a year.

I had enjoyed my work. The pupils were really cute, especially when they vied at the end of the period to be allowed to express a vote of thanks for teaching them, no matter what age they were. That's another aspect of the culture I like. They all wanted to make that wee speech thanking me for what I had done for them. But would I still enjoy being here so much if tied to a contract for a year? Or would I find it even more difficult to leave at the end of that year? The debate raged in my mind.

Freedom swung the argument. My freedom to roam at will, to visit other places, had become precious to me and I was reluctant to commit myself to a year's contract, so with many doubts, I declined the offer. I remained a terrestrial tramp.

My knowledge of the island was in demand again, guiding people on the trek through the jungle from coast to coast, teaching them how to husk, crack, drink and eat a coconut, and offering some bush medicine remedies: how to soothe away the inflammation caused by mosquito bites by the juice of a plant, which seeds to eat to cure diarrhoea and how to get rid of intestinal worms. I called it Papa John's Jungle Survival course.

During the hottest and most humid time of year the jungle was green and lush with huge ferns, vines and other creepers forming dense undergrowth. Trekking through the steamy forest was a sweaty business. The route involved one particularly steep scramble up to a volcanic pinnacle in the centre of the island where you have to use hands as well as feet. My two young companions were not very fit. Peter, looked up at me and told me with rasping breath, "I hope I'm half as fit as you, John, when I reach your age." He wasn't even half as fit in his mid-twenties, but it gave him something to aspire to.

Hassu, an Indian, had a particularly tough time on the uphill section, clutching his chest, gasping for breath. I was becoming concerned about him, but he made it to the top... gasp... swearing that he would now ... gasp... definitely... gasp...no buts or maybes... gasp... give up smoking.

Aye, right!

But, to give him his due, his resolve to give up smoking did last... until we reached the road on the other side of the island! There he lit up again as we waited for the bus.

No self discipline, these young guys!

The reward for the sweaty labour on this trek is a swim in the pool below the waterfall near the end. Descending the final slope through dense undergrowth, shirt and shorts cling wetly to your body, you strip off the shirt and leave it to dry in the sun and plunge headlong into the cool, refreshing water of the pool, luxuriating there for a while, then swim under the waterfall and feel the cold water pounding down on your scalp. It revives you so well that you feel you could walk all the way back over the mountain instead of taking the bus back home. Well, that's how I felt.

However, my party had no intention of becoming involved in such madness; they were relieved to have survived what they regarded as a challenging expedition and were quite happy to take transport home, so we walked the last mile down to the road to wait for the bus.

A group of people we had met in the jungle skipped the swim at the waterfall and were already there, eating sandwiches and drinking fruit drinks from two cars that were waiting for them. They immediately offered to share their food and drink, insisting that it was the least they could do as I had steered them on to the right track after they had been about to embark on what could have been a disastrous route. It is not unusual for people to get lost on this trek. Some have had to spend the night in the jungle before being found by a search party next day. The irony is that it took a Scot, from half way round the world, to guide them across their native island.

They were all Cook Islanders who now lived in New Zealand. Rarotonga was full of surprises with more to come.

Chapter 4

The Drover's Son and the Polynesian Princess

While driving around Rarotonga one sunny Sunday afternoon on my motorbike, a name seemed to thrust itself at me from a roadside gravestone - Duncan Munro. The grave was not in a cemetery, but that is not unusual. Internment on family land is normal here. Land cannot be bought or sold and, in a culture in which ancestors are revered, it means the descendants are always on hand to care for the graves. But that such a typically Scottish name should appear on a grave in the heart of an idyllic Polynesian island almost as far away from Scotland as you can get on this planet intrigued me. I stopped and read the inscription:

```
In Loving Memory
Of
Our Dear Dad
628048 Pte. DUNCAN MUNRO
47th Bat. Canadian Expeditionary Force
Beloved Husband of Teina J Tuka
Born Scotland 12/8/1880
Died Rarotonga 11/6/1954
```

I had an overwhelming feeling that Duncan Munro may have had connections with Easter Ross, the heartland of Clan Munro, a part of Scotland in which I had lived for several years before I retired. I also felt that behind the words on that headstone there might well be a story worth telling. I wanted to find some of his descendants to find out more.

Do you believe in coincidence? Well, it came to pass that a week or two later after playing spoons with the band at the Whatever bar, I was invited over to a group of patrons who had expressed an interest in seeing the spoons and talking about the kilt. They introduced themselves.

"I am so pleased to see you wearing your kilt," Anna Rasmussen told me. "I am part Scottish. My grandfather came from Scotland."

"Oh, that's interesting, what was his name?" I enquired.

"Duncan Munro."

"What! Duncan Munro whose grave is on the back road at Arorangi?"

"Yes, that's right. You've seen the grave then?"

"Aye! And I am really intrigued by it. I have been trying to find some of his descendants to learn more about him. I lived in the heart of Clan Munro territory for years. Can you tell me where in Scotland he was born?"

"I can't remember the name of the village, but I can give it to you if you come to my house tomorrow afternoon. I have some information about him there."

That gave me a great start. Anna had a heap of information, including her grandmother's family tree that went back about 800 years to the first Polynesian settlers who came to Rarotonga. She also gave me more contacts, other relatives who had information they might be willing to share. I did some further research in the Cook Islands before I left and on my return to Scotland, at both the Scottish and Canadian records offices and contacted the other descendants. There was indeed a story - a tale of adventure, drama and romance.

In 1916, lying in a military hospital in France, his body ripped apart by shellfire, this son of a humble Scottish cattle drover could never in his wildest dreams have imagined that one day he would marry into a royal family on the other side of the world in a place he had probably never even heard of - Rarotonga.

Born on 12 August 1880 at Achmelvich, a tiny community on the rugged northwest coast of Scotland, Duncan was the eldest of the thirteen children of cattle drover Donald Munro and Margaret MacLeod who later moved to Dornoch in the county of Sutherland. His grandfather, John Munro, had been born at Culcraggie, Alness in 1818, a mere stone's throw from where I had lived, and his great-grandfather Donald, son of Andrew was born at Glen Glass in 1789, right in the heart of Munro country so my hunch had been right.

Around the end of the 19th century, like many of his countrymen, Duncan reckoned that Canada might offer a more prosperous future and responded to a call for lumberjacks to harvest the vast forests of British Columbia. It was not an easy life in the Canadian logging camps. Felling huge trees with axe and crosscut saw was strenuous work. Usually in remote country, the territory of the grizzly bear, black bear, cougar and wolf, the camps offered little in the way of home comforts; a roof over your head, a deal board to sleep on and primitive cooking facilities. However, there was no shortage of work and it paid well. As a result of letters home, some of his brothers joined him in the early 1900s. This was male-only territory and it is little wonder that Duncan was still a bachelor, even in his mid-thirties.

But in 1914, in far off Sarajevo, a single assassin's bullet changed the course of world history - and Duncan's future - when Archduke Ferdinand of Austria was struck down. Within a few weeks Europe, and much of the rest of the world, was plunged into war. With such a horrific casualty rate in the trenches of France and Flanders, reinforcements were urgently required to support and relieve the regular battalions, and across the countries of the British Commonwealth men rallied to the call to arms. On 12th June in 1915, at Vernon, British Columbia, Duncan enlisted in the 47th (British Columbia) Battalion, Canadian Expeditionary Force. It was a 'hostilities only' battalion, a unit that existed only for the duration of the war, after which it would be disbanded and its men would return to civilian life, if they survived.

After initial training at the Royal Westminster Regiment headquarters near Vancouver, the 47th battalion sailed from Montreal on 13th November 1915 on the Canadian Pacific liner Missanabie. Nine days later the ship docked at Plymouth. Several months of further military training followed in England, until 10th August 1916 when the 47th were shipped across the English Channel to Le Havre and then transported to the trenches to join the Canadian 4th Division.

Arriving at the front, they were plunged into the thick of the action in the horrific and bloody Battle of the Somme.

On 11th November 1916, after months of deadlock, the 47th were dug in at Regina Trench when the order came to attack enemy lines. Going over the top, they were greeted by the clatter of enemy machine-gun fire and the boom of exploding mortars. Advancing into that deadly hail of fire with bayonets fixed, men fell, screaming, wounded or dying. Despite the carnage, the attack was successful and the months of deadlock were broken at last. But fate was yet to strike a cruel blow.

Duncan's war record reveals that he was struck by a fragment of shrapnel during this engagement. However, his eldest daughter in New Zealand gives a more graphic account of the events that were to change her father's life. Duncan was detailed to escort a group of German prisoners back to his own lines but, in the confusion of battle, seeing a group of Germans coming towards the Canadian lines, his own comrades opened fire. A mortar shell exploded behind him and the shrapnel struck with hideous force. It ripped through his lower back, took part of one of his lower vertebrae away, lacerated his bowel in several places, and passed right through the front of his abdomen. Duncan fell, bleeding profusely, into the mud.

Seeing his horrific wounds, with blood pouring from his body, some of his German prisoners came to his aid. They helped him to his feet and supported him back to the safety of his trench where they surrendered themselves.

Duncan's war now became a personal one, a battle against his debilitating injuries. After first aid in the field he was transferred a couple of days later to the military hospital at Camiers, on the coast near Boulogne. Following surgery there he was shipped back to England where he required further surgery and treatment for almost a year at hospitals in Norfolk, Hastings, Shoreham and finally The Duchess of Connaught Hospital at Taplow, Berkshire. After a short spell of leave to visit his widowed mother in Scotland, he was sent to Liverpool docks to embark on the Llandovery Castle on 19 September 1917. On his return to Canada, he had a further spell of hospital treatment in Victoria BC. He was finally discharged from military service on 6 July 1918.

As a token of gratitude for his war service, the Canadian government granted him 10 acres of undeveloped land on Vancouver Island. It wasn't a great deal. His land was mostly a shallow lake. Undaunted, he and his brother Findlay set about draining the lake and turned the land into a productive farm they called Summerland, but the demanding physical work and the damp climate of Vancouver Island did not suit Duncan's war wounds. He transferred the title to his land to his brother Findlay for a nominal fee of $1 and set sail for New Zealand to take up employment with the New Zealand Government. In 1919 Duncan was deployed in the Cook Islands, recording and shipping the copra harvest.

Duncan was now 39 years old and still unattached - but not for long. Soon after he arrived on Rarotonga, he caught the attention of 17 year-old Teina Tuka - and it is fairly certain that Teina's tall, striking figure also caught Duncan's eye. This was no ordinary girl. Teina, the understandably short form of her full name, Teinangaro Ki Raro Te Moana Matake'u Tuka, was a princess of the royal line, Te Ariki Marokura Arera Tuarea, a line of Arikis, or kings, who could trace their ancestry back 800 years to the famed Tangi'ia Nui, who around the year 1200, migrated across the Pacific from Raiatea near Tahiti and settled with his tribe on Rarotonga. Genealogy is important in Polynesian culture and Teina's family tree had been memorised and passed down with each succeeding generation in a fashion similar to the Celtic oral traditions of Scotland.

It is not known exactly when or how they met, but that there was a mutual attraction seems to be without doubt. However, Teina's association with Duncan caused her parents much consternation for she had already been betrothed to a suitable young Cook islander of similar importance; a prospective marriage not only of two people, but of their inherited lands. Land is wealth in Polynesian society and the joining of two young people, each with considerable lands, would bring more wealth and power to both families.

But Teina was a spirited lass with a mind of her own. She knew the man she wanted. In open defiance of her parent's wishes she eloped with Duncan on a vessel sailing to the small island of Manuae when he went to collect the copra harvest. Their first-born child, Peggy, was conceived during this voyage. In any family that is likely to have caused a furore, but Teina wasn't just from any family. She was from a family of considerable importance and her impetuous act in running off with Duncan had destroyed all prospects of a profitable marriage to her arranged suitor. That would not have enamoured her to anyone in either family. Furthermore, one set of grandparents had been missionaries to the outer islands at a time when the missionaries were trying to discourage cohabitation in favour of a formal Christian marriage, so her elopement would not have gone down well with them either.

Teina, now aged 18, gave birth to their daughter Peggy on 11 September 1920. As is not uncommon in Polynesian society, the child of the young mother was cared for by Duncan and Teina's very close friends, Mr and Mrs Hopkins, who looked after Peggy while Duncan and Teina continued to travel with his work among the outer islands. However, Mr & Mrs Hopkins could not bear to part with Peggy and she grew up with them, but always in close proximity to her real family. It wasn't until she was 14 years old that Peggy learned that her neighbours, Papa and Mama Munro, were actually her natural parents and the younger children with whom she had played happily were her brothers and sisters! This may seem strange to the western mind, but the concept of the extended family is very strong in Polynesian culture and, in cases like this, the notion of family can extend beyond blood relations. Older people are respected for their wisdom and knowledge, children are loved regardless of who gave birth to them and there is evidence that such domestic arrangements are capable of bringing considerable enrichment to young lives and a sense of belonging to an extended family community.

The strength of Duncan and Teina's love for each other enabled their relationship to survive the ructions caused by their elopement and three more children had arrived before they were eventually married at the registry office at Avarua, Rarotonga, on 6th December 1926. They had 10 children altogether, one of whom, Findlay, was stillborn.

At the time of his marriage, Duncan's occupation was given as trader. Teina sold the fruit and vegetables, water-melons, paw paws, mangoes, breadfruit and taro, grown on their land in the beautiful valley behind the village of Arorangi. He also developed a citrus plantation, growing lemons, limes and oranges and, around 1935, built a shop and traded at Tukavaine, behind Avarua, the main settlement on Rarotonga. The dramas were now over and Duncan and Teina lived the rest of their lives in conventional matrimony, working together to support their large family. Their children and grandchildren grew up and some migrated to New Zealand in search of a more prosperous life, just as Duncan had done half a century before, when he left Scotland for Canada.

Duncan died of heart failure in 1954 aged 78. Teina contracted elephantiasis from a mosquito bite and died three years later, aged 54. She was buried beside her beloved Scottish husband on the family land at Arorangi.

Today, the descendents of the Scottish cattle drover's son and the Cook Island princess are spread across the Cook Islands, New Zealand, Australia and Samoa. Intensely proud of their Scottish ancestry, they held a family gathering in December 2004 in Auckland. With over 100 descendents, the South Pacific branch of the Clan Munro is in robust health.

I am indebted to the following Offices and individuals who assisted me in my researches:

Cook Islands Registry Office
Johnnie Frisbie, Avarua Library, Rarotonga
General Registry Office of Scotland
National Archives of Canada
Military Service Record of Duncan Munro
Royal Westminster Regimental History
Munro family descendants: Peggy Rasmussen, New Zealand
                                   Anna Rasmussen, Rarotonga
                                   Rodney Rasmussen, New Zealand
                                   Kathleen Betham, Samoa
                                   Dr William Hunter, Europe

Chapter 5

Eruptions and Earthquakes

Ba-boooom... booom... boom... ba-boom...

It went on for several seconds. It couldn't be the deeply intense rumble of an approaching thunderstorm. Not on a cloudless, sunny day. And certainly not when your ears are 30 metres (about 100 feet) below the surface of the sea. It couldn't have been dynamite fishing either. That would have been one big bang followed by silence. Yet it continued to rumble and roar in waves, like a giant beast expressing its anger that divers should invade its territory here in the Solomon Islands.

It seemed to be coming from behind, the shock waves sweeping over me. I turned to satisfy my curiosity and faced westwards, hovering in a vertical position, full frontal towards the direction of the sound. Then it hit me: a shock wave, accompanied by another deep rumbling explosion. It felt as though a large hand, the size of a dinner plate, had thumped me flatly on the chest. My body reeled from the blow. My ears felt the pressure wave. Something big was happening out there in the blue void. We carried on diving and a few minutes later the rumbling eventually subsided.

Back aboard the dive boat, MV Bilikiki, all was explained. It was a large undersea volcano erupting. Its cone was just below the surface of the ocean out to the west of our position. The surprise was just how far to the west, about 60 miles no less. So the shock wave that thumped me on the chest and pushed me backwards and inch or two had travelled all that distance. It was my first encounter with the effects of an erupting underwater volcano. I must admit that, after feeling the shock wave and listening to the roaring, undersea explosions that accompanied the eruption, I was really quite happy to be 60 miles away. What it must feel like close up does not bear thinking about. We were told it throws up huge plumes of water, like a geyser, but at 60 miles distance on a hazy day there was no chance of seeing that, even from the masthead.

It was one of several interesting experiences in the Solomon Islands. The population here is mainly Melanesian, with the characteristic dark skin, fuzzy hair and (to European eyes) severe countenance that distinguishes them from the more gentle appearance of the Polynesians. Yet a significant proportion of the population has surprisingly fair hair. At first I thought it was a crude attempt at dying to get a blonde look, but it seems that it is completely natural. It is not what you would expect of such dark skinned people so it does make them look strikingly odd. A few thousand Polynesians live on six islands settled by that race of great ocean navigators who inhabit so many of the other South Pacific Islands.

During our voyage of exploration, on anchoring close to any village we were usually greeted by a flotilla of dugout canoes paddled out from the shore by women and children, all curious to see us and sell us fruits and vegetables. Rafts of canoes tied up alongside Bilikiki to display their produce and kept the ship supplied daily with deliciously fresh fruit and vegetables.

On a cultural visit to one village, the local gentlemen performed some warrior dances for us. We were advised to dress conservatively, as any display of bare skin was likely to offend. That was a wee bit ironic, for we were then entertained by some warriors clad only in the briefest of loincloths which offered more than a glimpse of bare-assed cheek as they pranced around covered in war-paint, knocking axes angrily against their shields.

In contrast to these almost naked 'savages', the ladies danced demurely, wearing long, ankle-length dresses. This is a relatively modern tradition resulting from the influence of the missionaries of the late 19th and early 20th century who decreed that it was sinful for women to wander around bare-breasted and insisted on imposing this ridiculously incongruous style of dress for the ladies, a style more suitable for a cold European climate than the steamy humidity of the Solomons. Formerly a land of headhunters where cannibalism was practised until the late 1800s, Christianity and the British influence in establishing laws, medical care and education have had benign effects.

Religion has a significant influence on their lives of people in these remote villages (perhaps a bit less so in the capital, Honoraria). Every morning and evening the villagers assemble in the meetinghouse under the leadership of the chief for prayers. Housing was simple; huts on stilts, constructed from bamboo and woven, dried leaves.

Diving in the Solomon Islands, while good, was not quite up to my expectations; there was not quite the diversity of marine life that I expected. However, the undersea topography proved interesting with some brilliant, sheer, vertical walls clothed in a dazzling array of colours offering some enjoyable swim-throughs. Caves there are aplenty, and in some you can penetrate a considerable way into the island and surface to find they have opened into the jungle with bats fluttering about above your head.

It was good, but just a bit disappointing in that I expected greater bio-diversity.

The most thrilling dive was in a narrow channel with a fierce current running, so powerful that it whipped off my mask as I rolled off the boat and entered the water. I managed to catch it before it was whisked away into the gloom, dived for the bottom where I hooked on, and managed to get the mask back on my face and cleared of water. Then I drifted along on the strong current until I met up with the rest of the group who were clinging to the reef by the side of the deep channel. These were the right conditions in which to view manta rays and we clung to the reef for an hour and watched nine large mantas perform an elegant and thrilling aquatic ballet as they fed on the plankton the current was bringing to their enormous wide-open mouths.

There are more than a few relics of the Second World War lying around the Solomons, both on land and on the seabed. These islands offered an ideal base from which the Japanese could harass the sea routes between Australia and the USA. Having built an airfield on Guadalcanal, amazingly they left it poorly defended and were taken by surprise when the US Marines made an amphibious assault and captured the airfield after only a couple of days, meeting relatively little resistance. However, the Japanese counter-attacked in what was mainly an air and seaborne campaign, each side inflicting heavy losses in ships, aircraft and men.

The sea between Guadalcanal and Savo, where the US navy suffered its worst combat defeat in the Pacific, is now littered with the wrecks of US, Japanese, Australian and New Zealand ships and planes and is now called Ironbottom Sound. The US navy was forced to withdraw support for the marines ashore on Guadalcanal for a spell. Despite this setback, the marines established their reputation as a formidable fighting force by overcoming odds of three to one to maintain control of the airfield, their only lifeline. The Japanese lost 33000 men, the Americans 7000 in the six months of intense fighting that followed before the Japanese were defeated.

Interestingly, there are no war graves here. Most of the bodies were either blown to pieces or left to be swallowed up by the jungles of Guadalcanal and the other islands. Putrefaction develops very quickly in these steamy jungles and a body would be soon be devoured by maggots. Around the islands lie abandoned tanks, guns, vehicles, parts of aircraft and along the shore lie the rusting hulls of ships, bombed or torpedoed and run ashore to try to salvage whatever could be saved. The American War Memorial is a beautiful and informative testimony to the young men who gave their lives in the struggle for freedom. Sadly the Japanese memorial has not been looked after. Weeds grow there and it is now vandalised with graffiti scrawled on its walls. Broken beer bottles litter the area, now used as a drinking den by young people.

Most divers who come here fly in, go aboard Bilikiki to dive and fly out again on the day they disembark. Very few stay around to have a look at the place. I came 8 days early to have a taste of Solomon Islands life with my dive buddy, Ray Casavant, from the USA. We had plenty of laughs chatting with the waitresses and housekeeping staff, practising the language and entertaining them with our heated arguments. There were not many tourists around, and even fewer who spent time talking to them, they told us, so word soon got about that if you want a laugh, go and talk to "the boys in triple 1" (our hotel room, 111). It became a daily routine for the housemaids to come and sit in our room for ten minutes or so, chatting to us, having a laugh, before carrying on cleaning the room and making the beds.

Each night at dinner we were entertained to some music by Robert, a largely self-taught and gifted guitarist. We got talking and he invited me to accompany him with my hand-crafted, wooden spoons. The effect was interesting. The group of noisy Australians at the bar suddenly stopped talking, bottles of beer suspended halfway to their lips, mouths open in anticipation. Out came the cook and the kitchen staff, in came the security guards from the front door and the receptionist from the front desk. When we finished playing I was immediately called up to the bar to show them what kind of instrument I was playing.

"Where can I buy them?" asked one of the Aussies.

"As far as I know there is only one man in the world who makes these," I said.

"How can I get in touch with him?"

"You are talking to him right now," I said and showed two spare sets I was carrying with me. They were both snapped up immediately. That paid my hotel bill for the week. I wish I had had time to make some more before I left home.

It would be interesting to see more of the Solomon Islands, a group of around a thousand islands, formerly a British Protectorate and now an independent member state within the British Commonwealth. There are over 900 different local languages. These are not just different dialects, but totally different languages, each with very little in common with the others. Few people can speak any of the local languages other than their own. This is not a desirable situation for government, education, trade and commerce and there are now only two approved official languages, English and Pidgin, a peculiar phonetic lingua franca devised by traders in the 1800s to facilitate their dealings with the Pacific islanders, not just here, but in other Pacific islands such as Papua New Guinea, Vanuatu and even in Hawaii. A universal language seemed the best way forward and this peculiar variation of English seemed to find acceptance, although there are variations from country to country as I found out later when I visited Papua New Guinea. It is a delight to learn and is very descriptive.

For example, in the Solomons, "I am very pleased to meet you" in Pidgin is Mi hapi tumas fo mitim yu. Now listen to the sound of that and you can get the meaning quite easily. Mi hapi tumas = me happy too much, therefore I am very pleased; fo mitim yu = for meeting you. Makes sense doesn't it?

Tanggio tumas = Thank you very much.

And how about, Wat nau nem blong yu? = what is your name? Literally, what now name belongs you? Nem blong mi, John = My name is John.

Lukim yu behine = See you later. Literally, looking you behind. What comes behind comes later than what comes first. Get it? Or in Pidgin, Yu save? = You savvy? Do you understand?

I loved talking this language. I loved it even more when the waitresses in the hotel were delighted that I should want to learn the language and greeted me each morning at breakfast with a big smile and said, Naes fo lukim yu, John (nice to see you, John) and gave me a lingering hug, and they were queuing up to do it too!

And of course I had to reply, Tanggio tumas. Mi hapi tumas fo lukim yu! (Thank you very much. I am very pleased to see you!). Well, who wouldn't be with a welcome each morning like that? Yes, mi hapi tumas!

However, dis fella sitim hea ritim tumas, so nomoa. Mi go baeleg. Lukim yu behine!

Yu save? This fellow is sitting here writing too much, so no more. I am going for a walk. See you later. You understand?

Leaving the Solomons, my flights to Brisbane, Port Moresby and New Britain all managed to stick to the scheduled times. Coming down through the cloud layer revealed the the volcanic landscape of New Britain and Kimbe Bay, my destination, a wide bay liberally sprinkled with reefs which offers many attractions for divers. The sunken caldera of an ancient volcano, it contains so many pinnacles of rock now encrusted with over 400 species of coral, representing 60% of all the indo-Pacific corals, and 860 different coral reef fish species have been identified there. Viewed from the air, it is spectacular. The multitude of shallow reefs present a kaleidoscope of colours to brighten up the dark blue of the ocean. My inbound flight took a wide sweep over the bay before touching down in mid-afternoon, offering me an alluring glimpse of what was in store for the next week. Well.... some of what was in store for me.

It was close to 3am when the earth moved for me. The bed was really bouncing up and down. But this wasn't a night of passion in Papua New Guinea (PNG). It was an earthquake. My bungalow was constructed of bamboo and thatch. There is a lot to be said for simple methods of construction in places where earthquakes are common. Easy and quick to build, their capability to flex helps them survive when concrete houses crack and fall down. Even if the roof fell in on me I didn't think it would do too much damage. It was only thatch tied to bamboo purlins. Reluctant to get up at that hour, I lay in bed and shook for a short time until the quake subsided and, after a few more tremors lasting only a few seconds, all became quiet again. In the eight days I stayed on the island of New Britain six earthquakes occurred, all between 4.8 and 5.8 on the Richter scale. These were pretty modest quakes, not strong enough to cause serious damage, but the phones were out of order for three days and the Internet was down too.

Some happened while I was diving, but the effect when floating in the sea was insignificant, just a low rumble. Most happened while I was ashore. You get used to the earth shuddering as you walk along, the leaves shaking on the trees and the buildings swaying. The locals didn't bother too much, so why should I? I didn't bother to get out of bed when they occurred at night. I just lay there being bounced around, listening to the bottles and cans in the fridge dancing with each other until it passed. It is just part of daily living there. I was soon asleep once more.

New Britain, just to the north of Papua, is a large mountainous island clothed in jungle. It is on a very active geological fault line so earthquakes and volcanic eruptions are common. The whole island is a series of volcanic peaks, many of which are dormant. Others can be violently active, like the one near the main township, Rabaul, which trashed it a few years ago. Rabaul was the provincial capital and most important settlement in the province until it was destroyed in 1994 by the falling ash of a volcanic eruption. During the eruption, ash was sent thousands of metres into the air and the subsequent rain of ash caused 80% of the buildings in Rabaul to collapse under its weight. After the eruption the capital was moved to Kokopo, about (12 miles) away. Despite several trashings in the 20th century, the people there are persistent. Rabaul is slowly being rebuilt.

At Kimbe Bay we had a volcano almost in our backyard. Its vents periodically threw up plumes of smoke and hydrogen sulphide gas which, when the wind was from the south, rolled down the mountainside and engulfed us in the awful stench of rotten eggs. This evil smelling, toxic gas, being denser than air, drops to the lowest level and the smell was quite intense, even three miles out at sea. Thankfully the wind was mainly northerly so it blew the smell away from us most days.

The diving was very good with everything from several kinds of shark, large schools of barracuda and trevally, rapaciously feeding tuna darting into shoals of smaller fish for dinner right down to the small stuff like pygmy seahorses and minute squat lobsters. The boat trips out to the widely scattered reefs also offered opportunities to watch whales and dolphins. The dolphins were there in dozens and the boat crew quickly slung booms over the side just aft of the bow with heavy cargo netting attached. The idea is to jump over the side, wearing your mask and snorkel, hang on to the netting with hands and feet and you can watch the dolphins.

Travelling at a modest 5 knots to keep the dolphins interested in playing in our bow wave, it is surprising how powerful the force of the water is as you are dragged along hanging grimly on to the net. Getting your feet locked into the net stops your arms being ripped out of their sockets, but even then it is tough and it was only with considerable difficulty that I managed to hang on with two feet and one hand, the other one holding and operating the camera underwater to get some pictures of the dolphins jostling for position in the bow wave.

Despite the earthquakes and the occasional thunderstorm, I enjoyed a very pleasant week there. Walking through the trees from my room at the extremity of the resort to the main building for dinner each evening, I was fascinated by the sounds of the jungle at night. The ever-present chatter of thousands of insects in the trees calling to one another with that peculiar castanet sound as they rattle whatever parts of their body together calling for a mate was at times deafening. Frogs were everywhere too, dark silent blobs jumping out of my way on the path that wound through the trees. My hair and face were covered in silky filaments of spiders' webs by the time I had walked the 200 metres to the restaurant.

I was sorry my schedule (I had a lot of diving and flights fitted in during that period) did not allow any time for exploring on land. It would have been interesting to explore the interior of PNG if I had had more time there. This is a country where people still live in primitive societies deep in the mountain valleys in dense jungle. It is a country that arouses a certain excitement and demands a sense of adventure. It is a country I would like to return to, but it is not the easiest place to get to, or from.

A minibus took me back to the airfield. I use the term airfield rather than airport because it was a wee bit on the primitive side. Built by the Japanese during World War Two, it has not been modernized very much since then. The runway has no lights which is awkward if the afternoon flight from Port Moresby, the capital of PNG, has been delayed and arrives over the airfield towards dusk on a cloudy evening. If the pilot considers that it will be too dark to see the runway clearly by the time he offloads his passengers and picks up those waiting below, he won't land and turns back to Port Moresby. So the inbound passengers get a 3 hour round trip from Port Moresby back to Port Moresby and spend another night there, and the outward bound passengers don't get out at all and are stuck in New Britain for another night. It is advisable to exercise some latitude when booking connecting flights and to allow some time for delays and last-minute cancellations.

I did not have much leeway, but to my relief the skies were clear and the flight was on time, well almost. Island time is infinitely flexible. I managed to get back to Port Moresby in plenty of time for my connection to Brisbane after which the colourful and exciting countries of South East Asia beckoned.

Chapter 6

South East Asia

My yearning to visit the islands of the South Pacific had been nourished by reading books when I was young. Delectable images formed in my mind then and have been reinforced by my travels there, described in my previous book, *The Virgin Backpacker – You Are Never too Old*. In contrast, having read relatively little about South East Asia, I was largely ignorant of countries like Thailand, Malaysia, Myanmar (formerly Burma), the Philippines and Indonesia. As a consequence, I had never felt the same desire to visit that area. Indeed the images I had in my mind were more of a negative nature gleaned from reading about World War Two. Then the allied forces had not only to fight a formidable Japanese enemy in dense jungles, there were also the diseases like malaria, typhoid, dysentery, dengue fever and so on, as well as the atrocities inflicted upon prisoners of war and indigenous people who were forced to work on the infamous, so-called Death Railway in Thailand and Burma.

In post-war years the British army engaged successfully in anti-terrorist activities in Malaysia, then came the ill-fated Vietnam War, political instability and corruption in the Philippines and Indonesia with outbursts of terrorist activity and kidnappings by separatist groups. It simply did not conjure up the same sort of idyllic and romantic visions I had developed of the South Pacific islands at all. It seemed an uneasy sort of place.

But how wrong that impression proved to be!

Of course, I know that in times gone by the South Pacific islanders were not averse to making the occasional human sacrifice or enjoying a bit of cannibalism, with Christian missionaries in particular seemingly offering themselves as a delicacy, but that all died out in the 19th century. Yet there are many reports that in some of the remote mountain valleys in Sumatra, Papua and Borneo, headhunters still practice their art, and even within the last few decades having you over for dinner meant that you could be on the menu. This was a fate that befell an over-zealous missionary in recent years when, ignoring all advice, he foolishly ventured into the interior of Papua to 'save' a tribe of cannibals - and helped to do just that by ensuring that they did not starve. They were very grateful. They ate not only him, but his wife and children as well. True but... gruesome!

However, travel is a great way to broaden the mind and, having listened to stories from other backpackers who had visited these countries about the friendly, welcoming people, great food, stunning scenery, superb diving....well, my education was being improved and I decided I had to do some exploring to find out more. While I had always enjoyed traveling independently, my experience the previous year of joining an adventure travel group to trek in the mountains of Patagonia had proved that it was a good way to gain some initial experience of a country where the language may present some difficulties. Having a local guide who knows the lingo and can manage the transport arrangements is a big advantage until you develop enough confidence in your ability to communicate and wrestle with such things yourself.

So, for my first visits to Indonesia, Borneo, Thailand and Myanmar, (English is spoken widely in the Philippines so I had no qualms about going there independently), I joined organized adventure tours and I recommend this as a good way to find your feet in such countries. After doing it once, I had no hesitation in returning as an independent traveller. You get a good look at the way of life of the indigenous people and their culture as well as having some fun, fit in some interesting exploring, see some fascinating sights and learn how to adapt to the peculiarities of this fascinating area. And there are plenty.

Crossing a street in any city in South East Asia is like walking on water. It seems impossible. Instant death stares you in the face as dense traffic hurtles along, motorcyclists weave in and out, avoiding death by millimetres, and no one seems to pay any attention to traffic lights, pedestrian crossings, or the rules of the road - except maybe in a one way street if it is really narrow: then if they want to go the wrong way they simply drive along the pavement forcing pedestrians on to the roadway, but that's fair play.

So, if you want to get to the other side of a street you simply have to have the kind of faith that enabled Jesus to walk on water, and would you believe it, it works! It takes some nerve to do it, but after a while you know you can do it and, as other newly arrived tourists stand shaking with fear, you boldly go where no sane man would attempt to go and step forward confidently. Tourists stand and hold their faces in their hands in horror at your madness, but somehow the attitude that shows the anarchic drivers that you are as crazy and anarchic as they are earns their respect and they dodge and weave around you as you cleave a path through the mass of steel that surges along the road. It is madness. But it works. Your faith in miracles is restored.

I had thought of hiring a motorbike to get around as I usually did in the Cook Islands. But here? No! There is just a trace of sanity left in me. Well, there may have been at first, but coming to the Philippines a few times dissipated any residual trace of sanity and, settling in one location for three months, it seemed to make sense to have a motorbike for getting around and I became as crazy and anarchic as the rest of them. On the roads you have to have be a committed anarchist or you go nowhere. There are no road manners other than the, "I'm not stopping for anyone or anything" attitude. My taxi driver once drove straight through a red light at a pedestrian crossing with people walking across it. I cringed in horror.

"Don't you ever stop when there is a red light and people crossing?" He shrugged his shoulders.

"There was enough space between them for me to drive through."

Standing at the side of the street at a crossing is futile. They will never stop to let you across. You have to exert your authority and step out. They may not stop, but they will try to avoid you - well usually. Maybe not by much, a few inches only perhaps, but that is enough for them, and you.

At cross roads the lights flash red and green in utter futility as drivers ignore them and barge their way into the scrum and somehow escape from it unscathed. Yes, sir, if you want adventure and a terror-stricken adrenalin rush, go driving in the cities of South East Asia.

It's all part of the anarchic way of life here. It's the same in the more provincial airports where organisation of passengers is seldom a feature. A queue? What's that? They just walk up to the desk and try to barge in beside the guy who is currently being checked in, hordes of them, whole families, barging in with their bags and cardboard boxes (they always travel with cardboard boxes!) with absolutely no respect for privacy, or orderliness. The line painted on the floor that tells you to Wait Here is treated like the traffic lights. It is of no consequence. So you have to become an anarchist in the airport too. You square your shoulders and barge in like the rest of them and once you get locked into the scrum you barge everybody else out using your baggage like a bulldozer to hold your place. I feel quite superior here where most people are small in stature and I can have a jolly time shoving them aside with my large dive bag on wheels.

It is a delightfully de-civilising experience.

Shopping? Labels with prices on them are meaningless. Everything is available at a price, but only the one on the price tag if you are very naïve - stupid is a better word. Haggle. If you keep shaking your head they will ask for your price. If they accept that immediately, even though it may be half the quoted price, then you have *still* been ripped off.

Thailand is a popular place for silly European tourists to come and fry themselves on the beaches. You can almost smell the flesh roasting. It's hard to believe after all the warnings about sunburn and skin cancer, but there they are turning lobster pink on sun-baked beaches. It is painful even to watch. They become very ugly, blister, peel and are very sick, unable to sleep, vomiting even, as the radiation from the sun has given them a dose of what it is like to survive a nuclear bomb. They suffer radiation sickness. And these are the same people who tell you they don't want nuclear power because of their fear of radiation, but they pay lots of money to go there and risk a good dose of skin cancer by lying in the blistering sun.

This is a popular area for Australian tourists (at least they have some respect for the sun, and paint their faces grotesquely white with sun block). Unfortunately, it seems to attract the less attractive kind of Australians; often over-sized, overweight, (you never see a small Aussie!) loud-mouthed, (is there such a thing as a quiet Aussie?) cursing, waddling along the street in a sagging sleeveless vest, exposing hairy armpits, with an inflated beer belly bulging at the waist, a cigarette in one hand and a beer bottle in the other - and the men look even worse!

It is also popular with Italians, also often loud, arrogant, with a permanent sneer under their aquiline noses, who seem to think they are superior to all others, but of course the Germans know better. And of course there is the daily parade of chemically dependent older men (like me? No!), who are attended by beautiful young ladies, but at a price. They are prey for the street touts selling condoms and Viagra.

"Viagra sir. I give you good price."

"I don't need Viagra!"

"Oh, you no have lady?"

You can see the pity in their eyes, but these guys are entrepreneurs, they see another opportunity for business. "I get you sexy lady, very cheap. Take to your hotel, no problem. Stay with you all night. Give you good service. I fix it for you." But not only does he offer to set you up for the night, he offers you the fuel to make it last all night long, a double deal! "You buy Viagra, sir, give you powah (power). I give you discount, very good price. Good for you, good for me!" They smile and wink at you. "Good for lady too. Make lady happy."

I smile and wink back. "No thank you. I don't want sexy lady."

"Oh, you prefer lady-boy! No problem, I can fix you up." It's hilarious. They never give up.

There are fixers everywhere, seeking to help anyone looking lost or bewildered. Whatever you want, wherever you are going, they always know someone who can provide, whether it be accommodation, transport, food, diving, a lady companion, you name it, they'll fix it for you and always there has to be a tip for the fixer - and he gets a commission from the service provider he puts you in touch with. They wait at the airport arrivals hall looking for the tourist with the lost look. "Taxi, sir? This way." They call the driver up on a mobile phone. What they don't tell you is that it will cost you at least twice what you would pay if you simply walked outside and took a metered taxi.

It can be very cheap to eat here and the choice of food is amazing. Just beware of those fiery Thai chillis though. I always ask when ordering, "Is this very spicy?" If the waitress shakes her head and says, "Only a little bit spicy," forget it. Swallow some sulphuric acid instead. It will be kinder to your stomach. Those little red Thai chillis are devastating. They will strip your tongue and lips of skin and burn out you innards. They go tearing through your digestive system like hot coals all night long and when you feel them burning their way out of your rear end in the morning, don't expect relief, for they'll burn you just as hotly there just as they did at the top end when they went in. The Thais love them, are addicted to them, and heap them into the food. So, pick out the red bits! And there are deadly green ones too! You may just be able to eat the rest. Thai food is very good and full of flavor. In the Philippines the attitude is 'anything will do', but the Thais really do have a passion for cooking. And the waitresses are usually charming. There are some waiters too, but I tend not to notice them.

Getting to South East Asia is relatively easy with flights from the UK and the rest of Europe to the major hubs: Hong Kong, Bangkok, Kula Lumpur, Singapore, from where you can go almost anywhere else. Getting around is quite easy too. There are plenty of bus services, although some journeys can be a bit of an adventure. Ferries to the islands? Sometimes it is the only way, but just don't expect the standards you would expect from shipping countries in Europe or North America. Many budget airlines operate in South East Asia now, offering really good value on both domestic and international routes. They offer the best value for getting around the Philippines, Thailand and Malaysia. However, Indonesian airline companies are something else! Published schedules, time keeping, standards of comfort, reliability of aircraft are often meaningless terms and when you see the cabin crews crossing themselves and praying before take-off, you know you have signed up for an adventure!

It may sound scary, but it is a fascinating region with friendly people, good food and plenty to arouse interest. It demands that you return again and again. And I did.

Chapter 7

Welcome To Jakarta

Some places immediately hit you, like a slap on the face, or a warm sensuous kiss from a beautiful stranger. (You haven't met any such beautiful strangers? Oh, OK, but it happens to me all the time!) That's how it was for me with Java, an island that has imprinted indelible images in my mind, aroused my emotions and given me the glow I always get when surrounded by cheerful, warm-hearted, friendly people. It's a place that has no half-measures, an all-or-nothing, right-in-your-face sort of place - and I liked it, very much.

As the big Boeing 777 murmured its way down over a flat, low-lying and very wet landscape in its approach to Jakarta airport, I thought it looked very much like the approach to Amsterdam. Dotted around this flat-as-a-pancake, rural landscape were small houses and farm buildings, brick-built with red, pantiled roofs, which I found surprising in the tropics where you become accustomed to a vernacular rural architecture of bamboo and thatch, or wood with tin roofs. It all looked very Dutch indeed, but then Java was a Dutch colony for a long time. Rather ominously, dotted around the landscape were several irregularly shaped lakes and what looked like long straight canals, but as the plane lost height I could see that it was not boats ploughing their way along the canals, it was cars and trucks driving on them! These 'canals' were, in fact, flooded roads.

On landing, I learned that the area had been severely affected by exceptionally heavy rains over the past twenty-four hours. The road from the airport into the city was a river of slow moving traffic, cars pushing through water up to their floor boards, even deeper in some places. A journey that normally takes about one hour took three.

Jakarta city centre was in utter chaos. Large areas were flooded so deeply that traffic could not navigate through some parts of the city and policemen directed traffic standing knee deep in water, in their bare feet with trouser legs rolled up. At other places, the local residents were in the middle of the road performing a useful service to motorists as they busily directed cars away from the deeper bits and controlled the merging of lines of traffic as three lanes were forced by depth of water into one passable lane due to the camber of the road on bends. These guys, often up to their mid-thighs in water, seemed to be enjoying it all and looked very self-important as their hands flailed about in the air holding lines of traffic up and then guiding them to safety. No mistake, they were important!

I don't know yet what Jakarta would be like in normal conditions, but on this occasion its traffic was in a state of total anarchy. Cars drove down one-way streets the wrong way, ignored red lights completely, executed U turns in traffic that was already grid-locked, forcing their way round and creating more mayhem. Even worse, cars drove along motorways in the wrong direction, with total disregard for their speed or that of the on-coming traffic. They simply put on their flashing indicators and flashed their headlights and the opposing traffic dodged out of their way. Motorcyclists, hordes of them, dodged in and out of the lanes of vehicles, squeezing daringly between cars and buses, coming within millimetres of being minced in the process. It was mayhem. It was crazy. It may have taken me nearly three hours to get to my hotel from the airport, but it was enthralling entertainment, and more than just a little exciting!

And the people? Despite being flooded out of their homes they seemed to be having fun. They were out, wading about, laughing, talking as they met others, children playing merrily, young men on the road sometimes up to their waists in water, pompously directing traffic.

I sat in my taxi, a 4-wheel drive Toyota Landcruiser. It was nice and high and had no trouble navigating the waters. It gave me a good platform from which to gaze in wonder at the scene. The locals, noticing a strange white face gazing at them from the open window, invariably gave me big welcoming smiles and one woman with a young child slung on her hip beamed and waved at me enthusiastically, calling out something I didn't understand, but which seemed friendly.

The welcome in their smiles made me quickly feel a sense of affection for this dirty, muddy, rain-soaked, crazy, chaotic city. Everywhere I went it was the same, with the usual curiosity, "Which country are you from? What are you doing in Jakarta? How old? Married? How many children?" The population may be 20 million or so, no one knows for sure, a seething, often under-nourished, mass of humanity living in the most appalling conditions in many parts, but it struck me as a place with a warm heart.

The people who lived along the riverbanks had it worst of all. Living in the worst possible housing conditions, their squatter shacks were made up of whatever material they could find; an odd assortment of wood, tarpaulin, corrugated iron, food sacks, with roofs not nailed down, but simply weighted down by old car tyres, lumps of concrete, heavy planks of wood or scrap iron. The people here waded about up to their waists in water, in some places up to their necks. Homes were awash as the muddy, brown floods surged through the narrow lanes, sweeping away the few possessions they had, and often entire houses.

But the following day I saw even worse. Our group had assembled at a hotel in a dry area of the city and we arrived at the station in the morning for what should have been a three-hour train journey followed by a seven-hour bus journey. The train was due to leave at 8.20am. It left at 11.30am. We crawled through Jakarta, stopping frequently for signals as trains queued in the opposite direction to make passage into the city, sometimes waiting for an hour or more before getting the green light to proceed. The reason for the delays of course was more flooding. There had been more torrential rain during the night and shortly after the train left the station we entered the flood zone. The railway was built mostly on an embankment, keeping us well above the waters in most places, just occasionally dipping to cross low bridges in which the tracks were submerged, but the massive girders supporting the sides of the bridges confirmed that there was still a bridge there.

The high viewpoint of the train offered some unforgettable sights. Large areas of the city were engulfed by swift-flowing, muddy brown water; water so deep that you could only see the roofs of the flimsy, single-storey houses. Some walls had already collapsed under the force of the flood, leaving tin roofs hanging at one end flapping about drunkenly in the surge of water. On the surface floated all sorts of household goods: tables, sofas, armchairs, all bobbing around gaily, bouncing from wall to wall along the rivers that had once been streets.

People waded in and out of houses trying to salvage what they could, carrying bundles of clothing and other possessions high above their heads. Ropes had been slung across the deeper waters from the houses to the railway embankment so that refugees from the flood could haul themselves along the ropes to the safety of the higher ground. Some enterprising lads had obtained inflated tyre inner tubes to act as vehicles for rescue and women and children were being ferried across the raging floods, clinging to the rope to stop themselves being swept away. The looks of relief and the cheers from the neighbours as a young mother, lying on her back in a rubber tube, cradling her baby in her arms, was hauled across the fast flowing waters to reach the safety of the railway embankment will remain forever in my mind.

In two-storey houses people stayed in their homes, confined to their upper floors. On many of the single storey houses people sat on the roofs, hoping that the floods would come no higher. A few military inflatable boats paddled around, rescuing folk from the predicament, helping terrified grannies, mothers and tearful young children down from their precarious perches on shaky roofs and into the rubber boats.

Perhaps the most amazing thing of all was that, among the thousands of homeless people who had sought refuge on the railway embankment, there was little evidence of misery. As the train crawled through the hordes of refugees, I took photographs at an open door (they don't bother to close the doors of the train – that is the air conditioning in the economy class carriages!) and they waved at me and shouted, "Welcome to Jakarta!" They smiled, laughed and posed for pictures for me. They cheered when people made it across to the safe ground, they laughed when people fell in, they splashed each other with the brown water. They were enjoying this as much as we do when we get a good fall of soft powdery snow. They didn't seem to mind at all. Whatever will be, will be, and let's just enjoy life, seemed to be the philosophy.

The saddest part of all was when the train stopped and a few men held up cans attached to the end of wooden sticks to the windows begging for money. I hate the begging mentality, but here was a scene of human tragedy that tugged at my heart. Yet how can you give to one and not all the others? But what annoyed me was that many of the men who were begging for money were also smoking cigarettes. That hardened my heart. I hate the thought that the money might be spent on cigarettes rather than buying food for their wives and children. We talked with Yude, our guide, about how we might contribute something in a responsible way, and he assured us there would be some kind of relief fund set up to organise help to which we could contribute. It was a deeply moving experience.

It took three hours just to get out of the city. Arriving at Bandung more than six hours late, we still faced a seven-hour bus journey to Pangandaran, our destination for that night; but as it was now 7pm, the last bus had long since left. Our tour guide, living up to the name of the company - Intrepid - left us at the restaurant in the station and disappeared for a while. He negotiated a deal with a minibus driver, and all we had to pay was an additional 10,000 rupiah per head (it sounds a lot, but it was only about 65 pence or $1 US.) to have an air-conditioned minibus for our exclusive use, and we would do the journey in five hours instead of seven. Good deal. We arrived just after mid-night.

On arrival at the hotel in Pangandaran we learned that we had been lucky. Our train was the last one to leave the city before the railway embankment collapsed due to flood erosion.

Chapter 8

What Earthquake?

A pleasant seaside town on Java's south coast, Pangandaran almost had the douce atmosphere of a quiet, middle-class British holiday resort. However, less than a year previously its tranquility was shattered by an offshore earthquake which created a tsunami that swept the south coast of Java. Houses and hotels fronting the beach stood forlorn with sea-facing walls stove in, roofs sagging drunkenly. Some were completely demolished, only a sad pile of rubble reminding us that this was once a home. Small fishing boats had been swept into the jungle, smashed to pieces against trees, some still perched high on massive tree boughs. Over 1000 victims lie buried in the town's cemetery, evidence of the awesome forces of nature.

But life goes on cheerfully. An open-air fund raising concert along the seafront attracted my attention, so I wandered along to have a look. Having the only white face in the crowd I was instantly noticeable. A man approached me and introduced himself. As the singer started to belt out a lively song he grabbed my hand and said, "Come, you are dancing with me." Now where I come from, dancing with a man is not the sort of game I play! We are a wee bit conservative about that kind of thing in the Highlands of Scotland, although since the advent of the disco things have changed a bit and it is normal to see groups of young men shuffling about together like clothes dangling on a washing line. Not my style, but that shows my age.

I felt distinctly uncomfortable about this. However, as I protested, a host of other men got up in the space between the audience and the stage and started gyrating to the sounds of the singer's lusty voice. Och well, in order to maintain diplomatic relations with the indigenous population, I relented and started swinging my hips with the rest of them. Ladies looked on admiringly. They smiled their approval. Then I really got into it and threw in some Cook Island warrior style dancing as well and that created a stir. Cameras clicked and suddenly there was a guy with a TV camera creeping up close to film the action.

Now what had surprised me was that all the dancers up to that point had been men. Usually it's the females who are uninhibited about dancing and get up first, but in this Muslim society the women sat shyly watching the men - until they saw what was happening. Then a group of them got up and elbowed my male partner out of the way and insisted I dance with them. It looked as if I had been the catalyst in stirring up a women's emancipation movement in a Muslim society. Would the men seize me, flog me, or stone me to death for inciting this revolution? But no, this was now good fun, and more was to come.

When the song ended and I walked off, the singer roared at me through her mike, "Hey Papa, don't go. Come up here and dance with me." I shook my head. The crowd cheered their encouragement and my male partner grabbed me once more and started to hoist my leg up on to the stage. Some things are just thrust upon you and you simply have to go with the flow. I went with the flow. The singer faced me and started, in best Tina Turner style, to rasp out another raunchy number, thrusting her hips at me suggestively, provocatively; so provocatively that I had to reply. I can play that game too and entered into the spirit of the thing with a few provocative thrusts of my own. The crowd cheered and clapped. The TV camera was running again, and I became a celebrity.

Next day when I went into the Internet café the boys sitting there gasped and pointed at me and then at the monitor screens. "It's him!" I went over to look and sure enough, there I was on the screen dancing on that stage. They'd obtained a copy of the video of the concert.

Pangandaran though very quiet, did provide an opportunity to get into the neighbouring jungle and meet its inhabitants; macaque monkeys, deer, scorpions and flying foxes. Our guide demonstrated how to "fish" for scorpions. Squatting beside a hole at the base of a rotting tree trunk, he dangled a string with small strip of chicken on the end of it into the hole. Within a few seconds the string twitched. He immediately gave a mighty yank and hauled out a hungry scorpion clinging to the piece of chicken. He already had a twig by his side and pressed that gently over the scorpion's claws. The tail with the sting was curled up ready to strike, but his right hand was out of reach holding the twig over the claws, rendering it immobile. From behind, he then took its tail between the thumb and forefinger of his left hand so that the sting was now immobilised, facing forwards. He placed his foot over the end of the twig and squeezed the trapped claws gently together with his right hand, released the twig from under his foot and lifted the scorpion up. Easy - when you know how!

Green Canyon, a deep, stalactite-dripping cleft in limestone rock way up the jungle, had an impressive Jurassic Park feel to it. Journeying through it by boat as far as a waterfall at the inner end of the canyon, we hooked up to a rock beside the falls, stripped off, and dived into the waterfall. It was gloriously cooling and invigorating after the steamy heat of the jungle. Swimming downriver in the powerful current, dodging rocks, swirling in eddies, we were showered by waterfalls that tumbled through the narrow slit in what, at one part, is virtually a cave where both sides of the canyon are so close you could almost step over it. Large monitor lizards gazed at us impassively from rocky perches. The opaque, muddy-brown waters made it impossible to see more than about two inches underwater and this lack of visibility created a sense of insecurity. It was impossible to see any rocks that might lurk under the surface, and it was impossible to know if there might be something lurking down there that might be tempted to have a nibble. However, our guide assured us that there were no crocodiles there. It was a sort of 'Indiana Jones' type of experience: adventurous, physical, thrilling, visually stimulating, and the cool waters were delightfully refreshing.

Yogyakarta, a sprawling city in central Java, and an eight-hour hour bus journey away was our next destination, a journey which offered more than the usual sense of anticipation. Gunung Merapi, the 9600 foot high Mountain of Fire, Indonesia's youngest (at 400,000 years) and most active volcano was having one of its very active periods. Located only 17 miles from Yogyakarta, warnings had been issued about threats to safety for those living in the vicinity.

We pushed on. At a distance of 17 miles away it was unlikely to pose too much of a threat to us and on the day we approached it had temporarily calmed down, which was a bit of an anti-climax really. I had been looking forward to some excitement and this most active volcano in one of the most volcanic regions of the world had seemed to promise some views of one of nature's most powerful phenomena, but it was not to be.

Yogya, the short form of the city's name, pronounced 'Joag-ja' by the locals, was another friendly place. Being in a city we were allowed free time for shopping, not an activity high on my list of pleasures. I elected to have lunch alone, away from the rest of our group as it is easier to meet the locals that way, and it proved to be so once again. I was the only customer in the small restaurant owned by a Dutchman and his Indonesian wife. The waitress, with no one else to serve became curious and sat and talked with me as I ate.

Then the owner and his wife, who hadn't much to do either, joined in the conversation as their sole customer seemed to offer an interesting diversion from doing nothing. By the time I had finished lunch I had been invited to join the owner, his wife and the waitress for dinner at his house that evening. See what I mean about travelling alone? It is much more fun and you get involved with people more easily.

Yogya's main tourist attractions are the Sultan's Palace, the extraordinary Prambanan Hindu temple, constructed in the 10th century, but currently cordoned off as a result of destabilising earthquake damage the previous May and, at nearby Magelang, the remarkable 9th century Buddhist monument of Borobudur, the decline of which is dated to around the 14th century when Java became predominantly Islamic. Yogya also provided an opportunity to see the ancient Indian legend of Ramayana portrayed in music and dance, in an open-air theatre, a colourful and spectacular event. Culture, palaces and temples are OK, but there was not enough excitement and adventure for me. Two days in a city is more than enough for me and I went to bed looking forward to getting up the jungle again next day and climbing Mount Bromo, an active volcano, the day after. That is more my kind of thing. This place was just too quiet for my liking.

The earthquake struck at 2.30am.

Only a few months previously Yogya and the surrounding area had been hit by an earthquake, which had caused 5,782 deaths, while 36,299 people were injured, 135,000 houses damaged, and an estimated 1.5 million left homeless. The evidence was everywhere. Like a city that had been bombed, temple walls had been cracked, some leaning perilously, and roofs had caved in. Rows of houses were punctuated by gaps piled with the rubble that once had been the homes where people had lived and died. Traumatised by that recent event, this latest quake understandably caused the population of Yogya some concern. Some earthquakes produce a sideways shaking effect. This time the vibration was mainly in a vertical plane, an up and down movement of the earth's crust, shaking people awake in their beds and when they stood on the floor they were bouncing up and down; ornaments danced on shelves and people rushed out to the streets for fear of the house falling down upon them. Parents grabbed their children and hauled them sleepily out of their beds to relative safety outside, with fearful faces traumatised by the memory of the quake just months before.

However, measuring 4.2 on the Richter scale, this was only a mild earthquake. It was big enough to shock, but not strong enough to damage or kill and after waiting sufficiently long to feel confident that no more tremors were imminent, people began to return indoors to try to sleep once more. It was the talk of the town next day. Everywhere people discussed it, how terrified they had been, how the children had been crying, how they couldn't sleep afterwards for fear of another tremor. And always they asked me, "How did you feel? Were you terrified?"

And my answer was always a perfectly honest, "No, not at all." The truth is that if they hadn't been so keen to talk about it I wouldn't have been able to tell you all this, for I had slept through the whole thing and felt absolutely nothing.

As I said before, this place was just too quiet for me!

The journey by bus from Yogyakarta to the Seloliman Nature Reserve, nestling in the foothills of the mountain range that spans Java from east to west, took all of ten hours. Nine months earlier it would have taken significantly less than that. We encountered several detours along the way as a result of another type of eruption. The problem this time was mud, lots of mud, pouring out of the biggest mud volcano in the world. It was created by the blowout of a natural gas well. Gas and hot mud started spewing from the well on May 28, 2006 when the drill penetrated a layer of liquid sediment. Attempts to pump concrete down the well did not stop the flow. While the company speculated that the earthquake that struck Yogyakarta on May 27, the day before the well erupted, might have cracked the ground, creating potential pathways for the mud to reach the surface, other reports have suggested that the drilling procedure was faulty. At its peak, 180,000 cubic metres of mud were spewing out daily. Barriers built to hold back the mud failed, resulting in the flooding of many villages. The mud, a hot, bubbling, grey substance with the consistency of wet concrete, had already wiped out 12 villages, killed 13 people and displaced more than 42,000.

More effective levees have now been erected to contain much of it in a huge lake covering an area of 7 square kilometres and 20 metres deep, which is now visible from space. Geologists say the mud volcano may be impossible to stop, but flow rates have reduced to around 10 000 cubic metres per day. All attempts to plug the geyser have failed, new spouts are opening up and there are indications that the void created by the loss of so much material has weakened the geological structure, with evidence of subsidence from around 0.5 to 14 metres deep. Such subsidence could result in the formation of a caldera if the ground collapses in on itself, leaving a large crater. Meanwhile, five years on, the mud still flows, threatening to destroy even more villages, homes and livelihoods in the East Java district of Sidoarjo.

There is always a bright side to these things if you look closely enough. Although a major disaster for the people living nearby, for the scientific community it was a chance to study the evolving geological process of a mud volcano. In the past, mud vulcanologists could only study existing or ancient mud volcanoes during dormant periods. This presented a unique opportunity to conduct scientific experiments on a developing mud volcano to further scientific understanding.

Even more outrageously optimistic however, was President Susilo Bambang Yudhoyono of Indonesia. Four years after this disaster, and with the mud still flowing incessantly, he enraged victims, who still had not been compensated for their loss of property, when he suggested that they should look on the bright side and develop the mud lake that had engulfed their homes and swallowed up their land and livelihoods as a tourist attraction!

Now, there's optimism for you - and a monumental lack of sensitivity.

Chapter 9

Eruption

From west to east, Java consists of a ridge of volcanic mountains that runs the length of the island. To the north and south of this ridge lie extensive, coastal plains. The land is fertile, with rice the main crop. It also has a good clay soil suitable for brick and tile-making which is another cottage industry, along with the crafts for which Indonesia is famous; wood-carving, silver-work, sculpture, puppet-making and batik. The brick-making clay is carved from riverbanks, watered down to the right consistency, and formed into bricks in simple rectangular moulds. Left to dry in the sun for a while, they become firmer and are then baked in wood-fired kilns, also stoked with the leftovers from the rice harvest. The result is that many houses in Java, in contrast to the neighbouring countries of South East Asia, are brick-built with red, pan-tiled roofs, rather than of wood construction with tin or thatch roofs. The result is a landscape of flat fertile fields dotted with red, brick houses and it all looks so similar to Holland, not surprisingly as the Dutch were colonial rulers here for 300 years. Eccentrically, the structures that house the kilns in which the bricks are baked are built of traditional thatch and bamboo.

Another surprise for me was the density of population. Java is the most densely populated island in the world with 115 million people crammed in to it. I expected long expanses of jungle with few inhabitants, but there are people everywhere and houses are jammed tightly together in the villages, probably to avoid taking over the good fertile ground in which grows the rice they depend upon so heavily for survival. Wages here are very low; the average monthly income is only about $20US, around UK£12. Yet the standard of housing across Java and Bali seems to be generally higher than in the Philippines, although the slums of Jakarta are just as squalid as those of Manila.

In the gentle foothills of Eastern java the rice fields are terraced on the slopes, offering a very attractive man-made landscape with the contours of each hill sculpted out in layers of narrow rice fields. The jungle presses in close here and the noise at night is deafening with cicadas screeching their high pitched whines and chirrups in the trees, querulous squirrels and monkeys having squabbles high above your head, and frogs croaking their mating calls incessantly. Huge black beetles fly about like bombs and this is a land of big spiders, some as big as your hand. This horrified some of our party, but they don't appear to be too dangerous. As always, it is the mosquitoes that are the biggest problem if you don't take appropriate precautions. Mosquito repellent is a must for travellers in this part of the world.

While trekking through the rice paddies and jungle our guide gathered a bundle of local herbs and made some herbal brew reputed to have great medicinal properties. This was an infusion of cardamom seed, lemon grass, ginger root, cinnamon, and palm sugar. It was delicious. I had three cups of it to ward off whatever ailments might be tempted to afflict me, for cardamom alone is used to treat a wide range of ailments such as infections in teeth and gums, to prevent and treat throat troubles, congestion of the lungs and pulmonary tuberculosis, inflammation of eyelids and also digestive disorders. It also is used to break up kidney stones and gallstones, and was reportedly used as an antidote for both snake and scorpion venom. I was comforted by the assurance that my three cups of the delicious brew had me pretty well fortified against whatever illness, bites or stings might come my way. Anything unpleasant that might get into my system would certainly have a fight on its hands. The large herb garden here is maintained to preserve the medicinal herbs used in traditional remedies. They even had one plant alleged to have the same properties as Viagra. And in case you are wondering, no, I did not grab some seeds to take home.

The next move was into the mountains, a long, uphill climb of about six thousand feet to some villages clinging to the slopes of some of Java's biggest volcanoes. The fresh, cool, mountain air and rich, fertile, volcanic soil creates ideal conditions for growing vegetables in the most amazing vegetable fields I have ever seen, plants growing in mathematically precise rows angled in herring-bone patterns, to avoid erosion by rainfall, along slopes of up to forty five degrees. No mechanisation is possible on these steep slopes so everything has to be done by hand. For mile after mile these incredibly steep slopes are cultivated, a beautiful patchwork of angled rows of vegetables in various shades of green: potatoes, cabbages, tomatoes and many more. It was astonishing in both the sheer scale of it and its aesthetic appeal.

A small hotel high up on the slopes was our resting place that night, or at least part of the night, for we were aroused at 3.15am. A winding journey by jeep, growling up the steep slopes of Mount Bromo took us to a high point on the edge of a massive caldera. Still active, Bromo had blown its neat conical top off a long time ago and it fell in on itself creating this vast caldera, a huge flat-bottomed crater several miles across. Our initial viewpoint was on the rim of the caldera from where the light of the rising sun revealed a remarkable landscape. To the southwest lay the most interesting view, slowly unclothed from its veil of darkness by the early morning light. This view looked directly into the vast, desert-like caldera of Bromo. After having collapsed inwards on itself, the pressure of escaping gasses built up from below and a new baby volcano began to emerge from the floor of the caldera, successive eruptions forming a beautifully neat cone of volcanic ash which has since been eroded by the rain and its sides are now riven with rain water fissures and gullies. As the early sunlight struck these it brought out in full three-dimensional relief, with light and shadow, the effect of these forces of nature. Eventually this cone had died out, but beside it Bromo had thrown up yet another young cone with a vast, smoking grey mouth out of which poured an incessant plume of white smoke.

A few miles beyond Bromo soared the towering Mount Semeru, an active volcano that has been in a state of almost incessant eruption since 1967, and the highest mountain in Java at around 12000 feet. Now illuminated by the sun it stood silently against a cloudless sky, a stark triangle against the clear, lightening blue of the sky. And then, as if to herald the dawn, it blew. A huge plume of brown smoke and ash emerged from its summit vent, growling and billowing up thousands of feet into the morning sky, eventually flattening its top like the anvil shape so characteristic of a massive thunderhead, but now illuminated into yellow, red and brown colours by the rising sun. Here were the primeval forces of nature at work, presenting an unforgettable image of fearsome beauty and energy. It was an awesome sight.

I had hoped I would see a volcanic eruption and now I had. It wasn't a lava eruption so I missed the sight of molten red rock flowing down the mountain's sides, but TV reports later revealed that vast clouds of hot ash and fine dust had settled over towns and villages downwind of the volcano. Plants had been covered in grey dust and people were seen sweeping it off their roofs.

Going down into the caldera of Mt Bromo, a desert with only a few pioneer plants colonising the volcanic ash that forms its flat floor, we arrived at the base of the new cone, smoking constantly above. From the base of the cone to the edge of the crater is about 500 feet, a steep climb up a grey ash slope. Looking into the crater of an active volcano for the first time is an awe-inspiring experience. Down there is a fearful-looking dark hole that penetrates the crust of the earth, grumbling quietly, hissing and venting off obnoxious smelling hydrogen sulphide gas and clouds of steam. That inward slope is very steep and smooth; stumble and fall into that and there would be little chance of escape. Down and down you would roll until you became suffocated or poisoned by the gas, if you weren't cooked by the heat first. It was a sobering thought. I walked carefully around the lip of the crater to get upwind of the smell and to get a good position relative to the sun for photos. On such a day the volcano looked almost benign, yet Bromo can turn nasty. Between November 2010 and the end of January 2011 it erupted ash continuously, with associated tremors and earthquakes. Tourists were excluded from the area and many airlines cancelled flights to Bali and Lombok as a result of the ash in the atmosphere which was reported as high as 18 000 feet and had seriously affected visibility.

Looking outward from this relatively young crater across the flat desert floor of the caldera to its high precipitous edges, you can only gasp at the colossal power that must have been released when the original mountain top blew itself to smithereens and collapsed inwards to create this desert bowl several miles across, already baking in the heat of the early morning sun. How high had Bromo been originally I wondered, before its towering cone could no longer be sustained by its relatively weak ash-like structure. That must have made quite a bang.

And now, as I gazed in awe-struck wonder, I thought about neighbouring Semeru, just a few miles away, still growling menacingly and pouring ash into the atmosphere. How strong is its structure and when is it likely to collapse inwards, or explode outwards, as most volcanoes do at some time, and with what devastating effect?

Here, on the crater edge of smoking Mt Bromo, I experienced another of the most powerful and enduring images of my journey through Java, and a sense of the immense power of nature's seismic forces and how they have shaped our world.

The final leg across east Java was a delight. It was another train journey. As soon as I sat down a family opposite me regarded me with great interest, especially a small girl about seven years old. Our group of five and another couple of Irish-born residents of Australia were the only ones with white faces on the train so it was not surprising that we aroused some curiosity. The wee girl looked at me. I looked at her and smiled. She hid behind her book and whispered something to her mother. Her mother smiled at me and I smiled back. Her father smiled at me and I smiled back and nodded. That was all the encouragement they needed and then the questions started to roll out. Where are you from? What is your name? All the usual stuff. I greeted them with a 'good morning,' spoken in fluent Indonesian, all two words of it, and managed to say a few more words in Indonesian which aroused even more interest. Unfortunately, as with all the other languages I have encountered I ran out of vocabulary after about thirty seconds, but that little bit makes an enormous difference and it always brings smiles and compliments.

The carriage was very hot and Yude, our Indonesian guide, then came along and told us there were empty seats in the first class, air-conditioned carriage. We could upgrade for 25 000 rupiah, not a lot to pay for the extra comfort, only about £1.50. The others got up to go, but I said, "Och no. I've just made some friends here. I'll stick around." That seemed to please my new Indonesian friends, and it pleased me to know that I hadn't spent 25 000 rupiah. Not spending money is one of my favourite hobbies. I had come here to savour an Indonesian experience and travelling in a steamy, hot train with new friends was all part of that experience. Eventually they got off and I went to cool off by the carriage door, which was permanently open. It was more refreshing standing there getting a blast of air, even if it was hot air, blowing around the body, enjoying the lovely pastoral scenes that flowed past me.

What was more interesting was the effect on the local population. Each village the train passed through, at every station, people looked up and when they saw my white face, they beamed with delight, waved and called, "Welcome!" I stood by the open door and waved back to them, like royalty. I felt like it too. They actually looked pleased to see me. Travelling by train always seems to let you see the back yards of towns and villages and this was no exception. Some of the poorer houses, little more than tin and plywood shanties, backed right on to the track, so close I could have shaken hands with the residents as I passed. This was a very rural excursion, no big cities, just small country towns and villages, rice fields and low, rolling hills fissured by deep gorges. It was a very attractive landscape and it provided some intimate glimpses of rural life.

Outside one village a stream flowed past a small cluster of houses. It passed through a concrete structure, with walls about six feet high, which had two separate chambers and was open-topped. The stream was split at the point of entry and flowed through both chambers. In one chamber stood three naked men, all having a bath. The other chamber was for the ladies. As the train passed by I had a most intimate view of this aspect of community life; men and women engaging in communal bathing at the end of a day's work, but with males and females separated, as is the custom in this Islamic society. From my elevated position high on the railway embankment I was able to admire the copper coloured bodies of the bathers. One of the women quickly crouched down, but it was too late; from my high viewpoint I could still see her squatting in the running water of the stream attempting to hide herself. It only lasted a few seconds and it was impossible not to notice, so I plead innocent to the possible charge of voyeurism. A few minutes later I spotted another elderly man having his bath in the river, stark naked, squatting in shallow water. It's the way they live here.

That was the last of my enduring images of Java, an island of so many welcomes and smiling people despite its floods, earthquakes, eruptions and tsunamis. It was a visit that helped put into perspective our moans about our bad weather back home. Maybe Scotland is not such a bad place to live after all.

Chapter 10

Bali

The ferry crossing to Bali only took about an hour, but it was great to be on the sea again, to smell the salt air once more, to feel the motion of a vessel on the ocean. The sea seemed to be caressing me, luring me to its bosom once more. It was irresistible. I simply had to get in the water again and organized some diving at Menjangan Island, a small island off the northwest tip of Bali with some good wall diving and lots of colourful corals. The following day, at Tulamben on the northeast edge of Bali, I was diving on a wreck, the USS Liberty, which was torpedoed in 1942. It was towed ashore before it sank and what could be salvaged was taken from her. She was left as a hulk in shallow water until 1963 when a volcanic eruption coincided with an earthquake. The tremors caused her to slide down a slope and she came to rest with her stern at 30 metres and her bow only 5 metres below the surface.

This depth range makes for an interesting dive. What you see at 5 metres is completely different from what you see at 30 metres as the species of marine life, coral and fish vary according to the depth. It is a big ship, 395 feet long, and the pounding of the sea over 65 years had broken her up so it made for an easy wreck dive and a very safe one too as the current is never more than slight and the ship is very open now. We did two dives on her, the first around the exterior and on the second dive we penetrated the structure, not that there was much penetration as it is so open now. What has become a useless wreck for man has become a marine community, home to so many beautiful fish, corals and sponges and anemones. A large turtle lurked in the gloom of the forward hold; on the stern clinging to a large Gorgonian fan coral was a tiny pygmy sea horse and above and around us swirled an enormous school of trevally with thousands of fish swirling in tight formation blotting out the sunlight as it passed above us. It was a delightful dive in perfect conditions.

I hadn't been expecting too much from the dive sites at Bali. However, I was pleasantly surprised with some memorable dives, none more so than at Gili Tepekong, a reef off the port of Padangbai. The gap between Bali and Lombok is a narrow funnel through which the current flows powerfully from the Pacific to the Indian Ocean and out there, about a couple of miles from the Bali shore at Padangbai, lies Gili Tepekong, a vicious, saw-toothed reef with two large black fangs sticking well out of the water and a rough rocky islet. As we approached in the boat it looked formidable in the big swell that drove large, white, breaking waves to foaming destruction on its dark crags. The Guide to Diving in Indonesia offers a cautionary note: 'a tricky dive with strong currents and powerful surges, it is one that should only be attempted by experienced divers.' The author was right. It was a challenging dive, but a very rewarding one with some really beautiful corals, anemones and sponges, some of the most colourful undersea rock gardens I have encountered yet, with sightings of sharks, barracuda and a host of smaller colourful reef fish.

But those currents were strong and tricky. One moment they tempt you into relaxing as they propel you along on the current, drifting effortlessly, enjoying the panorama of colours on the reef, then suddenly they become perverse and turn against you, forcing you to beat hard with your fins to keep control, sometimes driving you downwards in a rush, at other times thrusting you upwards towards the surface at an alarming rate. The big swell thrusts you sideways towards the reef threatening to dash bodies against hard black volcanic rock walls or coral pinnacles, then draws you back in a downwards rush as the swell, reflected back from its collision with rock, thrusts you in the opposite direction. It was like hanging on the end of a huge pendulum, a dive where constant vigilance, good timing, lots of fin work and excellent buoyancy control were essential. It was exciting, exhilarating at times, and called on all the experience gained in the past.

Bali is an island of contrasts. In the south around the Kuta area near the airport at Denpassar, it has become very commercialised, over-developed in a haphazard way, is choked with traffic and has lost much of its character. Far removed from the image of a tropical island paradise, this is a popular area with young Australians who enjoy surfing on the big waves that roll in from the ocean. The beaches are good and that means the tourists flock there, restaurants and bars abound, nightlife is characterized by loud noise masquerading as music, and drunkenness on the streets is commonplace at night. However, move a few miles around the coast and you enter a different world in which the Balinese people grow rice, engage in fishing or whatever their business may be. Tourism is more low-key, the towns and villages are quiet at night. This is not the kind of place to attract the raucous crowds of Kuta, but it offers a few glimpses of the lives of the Balinese people. And it is really beautiful in places. It is mellow, like the Balinese people.

The tourism trade in Bali had been devastated by the infamous nightclub bombing in November 2002 at Kuta Beach, in which over 200 lives were lost. This vile act, perpetrated by Malaysian Islamic terrorists, was so alien to the general attitudes of the famously friendly Balinese people who have suffered enormously since then as they depend so heavily on the tourist trade for survival. Although trade is recovering now, the hordes of Australians who once flocked to Bali dried up to a trickle for a year or two. Hotels, restaurants, tour operators, dive companies were all struggling to survive and the effect was felt right round the island. Lovina, a village on the north coast and our base for the first couple of days, was a pleasant wee place, but with no more than a handful of tourists. Indeed the arrival of our party of five probably increased the number of tourists by 100%.

Tertigangga and Ubud, the other two night stops were equally quiet. Warnings from the Australian government to travellers not to visit Indonesia were still being issued years later. The governments of Britain, Canada, USA were also advising against visiting this island of friendly people. Yet I never felt under any threat at any time in Indonesia, not in the streets of Jakarta at night, most certainly not on Bali, nor anywhere else. Universally I was greeted with warmth and friendship by lovely, smiling people, and never more so than on Bali. So many people I met pleaded with me to return.

On our final night, Yude, our guide, arranged for me to play the spoons with a band at the Jazz Café in Ubud where we had our last dinner together as a group. I had a brief audition with the boys in the band during an interval to find out how I sounded. That raised big smiles all round. "You're on!" was the unanimous verdict. At the end of the interval the compere called out: "Ladies and Gentlemen, tonight we have a special guest star to perform for you. Let's give a big welcome to Mr John from Scotland!" At the end of the set of tunes I got up to leave the stage, but there was a howl of protest from the audience. "No! More! More!"

"How about it, Mr John?" asked the compere.

"Aye, no problem." I grinned and sat down again.

These were good musicians. They played a lively Latino Jazz, most of which worked well with the spoons and, as is usual in a jazz band, each of the instruments gets a solo spot to improvise around the central theme. When my turn came the other instruments were muted, playing only a few skeletal notes in the background to allow me to dominate that part of the performance and demonstrate my virtuosity on my instrument. It's great what playing with good musicians can do to lift your performance. Their skill in improvisation inspired me; creativity took over and directed my hands to make sounds I'd never produced before. My mind was working on different levels. The conscious part recognised and marvelled at what was happening, but it was the music itself that had taken control at an entirely different level altogether. I just let it happen. I loved it. As the solo spot drew to a close and the rest of the band fell in behind me, picking up the tune again, the compere called out, "Mr John!" and the audience clapped and roared their appreciation. That's Jazz!

Afterwards the waiters and waitresses all wanted to try their hand, and several of the audience too. "Hey come and have a drink. I've never seen anything like that in my life." Our last night had developed into a party, at least for me.

That event ended my first Indonesian tour on a high note. I had no doubt Bali would see me again and it did, several times, as my gateway to several of Indonesia's other wonderful diving locations.

Chapter 11

A Trawangan Legend

"Stop the bus! Stop the Bus! FIRE! FIRE! FIRE! Everyone out! GO! GO! GO!" shrieked a panic-stricken Frenchman as he dashed from the back to the front of the bus to escape. The brakes went on, the bus pulled in to the side of the road and there was a mass exodus.

The first sign that something had gone wrong was when the air-conditioning in the bus packed in. There was an almost immediate rise in temperature and stuffiness. Outside, the sun was blazing hot overhead. I guess it must have been about 35 degrees Celsius in the shade and, under the relentless heat of the sun, the bus soon became like an oven. Hands reached up to fiddle with the air nozzles, but to no avail. I was just about to go to speak to the driver when the panicky shout came from the back of the bus and passengers rushed past me to get to the door. I looked round and smoke was belching upwards from under the rear seat, with a smell of rubber burning.

While all the others ran a long way from the bus and stood in a huddle on the roadside verge in the heat of the sun I went round to the back of the bus with the driver. He nervously opened the engine hatch. We both stood to the side in case of a sudden flashback as it opened and let the air in. Thick smoke belched out. I peered in. No flames, only sparking and smouldering around one of the battery terminals.

"Ah… The high-tension lead from the battery has been bent and is in contact with a metal bracket. It has short-circuited and is overheating. Have you anything to prise it off the terminal with?" He rummaged in a tool kit and brought out a long bar, and a pair of rubber gloves and managed to lever the lead off the terminal. The sparking and smouldering stopped. The smoke drifted away. We were stranded.

Luckily we had pulled in just beside a small roadside café and brought an interesting diversion to the dull lives these people lead as they wait optimistically for road travellers to stop for some refreshment. The owner kindly called us in to have a seat in the shade. The heat of the sun encouraged passengers to buy cold drinks. The owner smiled happily at our misfortune. Every cloud has its silver lining, if not for us then certainly for him as his sales soared. The driver called his base by mobile phone and a replacement bus was sent, arriving an hour later. I had booked a trip from Bali to Gili Trawangan, which involved this bus journey of about two hours, followed by a four-hour boat trip. That time scale had now been extended. Travel in this part of the world is often an adventure.

The replacement bus got us to Padangbai, a fishing village and ferry port on Bali, where we boarded a Phinisi Schooner, a traditional wooden-hulled vessel commonly found in these waters. She rolled a bit in the powerful currents and big ocean swells around Gili Tepekong, the black, fang-toothed reef that lies just offshore from Padangbai. The swirling tides around this rock reminded me of some of the seething, tortuous waters I had sailed in around the islands on Scotland's west coast. Seeing those powerful eddies from the deck of a boat and feeling them pull this seventy foot boat sideways made me realise just how strong were the currents I had been diving among there a few days earlier. It is little wonder that it felt sometimes like being in a washing machine. Four hours later I was stepping ashore from the small tender that took us from the big boat to the white, palm-fringed beach of Gili Trawangan, a great favourite with backpackers.

Many backpackers come here to learn to dive and in contrast with other places where I had been almost entirely in the company of experienced divers, here there were more young people learning, or gaining experience. On my first day, the dive guide was giving his briefing on board the boat just before we began the dive. He finished by saying the dive time would be about forty five minutes. My eyebrows shot up.

"Only forty five minutes?" I asked incredulously.

"If good on air, maybe fifty minutes."

I drew him another look. "Or more?"

Now his eyebrows shot up. "More than fifty minutes, John?"

"I'd be affronted if I couldn't."

"OK. Maybe 1 hour?"

"Aye, and a bit more still," I growled. "I want my money's worth." Well, I am a Scot after all and we like to get value for money.

"OK. We see how we go on air. If the others are low on air and have to go up, I will take them up and then come back to buddy with you."

All but one of the group were on their way up after forty minutes. One other diver was good on air and stayed with me while Kandar, our guide, shepherded the others back to the boat safely, then re-joined us down below to continue with the dive. The other guy was running low on air after sixty seven minutes, which was respectable, and by that time we had covered all of the dive site so I agreed to go up though I still had plenty of air left.

The following morning, Kandar took me aside and suggested an alternative to the planned dive with a group of people. A boat load of divers was headed to the west side of the island, but it could drop us off at the south end, just the two of us, and we could do a nice drift dive back, parallel to the shore, and finish our dive opposite the dive shop and just walk out. This would suit me better as it meant I wouldn't have to cope with inexperienced divers thrashing about, blowing out excessive bubbles and paddling with hands and feet and scaring fish, stirring up sand and occasionally kicking me on the head with their fins while I was hovering, lining up for a photo shot.

It also meant Kandar could have a nice easy dive escorting me and letting me take pictures without having to worry about anyone. And it would suit the others too as they would not have to sit waiting on the boat for me to surface when they had all finished their dives so much earlier. We dropped off first and had a lovely seventy five minute dive back to base, seeing lots of interesting things on the way.

When Kandar reported back to Ben, his boss, eyebrows were raised. "Seventy five minutes? Geez!"

This was just what I needed as Ben then suggested it would be better if I had my own personal guide in Kandar and we dived separately from the others from then on. Great! Our next dive lasted even longer - eighty four minutes.

Word got around and soon people began asking questions. One English guy met me next day and asked incredulously, "Is it true you did an eighty five minute dive yesterday, John?"

"Nooooo. That's an exaggeration."

"Yeah, I thought somebody must have got it wrong."

"Aye, it was only eighty four minutes." He nearly choked.

When we came ashore the following day Ben called out, "How long was it today, John?"

"Eighty one minutes."

"Oh, just a short one, was it?"

"Aye. My guide ran out of air."

Even the room cleaners heard the stories. It had now become a ritual. "How long you dive today, Mr John?" asked Ira, the housekeeper, and beamed at me proudly when I told her.

"Ooooooh, Mr John, you may be old man, but you very strong. Mr Alan, he young man, but only dive forty five minutes. Not good as you!" She giggled and gazed longingly at my manly, strong body.... OK, I am exaggerating now, just a little.... Maybe.

When I returned the following year Ben took me aside. "Look John, there is no point in you going with all these other divers. I need to get out of the office and take some pictures, so I will be your guide while you are here and we will drop off away from the crowds and do our own thing. I know where we can find some good specimens for photography. I have discovered a superb muck dive site over at Lombok. I keep quiet about it. It is only for experienced divers as the bottom is very soft, but there are loads of interesting critters living there."

So Ben and I, and Sue Lyn Lim, a Malaysian girl, formed a buddy team and had some gloriously long photographic dives, including the muck dive site at Lombok, under a jetty, which stretched to 91 minutes. Chatting to Sue on the way back, she had been impressed by the extent of my travels and remarked, "Hey, you are one cool dude, John." It's nice when young people think you are cool.

On our return that day we were comparing photographs on the laptops and identifying fish. Ben had captured a nice image of what we thought was a baby mimic octopus. I called up a photo of an adult I had taken the previous March for comparison while Ben had called over a Frenchman who was allegedly an expert. He looked at Ben's photo and was undecided. I offered my photo of the mature one.

"Ah yes, this is the one, Ben," he exclaimed. "It is a mimic octopus. Look at the Internet photo here, Ben, and you will see the similar features."

"That's not an Internet photo, that's John's photo," said Ben.

"No, that is an Internet photo he has downloaded," the Frenchman insisted.

Now when ignorance and arrogance are combined and expressed in such a loftily superior and dismissive manner, well, something deep stirs inside me. I felt my hackles rising. I was not so cool now. I stood up and growled into his face, "That is my photo."

"Noooo… You cannot take a photo of that quality with that little camera," he said scornfully, dismissing my claim with one of those disdainful, effeminate, sweeping gestures with his hand. "You have downloaded that from the Internet!"

So now he was insinuating that I was being dishonest. Well, we don't go in much for disdainful, effeminate, gestures in the Highlands of Scotland, nor do we take kindly to allegations of dishonesty and, as I was no longer cool, I came very near to slapping his stupid, arrogant, effeminate face. However, with my usual remarkable self-restraint, I growled again at him.

"Listen. That photo was taken wi' that wee camera!" I revert to my Scottish vernacular dialect when annoyed. "And the computer will show the details of where and when it was taken to prove it to you." I then drew his attention to the date, time, place, camera make and model, etc, all details that the computer stores with every photo taken from the camera. The evidence was overwhelming. His opposition crumbled, like Napoleon's army at the battle of Waterloo.

He backed off, muttering, "Oh. I could not imagine you could have taken a photo like that with that little camera. I was sure you must have downloaded it from the Internet"

"Aye, weel ye ken noo," I growled at him once again (Yes, well you know now, to phrase it in standard English).

However, inwardly I was smiling happily to myself. Not just because I had won the argument and punctured his unbearably self-opinionated, over-inflated ego, but because he had paid me the very best kind of compliment, a totally unintentional one. He really thought it was a professionally taken photograph. And that was really cool.

Gili Trawangan is only about three miles in circumference: low, sandy, with coconut palms and a hump in the middle. Life on all such islands is very laid-back. The locals are a happy-go-lucky bunch who take each day as it comes: don't worry, be happy and everything will be all right. They are always smiling, welcoming, easy-going, and very musical.

After dinner on my first night there, I walked along what passes for a roadway round the island; basically a sandy track, but paved with concrete blocks in the section where most of the dive shops and restaurants are located. The night was hot and dark. Street lighting is minimal here. With little else to do at night, a few young men were sitting by the roadside strumming guitars so I took my spoons and asked if I could join them. A couple of minutes later a bike bearing a rather hefty Australian woman stopped and she exclaimed, in typically cultured Australian tones, "Bloody Hell mate, that's brilliant! What's that you're playing?" She then went on to tell me I should be up at the Sama Sama Bar where they have nightly jam sessions. Some local musicians form the resident band and any visitors who can play or sing are invited to join in. "I can tell you right now, mate, if you go and play your spoons there, they'll love it. You'll be a Trawangan legend within 24 hours."

The boys I was playing with agreed and told me they would take me there. The band was having a break and they introduced me. "Let's hear you play," said one. I struck up, accompanying the recorded music that was being played. They all grinned, pearly white teeth in dark faces gleaming in the night, and muttered, "Hey, that's cool, man," followed by something in Indonesian to my friend who had brought me.

"They want you to play with them," he said.

The Sama Sama Bar was just a small, open, rectangular area under a thatched roof with picnic tables around it. The local boys play here and entertain the visitors who return night after night to hear live music performed, often with visitors who can play or sing joining in. It had a sort of Caribbean feel to it with rock and roll, rhythm and blues, and reggae, with Bob Marley songs particularly popular - he is an iconic figure throughout South East Asia. It was exciting, throbbing, lively music played under a thatched roof in the heat of the tropical night and it felt good.

The boys in the band were great to play with, really good musicians and vocalists. Two or three guitars, a bass guitar and a jimbe (a locally made drum played with the hands only) formed the core, and then there was me, adding my tippy-tappy sounds to the percussion section. The drummer and I very quickly established a musical rapport, almost a kind of telepathic communication, enabling us to compliment and inspire each other's percussive contributions to the music. This interaction generated a good feeling, blending in so quickly, and the guitarists all grinned their appreciation. The bassist's face was like the moon; big, round and chubby and when he liked something I had played well, he smiled, his eyes disappearing into creases in his big, ball-shaped face, white teeth shining against his dark skin.

They were musically creative and quickly realised the potential of the spoons to enhance some of the tunes. They asked me to do a percussion lead as an intro into one song, and in others, in the instrumental break, they gave me a solo spot, often impromptu, with a call from the vocalist to "Take it, Mistah John!" I belted out some lively improvisation, left hand whirling, working wonders with the sounds it created. How it does it I do not know, but if I think about my left hand everything goes to pot, if I let it do its own thing it makes magic. That really had the audience clapping their hands and cheering and at the end of the tune the vocalist called for another round of applause, "For Mistah John - what amazing playing."

Yes, it was just as the Australian woman had predicted. The boys in the band loved it, the audience loved it, and the owner of the bar loved it as more people crowded in to hear what was being played and the bar sales soared. And the more they drank, the better we sounded. The sound of the spoons carried well out across the beach, and three young Germans who heard it came to satisfy their curiosity. They stayed there till the bar closed at 2am and loved every moment. When I took a break they collared me and asked to see my instrument, telling me that was what had attracted them. Next day, on my way back up the beach from the dive boat after my early morning dive, voices called out, "Hey John, you playing tonight?" The news soon spread and some of the dive guides, all local lads, told me they had heard about it from their friends and they came along to hear me play in the nights that followed. So did the divers I was with. Tourists walking past as I was having lunch - it's all open-air restaurants here — smiled and waved, "Hi John," and flapped their hands, mimicking the playing of spoons. The bar takings increased and the bar owner expressed his appreciation. "Your drinks are on the house, John."

And so it went on every night of the week I was there. One night a young Irishman held out his hand in greeting. "That was absolutely bloody brilliant," he exclaimed in his rich southern Irish brogue. "Oi couldn't take me eyes off yer hands. The sounds ya get out of yer spoons, it's just amazin'! We've come here to watch ya this past three nights. When we arrived, people told us we had to go to the Sama Sama Bar to hear this fantastic reggae band wit' a Scottish guy called John, who plays the spoons. Ye're famous! Everybody on the island is talkin' abou' cha."

One night a guest band came over from Lombok to play the second half of the evening. Their style of music was different, slow romantic stuff, so I wasn't playing, just sitting with the resident band at the side to listen. A big Australian girl (I don't think such a thing as a small Australian girl exists, they all seem to be big) approached the stage and confronted the band.

"Where's John? Get John up there with his spoons!" She demanded.

When told their style of music was not appropriate for spoons, her face fell and she cried out in her cultured Aussie tones, "Aw faaack. I only came here to see John playing his faaacking spoons!"

As I left after my last performance the boys in the band thanked me and dedicated their next song to me. "I'm leaving on a jet plane, don't know when I'll be back again." The audience clapped and cheered and many shook my hand and wished me well. I have returned to that island three times now and each time had the same fantastic reception. On landing the following year, I had barely taken five steps from the boat when one guy approached me, held out his hand and said, "John, you have come back again! Did you bring your spoons?"

It seemed that the Australian woman that first night was right. I had become a Trawangan Legend.

Chapter 12

Komodo Dragons

The day started badly. I had ordered an early breakfast at my hotel in Bali, but the chef forgot my order. After I complained, there wasn't enough time to eat it. By the time it arrived I had already checked out and my taxi was waiting to take me to the airport. I departed hungry, and angry.

Getting to Komodo takes a wee bit of effort, even if you are already in Indonesia. Some live-aboard dive boats depart from Bali and offer a pleasant cruise for a day or two before actually getting to Komodo, or you can fly to Flores from Bali, which takes about an hour if all goes well, always a qualification that should be added when booking flights in Indonesia. All did not go well.

On arrival at the check-in desk I was told my flight to Flores had been cancelled due to a technical fault with the aircraft. My face fell. I had to connect with a live-aboard dive boat. Someone would be waiting at the airport to pick me up me and take me to the boat. The boat would have to sail without me, not a pleasant prospect to contemplate after paying in advance for the cruise. The girl told me she had tried to get me on a flight with another airline, but they hadn't enough room for me. I noticed on her list of names that mine was the last one. I queried this as I had booked the flight months before and I was certain that I was more likely to have been their first booking rather than their last. She had no answer to that as she had just been given the sheet with the unpleasant job of telling the few who were stranded what their fate would be.

A hungry man is an angry man - and I was both. In a polite, but hard voice, I asked her to allow me to use her phone. I called the local agency that had arranged the tickets for me (with some Indonesian airlines it is not possible to book online so you have to do it through a local agency), demanded the attention of the manager and let him have it right between the eyes. They had had my booking three months previously, but had only confirmed with the airline the day before, which is why I was last on the list. I told him about my awaiting dive boat connection and how much this trip had cost me and, if I missed the boat, I would be suing his agency for every penny plus additional costs for discomfort and disappointment. He assured me he would get his staff working on this immediately and asked me to wait. I sat in the Indonesia Air Transport office looking as grim as a fundamentalist Presbyterian minister preaching hell-fire and damnation to a sinful congregation on a wet and windswept Sunday in Stornoway - and if you have never been to Stornoway on a wet and windswept Sunday, believe me, it doesn't get much more grim than that.

Anyway, 30 minutes later the phone rang and I heard my name being mentioned. Another plane had been found and a short time later I boarded it with a few other castaways. After flying for an hour or so over the chain of volcanic islands that stretches eastwards from Java towards Timor, I landed at Labuan Bajo on the island of Flores, not much of a place to write home about, but that is where the airstrip is so there is no choice. From there I was bounced by fast boat about 20 miles through an archipelago of small islands to the traditional Indonesian Phinisi schooner, Mona Lisa, lying at anchor in a quiet bay. She would be my home for the next week. I was warmly welcomed aboard by Deirdre, our Irish divemaster, and one of the crew appeared with a tray laden with delicious fruit drinks. Things were looking up at last. This was more like it. I was afloat on a sturdy, wooden, sailing vessel, the food was good and there was plenty of it. The diving was eagerly anticipated, but so too was a run ashore to try to catch a glimpse of some of the world's largest venomous lizards, the Komodo Dragons.

From a mud pool in the otherwise dried-up riverbed, the water buffalo drew copious quantities of muddy black water into its mouth with a great sucking sound, swallowing slowly and relishing its coolness. Down went the head again and more of the filthy water entered its mouth until its thirst was slaked. Then it was time to lie down and cool off in the water. It lay there, refreshing itself in the shade of the trees that lined the banks of the dried-up creek, a welcome escape from the tyranny of the blistering sun.

Three small pools of spring water were the only wet parts of the entire watercourse. The rest was a dry, stony crack in the hillside lined by trees which drew their moisture from deep in the soil, their roots branching out from the base like the tentacles of an octopus, grey in colour, much the same as the soil. These few pools of water were essential for survival for the buffalo, pigs and deer that inhabit these islands, which are covered in a grassy savannah, with few places to shelter from the sun and few places to drink. But while the pools offered life-saving water, they also presented the most serious risk to the lives of the animals that drank there, for motionless among the stone-grey roots of the trees, and difficult to distinguish from them by their camouflage in the colour and texture of their skin, lay several large lizards up to 3 metres long and weighing about 200 pounds, the deadly Komodo Dragons.

They lay perfectly still, awaiting their chance: statuesque, sinister, opportunist killers, the world's largest venomous reptiles. When the buffalo lay down in the water and relaxed, eyes drowsy, enjoying the soothing relief of the water on its hot skin, the dreadful moment arrived. A large dragon stirred, waddled down the bank, then made a sudden lunge and plunged its teeth into the rump of the buffalo. One venomous bite was all that was necessary for a slow but certain death to follow, and it quickly withdrew as the buffalo bellowed in pain and thrashed its hooves around, struggling to get to its feet. By this time the dragon had retreated to the safety of its shady lair among the branching tree roots. All the dragons had to do now was wait. It could take a couple of weeks for the buffalo to weaken sufficiently before it would lie down in a panting heap. The dragons, which had stalked it patiently waiting for that fateful moment, could then move in for another bite or two to hasten the process. Then the feasting would begin. They would gorge themselves on the carcass, then rest for a month or so until another opportunist bite would bring another feast day. They eat only about 12 times per year.

It was long thought that it was the saliva of the dragon that injected a lethal cocktail of 57 types of bacteria into the bloodstream of its prey, causing blood poisoning and that, no doubt, has some effect. However, recent research has revealed that the Komodo Dragons have venom glands in their jaws. Within the venom is an anti-coagulant that prevents the blood from clotting, so the bite continues to bleed. The loss of blood weakens the prey and quite likely allows further infection to enter the blood stream: it also offers a scent which allows the dragons, which possess keen scent receptors in their long, forked tongues, to locate and follow their victim till it weakens sufficiently for it to drop. We saw two buffalo that day with the mark of death on them; the one in the pool of water with the fresh blood oozing from the bite on its rump, already crawling with flies, and another standing close by, quite severely weakened with its head hanging low, gasping in the heat of the mid-day sun. It probably only had another day or two left before being devoured. It is not a pleasant way to die.

This glimpse of nature in the raw was on Rinca, one of a handful of islands - Komodo, Rinca, Flores, Gili Motang and Gili Dasami - which are inhabited by Komodo Dragons. You are met by a local guide and taken on a two-hour trek to view the animals in their natural habitat. Except for one location. Near the landing stage a guest-house is provided for those who want to stay overnight. It is built on silts and in the shade underneath, lurked several large dragons attracted by the smell of cooking. This is not a place for the uninitiated to go wandering freely. It is mandatory to be accompanied by a local guide. At one point as we trekked up the side of the dried-out river, the guide stopped and whispered, "Look! Eight, no, nine dragons!"

"Where?" I gasped. I could see none. Such is the blend of their skin with the soil and tree roots they can be very difficult to spot and if you stumble along and unwittingly present yourself too close to these monsters you may just get something worse than a mosquito bite. The nearest monster was a mere five metres or so away, right in front of me, and I had not seen it! It amazed me how well they blended with the background of rock, earth and tree roots.

They are at their most active early in the morning after cooling down at night as they sleep. Being cold-blooded they need to lie in the warmth of the sun for a time. Living for up to fifty years they survive on a purely meat diet: mainly deer, pigs and water buffalo. They bite off large chunks of meat, skin and bones and swallow it whole. The digestive enzymes do the rest and when digestion is complete they regurgitate a solid mass of bone, skin, hoof and hair formed into a large pellet, in much the same way as an owl will cough up a pellet of the skin and bones of a mouse it has eaten. As there are only about 3000 of them alive they are a protected species. Males outnumber females by three to one. The females lay their eggs in burrows, digging several, all but one of which are decoys. She lays the eggs in only one, but neither predatory animal nor man knows which one, and she stands guard over her burrows to protect her eggs.

The guides all carry a stout stick, forked at one end, their protection against the dragons. If a dragon becomes aggressive they get a poke in the face to fend them off. They are rarely aggressive towards humans, although there are stories of children having been attacked near some of the villages. They are also reputed to have dug up and eaten the corpses of humans buried near the villages.

The islands here are hilly, savannah grasslands; but it is not lush green grass, more of a dull, dead-looking khaki colour, growing on free-draining volcanic ash or sandstone. There are only a few trees dotted around, except along the edges of the river valleys which at that time of year were mostly dried-up watercourses waiting for the rainy season. This is where the dragons lie in wait for the animals that come to drink, and perhaps to die soon after.

Our guide was well pleased with our trek. Altogether we spotted 26 dragons, 9 buffalo and a few eagles soaring overhead on the thermal currents. It had been a fascinating interlude in our diving programme, but after spending about three hours ashore in that blistering sun it was a relief to get back aboard Mona Lisa for lunch and to look forward to an afternoon and evening of diving, and there was no lack of adventure there too.

Chapter 13

Diving in That?

Mona Lisa was a sound boat, sturdy and comfortable. The food was good. The diving was not good - it was pure, dead brilliant! This was really world-class stuff, outstanding in terms of the colour, dramatic underwater landscapes and some ferociously strong currents which attract such a diversity of marine life with everything from sharks, mantas, dolphins and turtles to pygmy seahorses, ghost pipefish, blue ringed octopus and nudibranchs. It was simply fabulous.

And the renowned Komodo currents provided some adventure too. This was an area where four experienced divers had been swept away six months previously; their boat couldn't find them before darkness fell and they spent the night in the sea, eventually making their way ashore next morning on Rinca, the island I had explored to see the Komodo Dragons. After 36 hours adrift, they were spotted on a remote beach by an aircraft.

I dived that same site from where they had been swept into the falling darkness. A small rocky islet, wedge-shaped, sloping on the north side with a sheer vertical wall on the south side, it was just a bare rock above sea level. However, underwater it was stunningly beautiful. Covered in soft corals, sponges, anemones and marine algae, it was a riot of colour. We had timed our dive well, diving around slack water, that period of relative calm as the tide changed from the ebb to the flow, but even then the current still demanded respect. At the western corner Deirdre signalled for us to hang on while she checked the current round the corner. She peered over a rock wall and waved us on. You can see the effects of the current quite clearly underwater, everything bends to the force of the rushing water, the fish all head into it, their tails flapping like mad, and sometimes if it is fierce, they are propelled backwards, though still swimming forwards. At this time it was OK, a gentle drift, and we had a superb dive all round the island until the current suddenly picked up near the end.

The change was dramatic. One moment we were serenely gliding along, enjoying the amazing colours of a small bay, the next it felt as though a huge hand was shoving us backwards. The entire mass of water was moving and there was no fighting this. You simply had to go with the flow. We did, until we reached another bluff at the east end of the islet, when it suddenly came swirling round from the opposite direction. The collision of these conflicting currents resulted in a mighty push downwards. Kicking against it had no effect. We were still forced down. The ears began to ache under the pressure. It was time for action. Equalise the pressure on the ears by holding your nose and blowing and pump more air into your jacket to increase your buoyancy, and kick. We began to rise slowly, but it was like fighting against the flow of a sub-sea waterfall. We finned our way across the flow, hugging the rock face, and managed to get back round the corner and into a small, more sheltered bay to complete our 3-minute safety stop before rising to end the dive.

On breaking the surface, we could now see what we had been up against. The surface of the sea, which had been a slumbering, silky, smooth sheet when we went down had suddenly come alive, as though some monster was stirring it from below. It was now moving eastwards like a river in spate, a swirling, heaving mass, sometimes mushrooming upwards, pock-marked with eddies and whirlpools, contrary currents wrestling with each other, throwing up small waves, breaking white as they collided and refused to give way to each other. It was now a fearsome maelstrom.

Some new arrivals were waiting on Mona Lisa when we clambered aboard from the small boat. They looked incredulous: "Were you diving in THAT? What have we let ourselves in for?"

We were glad to be out of it now. Our timing had been perfect, offering us a memorable dive in serene conditions, but with a sting in the tail just to let us know what it could be like. Those currents were evil.

Other dives were fascinating. Two sites, Castle Rock and Crystal Rock, were beautiful pinnacles, with everything imaginable from dolphins and sharks to all the small stuff in attendance. A dive here late in the afternoon presented an incredible sight; what seemed like millions of fish, of all sizes, shapes and colours, milling around in a strong current laden with nutrients from deep in the ocean for their dinner. In the midst of all this we found a spot to hang on and wait. I slung my reef hook on a rock, paid out the 2 metres of line, inflated my jacket a little so I had slightly positive buoyancy, folded my arms and floated comfortably, hooked on and floating above the rock as though seated on an armchair, while the others hung on by their hands. And we simply gazed in wonder at it all.

The Cauldron... The name says it all. With a title like that a dive site must provide some seriously challenging diving and adventure. It is a narrow passage between two rocky islands into which the tide is funnelled and compressed, resulting in a very fast flowing river of ocean. Further complications arise because of the nature of the bottom and sides. It is not a smooth channel, but one in which the sea bottom rises from the depths to form a saddle over which all the water must flow. However, nature has thrown a joker into the pack in the shape of a large rectangular hole in the middle, maybe 20 metres across at 20 metres depth, with vertical sides so that the current drops into this giant pothole, and is deflected off the bottom, the sheer rocky sides and the wall at the end. The result is a veritable washing machine in which there are currents coming at you from every direction: up, down, sideways, forward, back, all without any degree of predictability.

And just to keep life interesting down there, on one side there is a canyon, a deep crevice about two metres wide in the rock wall with a steep downward slope. Swimming up the canyon into the flow of a full moon tide is impossible. You adapt, and become a lizard and literally claw your way up.

So this becomes not only a dive, but also an energy-sapping sort of exercise, more like rock-climbing-up-through-a-waterfall. When you reach the top of the canyon it widens into a circular hole, but don't expect any relief there. This is another smaller washing machine, in which the current will pick you up without warning and hurl you to the surface if you release your grip on the rock. Crawling across this hole, clutching at rocks, you find another smaller canyon leading back down to the main channel. Once in there you go down with the current as in a flume and get spat out into the main channel again by which time it is a case of spread your wings and fly. You just have to go with the flow. Zooming over the rocky saddle you are propelled down the other side into an open area scattered with large lumps of coral, behind which clusters of fish shelter from the torrent, snapping at the nutrients that come flying past them. That was more or less the gist of Dierdre's briefing to us prior to the dive, followed by the question, "Do you still want to go?" However, this is a dive you must do if you come here - if you are a wee bit crazy.

I did it twice.

Masochist!

The first dive was a gasping cracker of an adrenalin rush. The timing was such that we started the dive exactly mid-way between high and low water so the tide was in maximum flow and, with a full moon, the tides were running fast as they shifted more water through that gap in the available six hours of between high and low water. We dropped off the tender and headed straight for the bottom. There was no time to gather on the surface first as the current would have whipped us away, so it was over the side backwards and fin head-first to the bottom as fast as you can. We were well briefed by Deirdre. "Once you get to the bottom, grab a rock, hold on and have a look around for a few minutes to watch the fish."

Aye, right! She knows the site well and grabbed what seemed to be the only bit of rock attached to the sea bottom. I was left to grasp at rounded boulders about the size of watermelons and every one of them came loose in my hands. I dropped the first stone and grabbed at another. Same thing happened. The current was just too strong, effortlessly picking me up, and the stone with me. I was being slowly swept backwards with nothing firm to hold on to, finning like mad to stem the tide, but to no avail. There was only going to be one winner in this battle, and it wasn't going to be me. As I was forced to withdraw from the scene in reverse, Deirdre stopped admiring her fish to look round to see where I was and at that point I was drifting over a hump, was struck by a mighty upswelling and hoisted off the seabed with a boulder still in my hands. I started to ascend feet first. I was kicking like crazy to stay low, but was still going up faster than my air bubbles.

I had to drop my rock as I grabbed for the emergency dump valve in my buoyancy vest and yanked it hard. The air inside bubbled out and I managed at last to struggle back to the bottom where once again I could find nothing but rocks that came loose in my hands. Deirdre realised there was no way I could fight back against the current to where she was, relinquished her secure perch and we flew like birds through the channel to the cauldron, dropped down into the hole and clutched at the bottom which is all sand. All you can do here is dig your hands in like anchors. The sand is quite loose, like sugar. In this turmoil it never gets a chance to settle and consolidate. However, with the currents buffeting you from every direction you are forever being sucked out of the sand

and having to re-anchor and all the time using your fins to stabilise yourself. This was not easy diving; it was challenging, but it was fun.

Then came the canyon. The current tore at us with such ferocity we could only claw our way up the rock a few grasps at a time and hang on for dear life. It roared past our ears. It was like being in the middle of a waterfall. On reaching the small washing machine at the top, we then crabbed sideways and got ourselves out and over a reef into what was an amazing, tranquil little bay, a veritable Garden of Eden with the most beautiful corals and not a wisp of a current. The contrast was unbelievable, like a sweet dream following a nightmare. We hovered, like large dragon-flies, over the multi-coloured coral garden, gasping in air and relaxing and soon the dive was over. Back aboard the small boat we looked at each other.

"Well, what do you think?" Deirdre asked me, grinning.

"I think you are the most selfish, wicked, bitch alive, with an evil sense of humour to match!" I growled. "You went straight down there and snatched the only solid piece of rock on the bottom and sat there laughing at me fighting for my life with all these loose stones and up-currents."

She rocked with laughter. "Oh, I couldn't help it," she giggled. "It was so funny to see you raking every rock off the bottom and then reversing feet first to the surface, but you did all the right things and got back safely. But what did you think of the scenery?"

"Scenery? I never got the chance to see it!" I roared. "I was too intent on saving my life!"

She laughed again. "Oh well, we'll just have to do it again tomorrow so that you can have a proper look at it. What do you think of that for the first dive in the morning, before breakfast?"

"You are a sadist," I grunted.

"Och, I know," she replied in that disarmingly charming Irish accent, but the challenge in her smile was irresistible. There was no way I could back off and let this Irish slip-of-a-girl get the better of me. I looked her straight in the eye.

"Do it again? No problem. As often as you like."

"Great!" she grinned. "I just love that dive. That's it settled. First dive tomorrow morning it is then."

And so it came to pass that we did dive in the cauldron again. This time the current was not so fierce. It was towards the end of the ebb, so it was much more kindly; strong enough to make the dive interesting, but not so fiendishly ferocious as it had been the day before when we dived on the full force of the flood. This time I did see the scenery, and it was majestic, truly stunning in the early morning sunlight. And the fish too, lots of them. The cauldron and the canyon were both in a much more benign mood, simply glowing with a warm welcome. The day before it was as though they resented our intrusion: that day they enchanted us with their beauty and charm, with unforgettable images all around us.

"I love the Cauldron," said Deirdre afterwards as we sat on the wee boat taking us across to Mona Lisa lying peacefully on her mooring.

"Me, too," I grinned back. "It was fantastic, one of the most memorable dives ever."

After each dive, when we came back aboard Mona Lisa, the crew had set out delicious fresh fruit drinks or snacks like banana fritters to refresh us until lunch or dinner was served.   We ate on deck always; the weather was persistently fine and it was delightful sitting on deck dining in the warmth of the tropical night, watching the full moon rise over the islands, with its moonbeam, a brush stroke of pale gold, reflected on the surface of the sea.

Tired after four mostly energetic dives per day, well fed and thrilled by all we had seen, sleep came easily as we lay on the moorings that have been laid for such vessels so that they do not damage the marine environment by anchoring. This was a voyage that was worth every penny spent on it. A good ship, a good and helpful crew and Dierdre, an excellent divemaster who briefed us well and shepherded us around some potentially dangerous, but so beautiful and must-do dive sites which rank among the best to be found anywhere in the world. Komodo is a location for experienced divers; it is challenging, but well worth the effort if your experience is up to it.

At the end of the voyage we were each presented with a small map of the islands of Komodo National Park with our dive sites marked on it. On the back of mine, Deirdre had written a nice little testimonial:

```
Dear John
    It's been a pleasure diving with you throughout this
trip! It's been super-relaxing for me to dive with
somebody so competent and appreciative of the
underwater beauty of Komodo waters.
    Enjoy the rest of your trip - take care and dive
safely.
    Deirdre.
```

Chapter 14

Barefoot In Bat Shit

It does not sound like a great idea, but let me assure you, walking barefoot in bat shit proved to be a surprisingly pleasant experience. It was like parading over a soft, warm carpet, for that is exactly what it was, a carpet of dung, nicely composting away, generating a warmth that cossets your bare feet. It felt like the cave had underfloor heating.

Padding about barefoot in a huge cavern, home to millions of bats, on a small Indonesian island proved to be one of life's really interesting and enjoyable experiences. I had come to the Raja Ampat islands for some of the best diving in the world. At the eastern extremity of the massive archipelago of over 18 000 islands that is the state of Indonesia and about 30 miles south of the equator, you'll have trouble locating the Raja Ampat islands on a map, but they lie about 50 miles north-west of the western extremity of the large island of Papua to the north of Australia. The eastern half of the island, Papua New Guinea, is part of the British Commonwealth of Nations; the western part, until recently known as Irian Jaya, now simply called Papau, is part of Indonesia, the former Dutch East Indies. I like this part of the world. It is full of surprises.

It is not all that long since cannibalism was practiced in Papua, and there are still some primitive tribes living in inaccessible mountain valleys, some of which have only become known to the outside world within the past thirty years, so I would not rule out the possibility that you might appear on their menu if you were bold enough to venture in there and annoy them. Roads on Papua are few, usually only around the coast. The interior of this large island is still one of the least explored areas on the planet.

There were things other than diving to do. Taking a walk over Kri, the island I was living on, using a jungle trail, was a typically equatorial rain forest experience: dense foliage dripping wet in the almost 100% humidity, large colourful butterflies, the occasional snake, many lizards, some small and some not so small, strange birds, strange rustlings in the undergrowth. It was obvious that this was a little used trail. It was difficult enough at times to discern what was trail and what was not, and the conclusive evidence that it was not travelled often came in an intimate encounter with a large spider's web a metre or more across with strands like sticky wire, strung out across the pathway. This was a slightly disconcerting encounter as I blundered into one, and that stopped me in my tracks. The web was big and tough and that gave a hint that it must be home and trap for prey to a very large spider. It was.

The problem is that no matter how big the spider, when it is hanging there in the middle of its web it still blends so well with the dappled dark and light camouflage effect of the backcloth of jungle, you just don't see it until you can see the whites of its eyes. That is what makes it disconcerting.

To have that strong sticky web wrapped around your face is an arresting experience, let me tell you!

It was a huge, dark, long-legged spider that would have covered my hand, but it got more of a shock than I did, and went scuttling up one of the lines suspending the web from trees on either side of the trail and hid itself among the foliage as I tried to tear its exceptionally strong web from my face. It was like tearing off wire dipped in superglue, astonishingly sticky and strong. It gives you a kind of horror movie, panic feeling to be trapped in a web, but the 'keep cool' side of my brain kicked in and I took comfort from the thought that I looked even more terrifying to the spider than it did to me when it saw the whites of *my* eyes. After all, I did not look anything like a fly so it was unlikely to try to eat me.

This country is full of surprises and that was one of them - for both me and the spider.

Being under the sea is much more fun and after a few days of exploring the magnificent reefs near the small island of Kri, my base for this adventure, Maya, the manager of the Kri Eco Resort, suggested a day-trip to some further-off islands to have a conventional morning reef dive followed by a hair-raising, adrenalin-fuelling, underwater rush through 'The Passage.' This narrow limestone gorge between two islands is littered with underwater rocks and caves and the sea pours through here like a river in full flood. Impressive, some say terrifying, it feels like you are flying, such is the speed at which you hurtle along in the raging current, dodging the huge rocks that loom rapidly out of the gloom. It is more of a breathtaking rollercoaster ride than a serious dive, but it is a bit of fun. After that, the third event of the day was the visit to the bat cave.

This was a large A–shaped black hole, dripping with stalactites, in a sheer, limestone cliff. The long, white, fang-like appearance of the stalactites made it look like a gigantic, black mouth hung with rows of teeth, a bit like looking into a shark's mouth.

The boat eased its way inside the cavern and came to a halt against a pile of fallen rocks which blocked further access, a roof fall from a long time back. At the top of this heap of rocks was a dark hole leading to the inner chamber from which could be heard the squeaking of bats, lots of them. Snakes inhabit this cave too. They slither stealthily up the rough walls to feast on the bats. Our dive guide asked if anyone wanted to go in. Heads were shaken all round the boat. I couldn't believe it.

"Count me in," I said.

"OK, if you are going I will go too," said Joost, a Dutchman.

"No way am I going in there!" muttered a worried looking American from New York.

I don't get it. This guy scorned taking any precautions against potentially fatal malaria in one of the areas in the world in which it is endemic, yet he won't go into a cave to see some harmless bats? I think he got his risk assessments all wrong, but "Up to you," as they so often say in this part of the world. So Joost and I and Bija, our Papuan dive guide, prepared to step ashore on to the rocks to see what the cave held in store for us. Bija looked at us incredulously.

"Are you not putting on your diving bootees?"

"Maja said it was better to go barefoot, you are less likely to slip, she told us."

"But the cave is full of batshit!" he cried.

"That's what I would expect. Let's go." I stepped ashore and climbed up the rocks followed by Joost. Once we got over the top of the ridge and into the cavernous chamber in which the bats hung, our torch beams revealed an astonishing sight. Hanging from the roof were millions of black bats, their tiny eyes sparkling like diamonds in the light of our torches. It was like looking down on the lights of a huge city from a plane high up in the sky. Equally astonishing, the carpet of dung on which we stood and gazed at this sight felt just like peat compost, the stuff you put in your garden to improve the soil, same dark brown colour, same texture.

Bats are mostly very small creatures so their droppings are correspondingly small and, when the fresh bat droppings fall down to the floor, they are instantly devoured by the thousands of dark, fat beetles that scuttle about and pounce on any fresh dinner that rains down on them. So for your feet to find a warm, moist, smelly, fresh bat dropping is very rare indeed because the beetles get there first. Now what happens then is very similar to how earthworms process organic waste material in the garden. As they eat it, their digestive enzymes get to work, converting it from an unpleasant, smelly, sticky mess into crumbly compost which they then excrete from the rear end, dry and wholesome. And that is what the thousands of beetles that scuttle about your bare feet in here do too. Their digestive systems convert the bats' droppings into a carpet of warm, dry, crumbly material very much like the garden compost you buy for your pot plants.

It is remarkable. Even more so is the heat this process generates. That carpet is glowing warm as the composting generates heat, which then works its way up into the atmosphere. I would love to know how deep it is. It would make a lovely bed to lie on, apart from the fact that there would be a continuous rain of droppings on you, being pursued by hungry beetles which would crawl all over your face looking for their food as you slept.

It was incredibly warm and humid in the cave. There was a bit of an odour, but it was not sickening and you soon get used to it. In any case, you soon forget that as your torch beam illuminates the millions of bats hanging upside-down from the roof, some flying around squeaking; some large, some tiny shrew-like creatures. And the luxurious, warm carpet they and the beetles provided for us warmed the feet nicely after being soaked in seawater during our two dives. Fascinating.

The diving....aaaaahhh.... the diving is quite simply exceptional, breathtaking, fabulously colourful. This is undoubtedly one of the top locations in the world. The corals and sponges are in pristine condition, the reefs are teaming with fish. The diversity of marine life is incredible. Until recently, Cape Kri held the record for the highest number of different fish species recorded in one dive, 284, documented by an American scientist a few years ago. Tanjung Papisol in Triton Bay off West Papua, recently broke that record with 330! Add to that the many hundreds of different corals and sponges, the multi-coloured algae that clothe the rocks, the awesome limestone caves, canyons and cathedral-like overhangs festooned with marine growth of all sorts, in every texture and hue, and you have a truly amazing, undersea world.

Among these hundreds of islands, and even more reefs, the tide surges and swirls, producing some fiercely strong currents and that brings the nutrients that attract such a diverse range of fish, including some of the giants of the marine world; whales, sharks, manta rays, sting rays, napoleon wrasse and the odd-looking big bumphead parrot fish, turtles and dopey looking wobbegong sharks which lie lazily, well camouflaged, on the sea bed and let dinner come within range of their large, snapping jaws.

Dense schools of sardines, jacks, snappers and barracuda hover and circle in their hundreds and thousands; sleek, fast-moving fusiliers, large trevally, mackerel and tuna dart around like torpedoes, and among the corals are all the wee fish that glow in all the colours of the rainbow. All the small stuff, the pygmy seahorses, pipefish, sea-moths, nudibranchs etc are there too. It is a joy to dive in this pristine environment.

There are 110 dive sites all within a short distance of Kri island alone and there is so much more of this territory that has yet to be explored. For anyone who wants to experience some of the best diving the world has to offer my advice is, "Go to Kri, or take a live-aboard trip among the Raja Ampat Islands." It is not the easiest place in the world to get to, but it is worth the effort and expense. It is the kind of place you have to be really keen to get to, and that is good for the diving because the trouble and expense of getting there means that the relatively few divers who venture this far are generally experienced enthusiasts.

The resort at Kri is a cluster of traditional Papuan huts, constructed of bamboo poles and woven leaves, perched on stilts over the sea. The islands are all steep, limestone rock formations covered in dense rain forest so it is much easier to build over the water and that also has the advantage of taking your sleeping quarters away from the jungle and its mosquitoes. There is almost always a slight breeze over the sea so that there is no need for air-conditioning. Lift the covers over the hole in the wall that serves as a window (no glass required), and the air drifts through and allows you to sleep at a pleasant temperature.

The open-sided restaurant is also built over the water and serves the most delicious food. What the girls do in there with the most basic of cooking facilities is remarkable. The communal toilets, also built in Papuan style, are on the shore, but have western style flushing to a sceptic tank. They too are open-air style, with a space between the four walls and the roof to allow odours to escape, and that makes them very pleasant. Showers? You pour a pot of water over your head. Life is simple here, but surprisingly pleasant.

To get there you need to fly into Sorong on Papua and the resort boat takes you on a fast, bouncy 50-mile ride to Kri. There is really not much of any other kind of tourism in Papua. They get less than a thousand visitors per annum, virtually all divers, so pale-faced northerners like me are a bit of a rarity, arousing the interest of Papuans of all ages, who often stare at you in innocent curiosity, much as a child would do. Usually a smile to them, a wave, or a greeting, "Selamat pagi. Apa kabar?" (Good morning. How are you?) elicits the response, "Baik,"(I'm fine) accompanied by a warm smile. Others simply express their delight that you have come by waving to you, smiling big, beaming smiles and often calling out to you, "How are you mister?" (even if you are a woman!). Sorong, as a town, has little to commend it, yet it was a charming experience to go walkabout.

There are no other inhabitants on Kri apart from those who work at the two resorts owned by the same company, Papua Diving. They were forever laughing, joking, smiling and very friendly. The Papuan girls who work in the resort as chambermaids, waitresses and cooks were so much fun, always teasing me, each one telling me conspiratorially that one of the others wanted to marry me. Boya would sidle up to me and whisper, "John, you like Rina? She wants to marry you." Then Rina would approach me later and whisper, "John, you like Heni? She wants to marry you." Never in my life did I feel so desirable! They can speak only a little English and the resort management encourages them to learn and provides books for them to study, so I helped out with some informal lessons when I wasn't diving. I enjoyed it and so apparently did they. They were always crowding around me to practice their English.

This inevitably attracted the attention of some of the males. Bija, my dive guide, collared me on the last night and muttered incredulously, "Hey John, what's your secret? How come you always get all the girls around you?"

I shrugged my shoulders modestly. "Dunno. It beats me."

My departure was memorable too. When I appeared in the restaurant for the final lunch before departure, the girls in the kitchen, the waitresses and several of the male staff were seated all around the table and instantly broke out clapping as I entered. I left after lunch and when I arrived at the jetty there was the manager and the two assistant managers to see me off, as is normal, but this time the girls were all there too for the final farewell, an event marked by lots of hugs and joking and laughter as each one lined up, giggling nervously for her turn to hug me and say their goodbyes. The guys stood around grinning and winking, giving me the thumbs up sign. And as the boat eased away from the jetty they all waved and called out, "We never forget you, John. Hope you come back again."

After the 50-mile boat trip to Sorong, I had an overnight stay there and a morning flight direct to Manado, in north Sulawesi. The Lion Wings Airlines aircraft was an aged, twin-engined, propeller-driven thing with only limited luggage space and tiny cabin luggage bins, so even my hand luggage had to go in the hold. Thankfully I had my laptop in its own bag and that I could fit in with me. When the flight attendant sat down for take off she looked nervously out of the window, prayed, and crossed herself two or three times. That makes you think! She did the same when we were landing and the engines in reverse thrust sent the most alarming, teeth-rattling vibration through out the plane. When we arrived at Manado, about half the passengers' luggage did not come off the plane. The excuse was that the aircraft would have been overweight. The rest would come on the next day's flight.

I was not unduly troubled. I could rent a set of dive gear at the resort at Lembeh where I planned to spend the next few days and my luggage did arrive next day. A couple from the UK had connecting flights to Singapore that same day and then on to London. I wondered when their luggage would catch up with them.

Indonesia is a fascinating country and its people are friendly, but the local airlines must rank among the most shambolic in the world. They have a poor safety record. Planes seem to disappear regularly into the jungle never to be seen again. Ancient aircraft, with many bodywork patches, have worn-out seats salvaged from other scrapped aircraft judging by the number of logos of other world airlines stamped on their tired upholstery. The toilet door on this plane would not close so I had to stand with one foot back holding the door closed and pee into the bowl from afar, but with great accuracy. Luckily there was not too much turbulence at the time. The signs on the wall of the toilet were in Greek.

As I said before, this country is full of surprises, especially when you are travelling.

Chapter 15

Deceptions

Lembeh Strait, North Sulawesi, has the reputation of being the muck diving capital of the world. A narrow passage, it is a bustling shipping lane with container ships making for the nearby terminal and fishing vessels in all shapes and sizes rushing their catch to the fish dock for the early morning market. As you might expect with such activity, there is a fair bit of rubbish on the bottom; oil drums, bits of rope and netting tangled with isolated coral growths, bits of wreckage, banks of volcanic clinker and black, volcanic, coarse sand. Not quite the diver's dream of lush, colourful corals, anemones and sponges. For that you need only travel a few miles to Bunaken island a few miles off Manado, a wonderland of beautiful reefs, with sheer walls encrusted with all the colours of the rainbow and teeming with marine life. However, just round the corner on the east side of the peninsula, Lembeh offers a totally different kind of experience.

As you descend it looks a bit like a desert with bits of rubbish strewn around. Don't be deceived by its appearance, for this undersea junkyard is home to an astonishing variety of odd-looking creatures that find it easy to burrow or wriggle themselves into the loose sand, soft mud, or under the rubbish where they await the arrival of their unsuspecting prey.

The aptly named Stargazer, a sluggish looking, fat-bodied fish lies hidden in the sand except for its two eyes, as though looking up to the sky. Its mouth is facing upwards too, just waiting for a snack. Only the two eyes are visible, like pebbles on the bottom. Another deception. A small fish swims by and with amazing rapidity a jaw opens and snaps closed - dinner has been eaten. Sluggish? Not when food swims past. Not far away, what looks like a stone on the bottom is a large snake eel whose head appears like a small dark cone, just eyes, nose and mouth, the rest of the long body totally hidden in the sand. Weird-looking devilfish have pectoral fins they use as legs and walk, in a cumbersome gait, along the bottom. Extremely ugly, looking like an old piece of wreckage is their disguise, and despite their cumbersome plodding there is nothing slow about the speed with which those jaws open and close, faster than the eye can take in. Everything here seems to be deceptive. The flying gurnard is another that seems to prefer walking to swimming. Even when surrounded by strange beings like divers, they simply spread those elongated fins that look like wings out on either side like a fan, but still they run around on the mud rather than use the fins for swimming to escape. The markings on these large pectoral fins look remarkably like a large cat's face when they are opened fully, offering a startling defensive mimicry to deceive its pursuer.

Here too you can find the mimic octopus, a slim-line version that can mimic several other sea creatures. It will slither along the bottom and then oozes its infinitely flexible body and all those eight legs, or arms, into the sand and it disappears underground, like magic. The wunderpus is similar. There are various other cephalopods; octopus, cuttlefish and squid as well as the tiny blue ringed octopus, so cute in appearance, but deadly. These small octopuses - they can fit into the palm of your hand - flash blue rings on their skin when threatened. This makes them look deceptively pretty, but that warning should be taken seriously. An Australian is reported to have picked one up and brought it out of the water for his family to see. It wriggled up his arm and bit him on the neck. Bit by bit his body became paralysed. Limb by limb, organ by organ his entire body shut itself down. He was totally conscious the whole time until finally his brain closed down and he died. It took about 90 minutes for the bite from that one tiny creature to take him through that nightmare awareness of total paralysis and end his life. The golden rule is: look, don't touch. I wish more divers would observe that.

It only takes 1.5 milligrams of sea snake venom to kill a man. One bite from a sea snake will inject approximately 15 milligrams of venom into your blood stream, enough to kill you ten times over. You don't live long after that. This was one of the interesting facts I read in one of the books on the marine life of Indonesia. Thankfully, it is also well known that sea snakes are not aggressive creatures. The only fatalities from sea snake bites tend to be fishermen who may be a little careless in untangling the odd sea snake that gets caught up in their nets. Even though some divers like to show off by touching their tails, usually they pay no attention. They are remarkably unconcerned about divers and will often come close as they pass, intent on their own business. However, this book went to some length to amend the view that sea snakes are never aggressive, describing how one repeatedly attacked and tried to bite a floating oil drum as it was being hauled to the boat from the shore: so much for the docile reputation. The message was clear. Never take things for granted.

Now all this rapidly flashed through my mind two days later when I came, quite literally, face to face with a sea snake. It was just at the end of a dive as we were having our three-minute safety stop at five metres depth before surfacing. I spotted a large sea snake exploring the coral underneath me. I followed it as it wound its way through the corals, taking photos. I wanted a good picture of its face so I hovered about a metre above an opening where I expected it would reappear. My patience was rewarded. It suddenly emerged, looked up at me, and made straight for me. Instantly, the passage in that book came into mind, that perhaps sea snakes might occasionally be aggressive. This one certainly had a determined gleam in its eye as it shot up to face me.

An animal may approach you if it is hungry and sees you as food, but I don't look much like the small crustaceans and fish that sea snakes normally eat so it wasn't likely to want to eat me. An animal may become aggressive if it feels you are invading its territory, but sea snakes are not territorial creatures and often mingle comfortably with divers. An animal may become aggressive if it feels threatened, acting in a defensive manner, striking out at you: that seemed a possibility. I had been hovering above it for some time like the paparazzi that follow the rich and famous and intrude upon their privacy to sneak a quick photo. There was one other explanation, it was merely curious and wanted to investigate this black, bubbling creature with a camera in its hands.

All these thoughts flashed rapidly through my mind in the short time that it took to get from its coral labyrinth to within kissing distance, plus the fact that if it was intent on biting me, I was unlikely to live to see dry land again. Images of my family flashed through my mind like a whirlwind, and my mother sitting there shaking her head and sighing, "Oh, THAT boy!" But there is no need to worry. You wouldn't be reading this if I had been bitten.

Escape was out of the question as I could never move faster than it could. I could only sit and wait for whatever fate had in store for me. And after all my escapades with typhoons and floods and landslides and earthquakes and volcanic eruptions, I was trying to count to see if, like a lucky cat, I had reached the end of my mythical nine lives.

It pushed its face right against the camera lens, turning its head slightly to look inside the lens. Maybe it saw a reflection. I don't know, but it paused there, poking at the lens with its nose, as if trying to get inside this strange hole that was in front of it. This was the picture I had wanted of a potentially deadly sea snake, close-up, but not that close. Not within a few millimetres of my delicate, soft skin.

I couldn't even adjust the camera to put it into macro mode, allowing me to take a close-up photo. I dared not move. Any movement of my hand might trigger an alarm in the snake, perhaps causing it to bite defensively, and that would have been the end of me. This was not a time for panic. So I just hovered there, face to face, or more accurately, camera to face with the most venomous creature in the sea, hardly daring to breathe until it had satisfied its curiosity and then, with a rapid flick it was off, making for the surface to breathe. I too flicked round and managed to get another picture of its full length just ahead of me as I followed it to the surface. I had also managed to get two shots of it approaching me in the couple of seconds it took to leave the coral and get intimate with me. It was a great way to end the dive.

There are some small, colourful reefs at Lembeh where the large gorgonian fans offer a habitat for minute pygmy seahorses, no more than about 2cms long, cute wee things and so well camouflaged to blend in with the knobs and warts on the coral, that they are extremely difficult to detect. The dive guides know their patch well though and can always find them for you.

There is a myth that these creatures were only discovered in the 1990s when the first photos of pygmy seahorses appeared in the dive magazines. However, although the diving community at large only seemed to become aware of these tiny creatures then, they were actually discovered in 1960 by divers working at the Aquarium of Noumea in New Caledonia. It wasn't until 1970 that Gilbert Whitley, then Curator of Fishes at the Australian Museum, first described Bargibanti's Pygmy Sea Horse (Hippocampus bargibanti) to the scientific world: it was just another scientific event and not much note was taken. It was the first pygmy sea horse to be named until Alan Power found another one at 50 metres on a sea fan at Santo, Vanuatu, in the early 1970s. Of course then there were not many underwater photographers around; travel was relatively expensive, cameras were not so brilliant as they are now, and divers were still relatively rare. Still not much excitement was aroused and the pygmy seahorse remained virtually unknown until more specimens were discovered throughout Papua

New Guinea and a few other places within the last 20 years.

The late Larry Smith, then manager of the Kungkungan Bay Resort in Lembeh is accredited with finding the first pygmy seahorses in Indonesia in 1995. Within weeks numerous locations for pygmy seahorses were charted, more species were discovered and now they are highly sought-after, but very challenging, subjects for photographers.

Being so small is part of the problem. Only about 2cms, (three quarters of an inch) from nose to tail, when the tail curls round the coral to anchor them in position, there is not much left to see. They blend so well with the corals and they are extremely camera shy and invariably turn away, so you usually get shots of their backs. Just once in a while you get a good profile shot, and that makes you glow with satisfaction. As with other seahorses, the female deposits her eggs in the male's pouch. He then fertilises them and carries them through the gestation period of about two weeks till they hatch. One male has been observed giving birth to 34 babies.

The electric clam is another dazzling performer. Secreting itself in crevices in caves or under overhangs, it is bright red, with hair-like fronds over the membrane between the two shells. Whenever you approach closely, it starts flashing what looks like blue streaks of lighting from one end of the membrane to the other. The light is not electricity though: it is a form of bioluminescence created by a chemical reaction involving a pigment and an enzyme. The pigment reacts with oxygen to produce light and the enzyme acts as a catalyst to speed up the process. This results in the release of energy in the form of flashing light. Though research has not yet proved conclusively why they do this, it seems as though they detect changes in the light as a potential predator approaches and this triggers the chemical secretions that produce the lightning effect. It is an effective deterrent, enough to startle the observer and some divers have wondered if they'll get a shock from it. However, being bioluminescence, not electricity, there's no risk of that.

Each night at dusk, the mandarin fish become active and emerge from their hiding places among the broken coral rubble that lies close to the shore in about six metres of water. They are small, about the size of your little finger, but so exotically coloured in the dark green and orange colours like a mandarin's cloak, they are difficult to spot in the gloom as night begins to fall. These are very shy creatures and if you use too much torchlight they hide away. Cover the torch beam with your fingers, letting just a little light through and they tolerate your presence. Then the excitement begins. The males come out looking for a female, with whom to go roaming in the gloaming. As with humans, the twilight hours, as the sun goes down, seems to evoke a sense of romance. It is a time for courtship.

The mandarin fish pair up, aligning themselves side-by-side in a vertical position. The male and female then wrap themselves around each other in the most tender, loving embrace and they spiral upwards together, as if they were soaring up to the heavens in an ecstasy of passion. This only lasts for a few moments, but is so utterly beautiful to watch it is mesmerising and it would be a hard-hearted observer indeed who would not have his emotions stirred by such a display of tenderness.

We were all there, voyeurs, trying to capture these two tiny fish making such tender and passionate love on camera. Unfortunately, I had mixed up my batteries and inserted the ones I had used in the earlier dive back in the camera instead of the newly charged ones. My batteries were running so low on power so I had to keep the camera switched off until I saw a union likely to happen, switch on and get into focus and by the time I had done that the moment had passed and the lovers had split and dived back among the coral.

Kungkungan Bay Resort was excellent: great service, good food, comfy rooms, with waitresses, sweet and ever smiling, helpful and charming in the extreme. If I had only been forty years younger I may never have left.

Richard, one of my dive buddies, a 67 years old diver from Las Vegas, Nevada had been there seven times. He enjoys a glass of Scotch whisky and told me at dinner one night that he had a bottle of Johnnie Walker stashed away in his room and he would like me to share a glass with him on my last night there. He chose a table out on the verandah, explaining that the rules were that if you bring your own drink, they levy a corkage charge, but having been there so often, he had charmed the waitresses. They would smuggle the bottle out to the verandah for us to enjoy. So the two of us chose our table outside and one of the waitresses collected the bottle from the cash desk where it had been hidden, covered it up, and brought it to our table where we were able to enjoy a quiet dram and good conversation ranging over many topics, one of which happened to be the waitresses.

As they served customers at the far end of the verandah they had to pass our table. You could not be human if your eye was not drawn to them. They were beautifully dressed in traditional long, silken dresses, clothed from the neck to the ankle, but with a slit on the left from ankle to mid-thigh, offering an alluring glimpse of shapely leg.

As each of them passed I got the usual dazzling smile and he got the rear view. I grinned as the conversation faltered while his eyes flicked towards the retreating girl's rear end. When he looked back at me, with a twinkle in his eye, he muttered, "That's the most darned, neat, little ass. When it walks past it reminds me of two jack rabbits in a sack."

In order to get maximum benefit from a visit to North Sulawesi a diver ought to consider spending a few days at both Lembeh and Bunaken National Park. The contrast between the two environments is great with Lembeh essentially a muck diving destination, while Bunaken offers spectacular reef diving with reefs surrounding the volcanic islands that lie close to Manado. I was also well served at Tasik Ria Resort while there.

My final day before leaving Taski Ria was spent touring the Minahasa Highlands in North Sulawesi, to get some images of traditional life in this part of Indonesia. The resort offered tours, but it was not economical for only one person. Merri, one of the receptionists, suggested it would be much cheaper for me to hire a car and driver privately and she volunteered to give up her day off to come and act as my guide and interpreter. Bright, intelligent and very knowledgeable about local customs, she was an excellent companion and I had a great day out with her.

The culture here in this remote peninsula is distinct from that of Java,

Sumatra or Bali. While Indonesia is predominantly Moslem, with Bali being mainly Hindu, in North Sulawesi they are mainly Christian and very tolerant of the other religions. Spices were what attracted the Dutch here. They have a bewildering array of spices for cooking and health and can use certain spices for embalming to help prevent a corpse from decaying rapidly, even in the steamy tropical heat. I had no idea how much wealth could be generated by cloves. Those who owned clove plantations were the wealthiest in the district. There were villages in which everyone seemed to be employed in building wooden houses, some very beautiful. It is a form of shopping. You go there and select the house you want. They dismantle it and re-erect it on the site of your choice. Some villages specialise in pottery. Others along the lake-side, or more accurately actually on the lake, where villages on stilts over the water are common, go in for fishing.

A visit to a traditional market in one village provided some shocking images. A cage held some moderately sized dogs. They were not for sale as pets. They were waiting to be killed, the hair removed by singeing and then they are laid out on a slab as meat for human consumption. Also on display were wild pigs, bats and a kind of white-tailed rat from the rice fields, waiting for some hungry buyer. Butchering was primitive. The chopping up of carcasses was done on large blocks of wood deeply saturated with the blood of hundreds of other animal dissections and crawling with flies. Blood flowed freely along porcelain-tiled worktops and dripped onto the floors, forming puddles, which people walked through. Beside the dog stall, dog tail ends and the bottom parts of legs with the paws on were tossed aside, strewn on the ground beside the stall. The flies had a feast here every day. The rats took care of the rest at night. It was perhaps the most nauseating sight and smell I have encountered on all my travels. Of course, why should we baulk at eating dogs when we eat other animals like sheep, pigs and cattle? The dog is eaten in many countries and islands around the ring of fire. We eat birds, so why not bats, rats, cockroaches etc, all potential sources of protein.

As Merri, my guide, explained, "In Indonesia we eat everything, Scooby Doo, Mickey Mouse and Batman."

Chapter 16

After The Tsunami

Try to imagine it: a huge, 2300 ton, sea-going barge sitting in the middle of a city, but not in a canal. It is sitting on dry land five kilometres inland from the sea! How did such a monster get there? Nearby, a fishing boat sits upright on the roof of an empty shell of a house whose doors and windows were smashed to smithereens.

It is almost impossible for the mind to grasp the enormity of what happened in Banda Aceh, Sumatra, on that horrific morning of Dec 26th 2004 when the infamous tsunami struck.

Banda Aceh, at the northern tip of Sumatra, was a city devastated by that colossal tsunami. Stirred up by a massive earthquake measuring 9.1 on the Richter scale, that enormous tidal wave swept in from the sea like a bulldozer and swept away thousands of dwellings and the people who lived in them to a horrific death. No one knows how many people died that day along the coasts of Sumatra and Thailand. It is a death toll in the hundreds of thousands.

Few places in the world are so well placed for destruction by a tsunami. Flying over the city and its surrounding area on our approach showed just how flat and waterlogged the area is. It is scarcely above sea level at all, so when that earthquake's shock waves threw up a series of huge tidal waves, they could sweep unhindered through the city and penetrate far inland, crushing houses, shops and people, tossing cars around like toys. There was little hope of survival in the face of such a powerful onslaught.

Standing beside that huge barge that was carried inland for 5 km, an incredible monument to the awesome power of the sea on that day of death, I marvelled at the resilience of the people of Indonesia. It is only in a few spots like this where the barge has been left (it would hardly feasible to move it back 5 km to the sea) that there is any evidence left of the awful disaster. It remains there as a monument to the people who suffered and lost their lives and to the massive international support that the world gave in their time of need, something that the people of that city have not forgotten.

So what do you do with a very large barge sitting in the middle of a city five kilometres from the sea? Convert it to a power station and make it an asset. It now supplies electricity. I liked that. Rather than waste energy breaking it up for scrap they have utilised it as a force for good and, by its sheer incongruity, it still serves as a dramatic reminder of what happened here.

A small museum to the tsunami stands a short distance from the barge and the fishing boat on the roof. There, in its collection of photographs, the visitor can see horrific images of the scenes of devastation and death. Nothing is left out. It is there in all its gory detail, shocking photos of the torn bodies piled up among the flotsam of broken houses. Shocking yes, but I believe there is nothing wrong with that for it brings home to us just how these people suffered. It would be too easy to forget when you see how the city has recovered, and it brings home the colossal challenge faced by the relief agencies in bringing in food, medical supplies, clothing and all the essentials of life in a city of hundreds of thousands who have lost everything.

In a park in the city centre is another monument, a veteran aircraft, a Douglas DC3. Often called the Dakota, a type of aircraft which first flew away back in 1935, these aircraft saw sterling wartime service as transport planes and when the Russians blockaded the city of Berlin in 1948 and refused to let supplies through by road or canal barge, it was the Dakotas that flew in supplies on a daily basis, hundreds of them, landing and taking off from Templehof Airport every minute or so. In both wartime and in these so-called cold war political events, the Dakotas became a symbol of relief, bringing aid to those in need and one now sits on a plinth here in Banda Aceh, a testimonial to the flights bringing aid to that beleaguered city.

That particular memorial held some significance for me as a sort of metaphor. Age does not necessarily mean decrepitude. These veteran aircraft with a maximum speed of only around 350 miles an hour can still offer sterling service 75 years since the first one flew - and I am not ready for the scrapheap either!

The citizens of Banda Aceh have bounced back and are as cheerful as you will find anywhere. Their city bears only these few scars to remind us. They are smiling, friendly and welcoming. Their positive attitude, combined with what I saw there, had an emotional effect on me. It is difficult to be immune to such pictures of human suffering and you cannot fail to be inspired by the way they have recovered from the most awful natural disaster in recorded history.

Now, six years on, Aceh is once again a bustling modern city. Its people have rebuilt their homes and, on a superficial level at least, appear to behave as though nothing had ever happened. But no one in this city was untouched these events. The memories remain. The losses are permanent. Nothing can erase the horror of that fearful day. And that barge isn't going anywhere. It will remain the most startling reminder of the most awesome power of the sea and a monument to the tens of thousands who died in this city on that one day.

"Pulau Weh? Where is that?" was the usual response when I mentioned I was going there to anyone. It is a small island just off the northern tip of Sumatra. Very few people had ever heard of it, even among the diving fraternity, yet the diving there ranks among the best I have experienced.

Perhaps there was an excuse a few years back for not going there. It involved a flight to Medan followed by a long bus ride to Banda Aceh, followed by a ferry to the island. Now you can fly into Banda Aceh from Malaysia or Singapore with a one hour ferry ride to follow, which makes it much more accessible.

Indonesia has the largest Moslem population in the Islamic world, but most regions exercise tolerance and Moslem, Hindu and Christian religions all co-exist peacefully. However, this northern province of Sumatra is the most fundamental: religion dominates daily life here. The women all wear the burkha.

Alcoholic drinks are forbidden. In the provincial capital, Banda Aceh, city people socialise in coffee bars with free wi-fi Internet access. Everyone seems to be on Facebook, that world-wide form of "socializing." They all seem to be enjoying themselves without getting drunk, something I would like to see more of in western societies. I can never see the point of getting drunk as a way of enjoying yourself.

As a result of political unrest over the past thirty years, many western governments have advised travellers against travelling here, and some still issue warnings. However, a peace has been settled in recent years between the guerrilla rebels and government. Since the tsunami in 2004, the people here have seen the compassionate side of the western world, and I found nothing but friendship and welcoming attitudes when we walked through the city streets at night after dinner. People made eye contact and smiled, often speaking to us, asking where we were from, and they all seemed genuinely pleased that we were visiting their province.

I had met up at Kuala Lumpur with Roger Talbot who had been my dive guide on my last trip to Burma and we flew on to Banda Aceh together. However, a couple of weeks before we were due to fly, Air Asia changed the flight schedule to a later time which meant we could not get the afternoon ferry to Pulau Weh and had to spend a night in Banda Aceh, a bit of a nuisance, but an interesting experience nonetheless. The chilli sauce I had with my dinner was pleasing to the palate, but less so to the stomach. At 2am it was still raging hot and felt pretty raw for the next three days.

In the morning, a fast ferry whisked us over to the island in an hour and a taxi was there to transport us over steep and tortuously winding mountain roads to the Lumba Lumba Dive Centre. The island is densely covered in jungle. On one hill, the road was swarming with a clan of monkeys, cute babies playing with each other, tolerant parents and elders strolling down the highway quite unconcerned about the traffic, not that there was much. They were just like an extended family out for the day, all seemingly enjoying themselves. The dense jungle greenery obscured any view until we got to the coast again and had occasional glimpses of the large bay that was to be our location for diving for the next week.

In a small bay within that, Lumba Lumba Dive Centre snuggled cosily against the steep, tree-covered hillside with a sweep of sandy bay before it. It looked idyllic. It was hard to believe that it too had been trashed when the tsunami struck. However, as most of it is located on a steep slope, it had been possible for everyone to escape. Now rebuilt, it is a very pleasant cluster of comfortable bungalows and dive centre. You have to be prepared to exercise some tolerance if planning to go there. The dive centre does not have its own restaurant so catering is provided by a few small, locally owned restaurants strung out along the beach, no more than shacks really. The cooking is done on small gas stoves. That means it takes a long time from ordering until the food is on the table. They did not keep much of a stock of food; certain dishes had to be ordered the day before. The choice was pretty limited, even more so as they continually ran out of things. I ordered toast and honey at breakfast. Back came the waiter.

"No Honey." So I had toast without honey. The next customer ordered toast too. Back came the waiter.

"No toast. Bread finished." The old proverb, the early bird catches the worm, was so true here. One good thing though was the daily visit by Mama Doughnut who brought along a box of freshly cooked doughnuts with various fillings at the end of the day's diving. They were irresistible.

It was a quiet place until nightfall, which was heralded by the sounds of the jungle: the incessant din of cicadas, the croaking of frogs, the flutter of bats and all the other rustling sounds of the night. Oddly enough, there was the occasional "Mooo" as well, as a few cattle wandered around unfettered along the beach and through the resort grounds. Goats pranced about as well, browsing among the foliage.

The diving was superb. Being on the edge of the Indian Ocean the bay receives some fairly strong, deep-water currents bringing lots of nutrients so there is a wide variety of fish to be found here: sharks, large rays, turtles, schools of barracuda, tuna, trevally and all the usual reef fish as well as nudibranchs I had never seen before. In stark contrast to the previous two weeks of muck diving where the emphasis was on finding critters in the mud and sand and among the rubbish, here it was underwater spectacle on a grand scale. The landscape is one of huge rocks, the remnants of geological upheaval, for this is right on the edge of the fault where two tectonic plates of the earth's surface are pushing against each other. The Indian Ocean plate is thrusting itself under the Sumatra coastline, which is why there are so many earthquakes in this region. As the ground is forced upwards it breaks and this island is a jumble of broken rock, tumbling down into a deep bay, presenting a rugged underwater landscape covered in colourful marine algae, anemones, sponges, corals and offering shelter and food for many species of fish.

Dives usually started deep at around 30 to 40 metres and ended up close to the rocky shore. Close inshore where we usually did our 5 metre safety stop there was plenty of interest with a considerable surge from the big Indian Ocean swells that sweep into the bay. You swing back and forth in the surge among those big rocks as though dangling on a pendulum. It was fun. Fish are often found in large schools there, as though they too enjoyed swinging back and forth. I have never seen so many powder blue surgeonfish packed together in one place. Usually you see them singly, but here there were hundreds of them schooling together, all swinging in the surge among the huge boulders, like I was. They were clustered together so densely that it was almost impossible to see through them. The reason was food. A school of sergeant majors, small striped fish, were having a mass egg-laying session among the rocks, and as quick as the eggs were being laid, the surgeonfish were swooping in and eating them. The eggs were being spewed out in swarms: there must have been millions of them, nature's way of ensuring that at least some would escape and hatch out.

Everywhere, the variety and density of marine life was impressive, as was the beauty of the undersea landscape. It is teeming with marine life. It is rugged, very colourful and every dive was a delight. There was no pressure to end the dives early and most dives were between 60 and 78 minutes duration, so that was good value for money - and good value for money always makes me happy.

Socially, it was very pleasant too. Considering how seemingly unknown it appeared to be before I arrived, the place was virtually running at full capacity. Among the divers were some airline pilots flying Boeing 767s with Thomson Air who were operating on charter to Garuda, the Indonesian flag carrier. At that time of year thousands of Moslems fly from Indonesia to Jeddah to make their pilgrimage to Mecca, the Hajj, which all able bodied Moslems are obliged to do at least once in their lifetime. Extra planes are flown in to cope with the demand and these pilots were using their off-duty time to enjoy some world class diving. Thousands of Indonesians want to make this pilgrimage before they die and many are on the brink of death before they set off. Each year around 200 deaths occur on these flights, so they always carry plenty of coffins. I enjoyed talking with the pilots, one of whom was a Scot, comparing aircraft handling and navigation in the air with my seafaring navigational experiences.

Also diving with us were Jeannie, Janice and Caviner, three young Singaporean teachers starting out on their careers. They were great company, always laughing, and had somehow learned that Roger's birthday was on 13 Dec and mine on 16 Dec, so they had secretly commissioned one of the restaurants to bake a birthday cake for us. On the last night before our departure they insisted we join them for a farewell drink and then miraculously produced the cake from somewhere and set up a wee party for us.

It was a couple of days early, but who cares?

Chapter 17

On Top Of The World

The third largest island in the world, Borneo is a huge landmass of mountains, plains, and the oldest tropical rainforest in the world. Estimated to be 130 million years old, it is 70 million years older than the Amazon rainforest. However, in the last few decades much of that rainforest has been heavily logged to supply the Malaysian plywood industry, and more recently the natural forest has been replaced with an enormous expanse of palm oil plantations. These undoubtedly bring economic benefits, but at the expense of the loss of a vast natural resource.

The jungle - dense, tangled, steamy - is full of exotic creatures: orangutans, screeching monkeys, snakes, strange insects, beetles as big as your hand and, of course, mosquitoes. Some of these, such as the orangutans. have become endangered species as commercial exploitation has destroyed so much of their natural habitat, as well as a source of plants of importance for their medicinal properties.

After a bumpy flight from Kuala Lumpur, I arrived at Kota Kinabalu, the capital of the province of Sabah in the north of Borneo. It is part of Malaysia along with its southern neighbour, Sarawak. Surrounded completely by Sarwak lies the tiny, independent, but incredibly oil-rich Sultanate of Brunei, the fifth richest nation in the world. These three all lie along the west and north coasts of Borneo in a relatively narrow strip. The rest of Borneo, called Kalimantan, is largely undeveloped and is part of the state of Indonesia.

The first thing that impressed me about Kota Kinabalu, or KK as everyone seems to call it, was the friendliness of the people. People smile at you in the street and speak to you with that same curiosity common in other friendly places like the Philippines, Cook Islands, Fiji. My abiding memory of KK is that it is a city of smiles, a comfortable place. I also discovered that it has a significant population of Filipinos, many of whom I met and who beamed with delight when they discovered I could speak some of their language and had spent so much time in their homeland. More smiles.

On my first visit here I joined a group of 10 other like-minded travellers taking part in an adventure tour organised by Intrepid Travel, an Australian company. They were all between 20 and 30 years old with one exception aged 40, and then there was me, the grandfather of the group at 65. A two-hour journey by road and rough mountain track in a four-wheel drive truck took us from modern, bustling KK to Kiau Nulu, at an altitude of about 3000 feet, a mountain village of some 70 families. That doesn't sound a lot, but it represents a population of about 700. Big families are the norm here, with women giving birth to as many as 12, 14, even 16 children. One 50 year-old woman I met was married at the age of 14, became a mother at the age of 15, and had 14 children.

Older children help the mother with the younger children, the cooking and the never-ending task of washing the family's clothes. Every house is festooned with garments drying in the sun. The boys help the father on the family land, planting and harvesting fruit and vegetables. They are part of a tribe called the Dusun people and have their own language. A small bunkhouse owned by the Catholic Church was where we slept. The difficult nature of the terrain is perhaps the reason why Christianity only arrived here in the 1960s.

Following a welcome by the headman of the village, a dance troup from the primary school performed some traditional dances to the sound of music made by adults playing different sizes of gongs. They then invited us to try to play. As each gong has to be struck with a different number of beats from all the others, our efforts resulted in not so much music, more a breach of the peace. However, I decided to play the same game and invited the villagers to try to play the spoons after joining them in one tune. They were totally perplexed when they discovered that what looked so easy in my hands, defied all their best efforts.

Food was provided by some of the ladies of the village. Meals were served and eaten sitting cross-legged on the floor of the kitchen of one house; chairs and tables don't seem to matter here. The food was good, rice with various other dishes, usually concocted from chicken, vegetables and mountain herbs.

After dinner several of the men of the village arrived with a supply of homemade rice wine. Their custom is to celebrate the Sabbath by drinking plenty of rice wine after the church services are over. Protocol dictated that you had to drink a cup of the stuff without stopping and not leave a drop in the cup, demonstrated by turning it upside down over your head. If one drop fell out you had to drink another cup. It wasn't the best tasting wine I have ever drunk, so I made sure one cup was enough for me. After that we each had to introduce ourselves, then the music started.

The headman had told me to bring the spoons over to join in and this thrilled the local lads who all wanted to try to play, but were no more successful than the others had been earlier. That however earned me some respect as they expressed their admiration of my playing. They were all mountain guides or porters, several of whom I met a couple of days later on my ascent of the mountain and who greeted me so cheerily with their hands imitating the playing of the spoons. Mount Kinabalu has brought significant employment to the people who live in its foothills and tourism is developing as this mountain is becoming a magnet for trekkers from all over the world. It was included in a book I read in Scotland the previous summer listing the best mountain trails in the world.

Our attempt at an ascent of Mount Kinabalu was well planned with no rushing so we could get accustomed to the altitude gradually to avoid the risk of altitude sickness. The following night we spent further up at an altitude of about 6000 feet at the base of the mountain, where it becomes distinctive from all the others around it, rearing its massive, rocky head high above the multitude of ridges clothed in jungle that stretch as far as the eye can see. This was a good place for a warm-up before tackling the ascent of the mountain itself and I took the opportunity to trek some of the trails that are kept clear in the jungles here. There's not much fear of getting lost. It is almost impossible to wander off the trail so thick is the vegetation around you and so steep are the mountain slopes.

In the morning we got kitted up for the ascent proper, a two-day climb to the summit. Our packs contained changes of clothing and footwear, rainproof gear, toiletries and towel, toilet paper, insect repellent, first aid kit, hats, one for shade from the tropical heat and the other protection against cold weather, cold weather fleece tops or jackets, gloves, wind proof jackets for the night climb and at the summit, sunglasses, cameras, high energy food for snacking and, heaviest of all, water, plenty of water.

The plan was to climb up to a bunkhouse at 11000 feet, sleep there that night and get up at 2am for breakfast before leaving at 3am for the final push to the summit in darkness, the aim being to arrive on the top at 4095 meters (about 13435 feet) just as dawn was breaking, the best time of day to be there. Usually the night sky at the summit is clear, with clear mornings. Then, as the sun gets higher, it becomes blisteringly hot with the risk of heatstroke and severe sunburn. Clouds tend to build up in the afternoons and that can mean torrential rain, thunder and lightning. So, if you want to climb this particular mountain you get out of your bed at 2am, climb in darkness and see it at its best in early morning, then scarper off the baking rocks of the summit plateau and into the shade of the forest once more as you descend. And if you are lucky, you might get back dry. Well, no, that's not quite accurate, you may escape before the rain comes, but you will sweat buckets and your clothing will be drenched anyway, but somehow that doesn't count as being wet.

I declined the offer of a porter to carry my backpack. This mountain is high and it's uphill all the way, steeply uphill at times, by a rough and rocky trail, so our guide strongly recommended hiring a porter to carry our packs. I was 65 at the time, a pensioner, senior citizen, old man, call it what you like, but for me it was a matter of self-respect, or just being thrawn, (for the non-Scottish readers that means stubborn, but with added attitude!). I intended to do this climb carrying everything myself. My room-mate, an Australian in his late twenties, thought likewise; the rest hired porters and travelled light. There were certain looks from some of the others that said, "He'll never make it." About a third of those who attempt this climb fail to get to the summit. I had other thoughts. Only three young guys in their early twenties got to the top before me, by a mere ten minutes, and they had porters carrying their baggage. The rest of the group was a long way behind. Being thrawn can be satisfying.

The climb from the National Park Headquarters gate at 6000 feet took us up through jungle and then smaller scrub trees on the higher slopes to Laban Rata Resthouse at 11000 feet where we would bunk for the night. The canopy of the jungle trees kept some of the heat of the sun off, but the steep climb up an increasingly rocky trail was enough to generate gallons of sweat and it wasn't long before the group began to spread out. The trail is well maintained - it's virtually impossible to get lost - and the guide allowed some of us to go on ahead at out own pace while he stayed with the main group. The three young guys, unencumbered by any baggage, galloped off ahead. I plodded along at a steady pace, but gradually left the others behind.

From Laban Rata, the view was interesting. By late afternoon the clouds are usually well below this level so the evening scene was one of a clear sky above with a sea of cloud obscuring everything below, apart from a few distant mountain peaks which, like islands, penetrated the cloud blanket.

Immediately after dinner we climbed into our bunks to catch some sleep. At 2am we were up again. After a light breakfast, we were on our way, head torches lighting the way ahead. An agonising start saw us climb up some very steep slopes to the end of the tree line and then the rope work began. From here on it was all bare rock, a landscape devoid of vegetation, apart for a few hardy alpine plants clinging to crevices between massive rock slabs. The rock here was smooth and steep, too steep and smooth to tackle without the use of a rope. However, anchored into the rock, there was a rope, strong and white, all the way to the summit. On the steep sections it offered itself as an aide to get yourself up; on the more gentle slopes of the summit plateau its white line was a marker to guide you to the top, Low's Peak, the highest of Kinabalu's several summits.

I grabbed the rope, leaned back and with its aid walked my way up the steep first section. After that there were sections you could simply walk following the white line of rope, but periodically you blessed the guys who had laid that rope to get you over the difficult scrambling sections and especially the last few hundred feet which was the roughest and the most demanding as by then the air was pretty thin and your tired muscles were begging for more oxygen.

Dawn was not far from breaking as I reached the peak, with just enough light to reveal the nature of the landscape around us. On the way up it had been a dark, moonless night, a night sparkling with stars, but our heads were focused on the light beam from our head torches showing us where to tread on the rough ground. Only dark shadows appeared from time to time to indicate the presence of large rocky outcrops along the way: everything else was obscured by darkness. But now the features of the landscape were slowly released from the dark shrouds of night, and what was revealed was breathtaking.

At first, before the sun had appeared above the horizon, a greyish light allowed us a glimpse of where we were. Steep precipices, dropped down a thousand feet or more; around us lay a kind of greyish moonscape of barren rock, a landscape of grotesque peaks of the sort that illustrate the fantastical fables of children's books, a landscape sculpted by nature in her most surreal mood. It was like being on another planet. Then, miraculously, as the first reddish light from the sun struck these surrounding peaks, they glowed red like embers on a fire. It was, quite simply, a wonderful, warming sight. More and more features were revealed as the sun rose, warming our chilled bodies, enabling us to forget the agonies endured in the climb to be here at this time. It was worth getting out of bed at 2am to see this.

It had been a fairly demanding climb. Muscles had ached, legs had trembled as breathing became harder in the rarefied atmosphere above 12000 feet. The body had to work harder to take every step upwards, always upwards, with never a level stretch to ease the pain a little, and the heart pumped faster. The last few hundred feet were the roughest and toughest of all, scrambling up a jumble of large rocks, some the size of a small house, heaving your tired body up on the rope, having to stop every few feet to gulp in more air for the heart to pump that much needed oxygen to tired, trembling muscles.

But the warmth of the rising sun, revealing the amazing scene around us, dispelled the tiredness and, with some reluctance on my part, we started our descent, not just back to Laban Rata where we had slept, but all the way back down to the National Park HQ. Having already climbed up nearly 3000 feet that morning, we now had to descend over 7000 feet, and that was going to put some stress on the knees and thigh muscles. I had my trekking poles with me however and, as always, they proved invaluable, taking so much of the strain off the legs. After a brief stop at Laban Rata to have a second breakfast, we carried on down and arrived back at base at 2.30pm.

A short journey by road took us to Poring Hot Springs, the perfect place to soak after such a strenuous day. The springs were hot, but what a relief they were to the aching legs. I had struggled through the heat of the jungle and the chill of the steep rocky upper slopes to get to the top at 13435 feet. I had carried my own pack and had outperformed most of the youngsters with me. I didn't feel tired. I felt good.

No... I felt great... I felt on top of the world.

Chapter 18

Bloodsuckers

A long bus ride of about 200 miles from the mountainous interior around Mt Kinabalu over the broad northeastern lowlands took us to the banks of the Kinabatangan River. The magnitude of the jungle clearance that has taken place here in the last twenty to thirty years is staggering, the rainforest having been cleared and replaced with palm-oil trees, millions of them. For at least four of the five hours of the journey that was all you could see; palm-oil trees, planted in straight rows for mile after mile, literally thousands of square miles of monoculture.

Palm oil earns a lot of money for the area. It has brought prosperity and provided work not only for the locals, but also for many immigrant workers from Indonesia. The scale of it is staggering, but I wonder what may be the long-term effects of only one kind of tree growing over such a large area. The risk of disease striking the trees could have a devastating effect, laying waste to such a large area and the effect on the economy would be disastrous. So much here depends on palm-oil production now; planting, harvesting, transporting, processing, sales, marketing, exports, and the people employed in this work have to have homes, transport and food etc so there is so much ancillary activity dependent on these palm trees remaining healthy. And, as always, the real wealth belongs not to the local people, but goes to the wealthy merchants and foreign investors who drive the commerce forward.

Living in a village on the banks of the river, staying in the homes of a tribe of river people whose lives for centuries past have depended on the river, offered an opportunity to savour some local culture. The villagers were very hospitable, welcoming us into their homes. Dinner meant sitting cross-legged on the floor eating traditional food, eating only with hands. No forks, knives or spoons are used here except for serving the food on the plate. A bowl of water is offered prior to eating to wash the hands. They eat with only the right hand, never the left, which traditionally was used for cleaning one's private parts.

I needed two hands, regardless of how I cleaned my private parts. Try eating rice and curry with only your right hand, sitting on the floor, and you are not allowed to have your legs pointing out in front of you either as that is regarded as very offensive body language, they must be crossed or tucked in behind you. For those unaccustomed to sitting like this, it is very uncomfortable after a few moments, and my attempts at eating in this fashion had my rice dribbling down my chin and scattering over the rug. I muttered an apology and spat out more rice all over the rug. They just laughed. I had to lift the plate up close to my mouth with my left hand and then shovel the rice in with the right from close quarters. The correct technique is to scoop together a portion of rice, compact it with your fingers, gather it up with your fingers and then flick it into your mouth with your thumb. Sounds easy. Go on. Try it.

They didn't speak much English either, understanding only the occasional word. Not that it mattered. With a bit of sign language and appropriate body language we enjoyed ourselves and sustained some strangely convoluted conversations. Like the mountain people we had visited a few days earlier, the river people had their own distinct language and spoke that at home as well as the national language, Bhahasa Melayu, or simply Malay.

I had a very comfortable bed and slept well. Next door was the bathroom. It was not so comfortable. It had a concrete floor with a drain hole at one corner and a huge drum of rainwater and a scoop to pour cold water over your head. That was your bath. Here they use squat toilets. You squat over another hole in the floor with a long drop. A large bucket of rainwater with a scoop is used for cleaning. It's OK after you set your mind to it.

The orangutans and monkeys are sensible and hide away from the heat of the sun in the middle of the day so the best time to see them feeding and socialising is in the morning or evening. The jungle is very dense so this meant rising at 5.30am for a boat trip up the river, the best way to see the wildlife in its natural habitat. And we did see them, three orangutans, one mother with a cute baby clinging to her as she swung casually from branch to branch, about 50 feet up in the canopy, and several varieties of monkey; macaques, both short and long tailed, and the rather comical looking proboscis monkeys with their long drooping noses. The locals call them 'English' monkeys on account of the English settlers here having much bigger noses than the typical small, almost flat, noses of the indigenous population. Elegant, statuesque egrets posed along the river banks and hornbills with their amazingly large beaks fluttered around on the high branches of trees. It made an interesting start to the day.

After returning to the village for breakfast they showed us how to fish using traditional traps made of rattan and bamboo and a bell shaped net, which required an interesting technique to cast it out on the water and draw the catch in. The community centre in the village had a large enough kitchen to allow us to have a cooking lesson, sitting on the floor as usual, chopping up meat and vegetables and then cooking in a wok. I really enjoyed that and spent some time discussing cooking with a couple of the girls who taught us. They were as keen to learn from me as I was from them and we swapped recipes. They now know how to make Scottish Shortbread. The food we cooked was eaten for lunch after which they put on a display of dancing wearing colourful traditional costumes and invited us to join in.

The original plan to go trekking and camp in the jungle had been cancelled due to the heavy rains they had experienced in the previous week. The river level had risen about 10 feet higher than normal and a large area of the flood plain where we should have been walking and camping was still underwater. In flood conditions the crocodiles move out of the strong river current and into the more still waters of the flooded areas of jungle looking for food and dry banks to rest on, so it was not considered safe to go wandering about the jungle and wading through muddy waters for fear of encountering hungry crocodiles. They grow to about 20 feet in length here and are definitely not to be tangled with. That was a disappointment and it was back to the homestay for another night of sitting cross-legged on the floor, shovelling rice into your mouth, up your nose, down your chin and all over the carpet once again. Our hosts didn't mind the mess. It was entertainment for them.

An hour-long boat trip in a fast, bumpy boat from Sandakan to a tiny island, Pulau Selingaan, provided the most uncomfortable voyage I have ever endured. Going flat out, the boatman in his hydraulically dampened chair never seemed to consider the discomfort the passengers had to endure sitting on a hard seat. In what was a pretty choppy sea he battered into every wave in a bone-crushing crash with such force that my vertebrae were playing against each other like castanets and my brain was rattling against my skull. It was not nice at all. I considered killing him.

Pulau Selingaan, a tiny island you could walk around in about twenty minutes, is also known as Turtle Island on account of the nesting habits of the turtles which lay their eggs in the sand here. At night the turtles come ashore to lay their eggs in large holes they dig in the sand. The beaches are cleared each day at 6pm to give the turtles priority. At about 9pm we received a call from the beach rangers informing us that we could go and view a mother laying her eggs. She was a big turtle about 15 years old and laid 82 eggs, all of which were collected in a bucket as there is a turtle conservation project in operation here. The eggs, collected by the ranger as the mother lays them, are then placed in holes dug in a protected hatchery to protect them from predators. Each hole is marked with a stick, which tells the date and the number of eggs.

Two months later when the babies hatch - they are about the size of the palm of your hand - they force their way up through the sand from the bottom of the hole with all the eggs in it and, once on the surface, make a dash for the sea. They all seem to hatch at the same time so there are hordes of tiny turtles all desperate for a swim and plenty of predatory birds awaiting them. It is an amazing sight to see the earth suddenly erupt with hordes of tiny turtles. How do they know which way to dig to get out? Contained by a fence in the hatchery, they are collected and taken to the beach in a box to protect them from the predatory birds that are always around to feed on them and then released close to the water's edge. They run to the water. A wave comes in and they get swept back again. Undaunted they make another determined rush for the sea and then get swept back and forth in the surf as waves sweep the shore, but they are the most determined wee things and plunge back into the sea until they disappear from view. Most will get eaten; only a very small percentage will attain maturity. It was a memorable sight to see these cute wee things, running along on their flippers with their heads held high, making their dash for the sea, surely one of nature's most endearing sights.

Not far from Sandakan is the Orangutan Rehabilitation Centre at Sepilok, where injured or orphaned animals are cared for and released again into the jungle when they are able to fend for themselves. Twice each day they are assisted in their feeding. Bananas and young bamboo shoots are laid out on a feeding platform in the jungle with ropes leading to it attached to some distant trees. An empty oil drum is banged at 10am and 3pm and shortly afterwards the orangutans swing in from the jungle and along the ropes to have their meal. They are amazing creatures, so agile and effortless in their movements, their facial expressions so cute. A tribe of cheeky macaque monkeys also joined in after the orangutans had had their fill, forever squabbling and fighting, like monkeys.

Having seen that, the jungle awaited us. This was a good opportunity to do some trekking in dense tropical rain forest. To my astonishment, my Australian room-mate and I were the only ones game for trekking in the jungle that day. The others, all in their twenties, took a taxi back to the town and went to a cinema! I couldn't believe it. What were they thinking of? How could they prefer watching a film they could see back home to ploutering through the mud in the dripping, steamy jungle, seeing armies of enormous black ants on the march, hearing monkeys screeching and crashing among the trees high above, listening to strange rustlings in the undergrowth, seeing snakes slither away silently, getting huge sticky spiders webs wrapped around your face, and finding yourself on the menu for hordes of bloodthirsty leeches? After all the heavy rain of the previous couple of days the jungle was really humid and steamy, every leaf dripping with moisture. The trails, such as they were, were mostly ankle deep in soft mud, water and rotting leaves. In conditions like these there is no evaporation of the sweat on your body, you just get damper and damper. You can almost imagine the green mould growing on your skin. And, of course, these are the kind of conditions so beloved by leeches.

It wasn't long before regiments of the damned things were swarming up our legs in that peculiar top to bottom flick-over motion they have when head and tail alternate in sticking persistently to your skin. They do this walk up your body until they find the right spot. Soft, smooth skin is preferred to the scrub-like hair that grows on my legs. They dropped off leaves on to arms and clothing as well, and hordes of the little blighters came swarming up the leather of my boots from the carpet of leaves and mud and puddles of the jungle floor. This was the stuff of horror movies. With almost every step, hordes of the black marauders jumped aboard, intent on sucking your blood. We were kept busy every couple of minutes removing them. I use the back of my thumbnail in a scraping movement and this usually gets them off though it may take several scrapes to get them away as they will flick their tails over and stick fast again just as you clear the head. They are thrawn.

The trouble with leeches is that you don't feel them, neither when they climb up your leg, nor when they painlessly suck your precious blood. They anaesthetize your skin first and inject an anticoagulant substance into the blood, thinning it and making it easy for them to suck it out of you and into their stomachs. When they climb on they are usually as thin as fine string. After a few minutes sucking your blood into their long empty stomachs they swell up and fall off. By this time they can be the size of the large black slugs we get in our gardens in Europe. They are quite clean however and are used in hospitals to thin the blood of some patients with their anti-coagulant. However, it is after they have gone and your blood continues to flow freely from the wound that there is a risk of infection. I thought I was doing fine keeping myself clear of them until, near the end of our trek, I thought I felt something inside my sock at my right ankle. I stretched the sock out and there was a leech as big as my thumb. It had dined royally on me.

Paul, my companion, had found one under his shirt on his stomach, just above his belt. I checked in that area too and as I lifted my shirt, which I had been wearing outside my shorts, I was horrified to see that the groin area of my shorts was extensively dyed red. I looked inside and I was covered in blood. Two leeches had been in there, dangling from my scrotum, feasting on the blood supply to my private parts. I could only laugh at the thought of two leeches, swinging gaily back and forth as I trod through the jungle, blissfully unaware that I was host to some uninvited guests gorging themselves unashamedly on the lifeblood of my testicles. And once they were gone the blood just kept on flowing, like water from a tap. I began to worry about losing so much blood. What if I became weak through loss of blood and fainted? Then they could all descend on me and suck every last drop out of me. This was no time to start panicking and I quickly regained my self-composure. I had plenty of blood left, but what a mess I was in.

But more was yet to come. Soon after we emerged from the jungle, we found a small restaurant by the roadside as we made our way back to the bunkhouse. We needed food and drink so we stopped, dripping with sweat and mud and blood, but regardless of our bedraggled state, we went in and ordered food and drink. The other diners regarded us with some bemusement/distaste/disgust: choose your word, any one will do. Then, as I supped my deliciously cool, fresh orange juice, I heard gasps of horror from the group at the next table. Wide-eyed with amazement and speechless, their fingers were pointing at my left foot. I put my glass of juice down and looked. A big, fat leech was squirming its way out of my sock. I bent down and picked it up and took it over to let them see it.

Panic! Chairs were pushed aside and folk fled from me as if I were diseased. I shrugged my shoulders. I can take a hint. I won't stop where I'm not wanted. I took it to the door and threw it out, then went back to my chair and supped my juice again. The diners nervously returned to their seats too. Then I thought I'd better check to see if there were any more and bent down to take off my boot. As I did so, two more fatties emerged. I deposited the leeches safely outside once more, then took my sock off. There were another two still in there, still feasting on my ankle, and I never felt a thing. They are so flexible that even when walking they just get squeezed in and out like a soft balloon and get fatter and fatter till they decide to leave. My sock was absolutely saturated in blood so I put it back on to help contain the flow that was turning the floor of the restaurant bright red. I put the serviettes on the table to good use to soak the blood up.

I then checked my right boot and sure enough there were two in there as well. Paul also had managed to dig out a couple from his footwear. Our flock of leeches were now hopping across the restaurant floor towards the other tables, clearing a crowd of diners before them like a tsunami. People were clinging to the walls and were frantically clawing at each other to get out by the back door as we were seated right at the front door. No one would come near us. I looked quizzically at Paul. "Do we have a body odour problem?" I put my boots on again and our food was delivered. The waitress took the salt from the table and poured some on each of the leeches. They shrivelled up. She then got a brush and swept them out. Peace was restored, though few people wanted to sit anywhere near us after that. It was like a nuclear fallout area. No one entered. Not that it bothered us. We were too hungry to care and now it was our turn to feast.

Back at the bunkhouse, I couldn't get the bleeding to stop. After showering, I put on a dressing, covered it and taped it down all round with surgical tape to make a seal. Then I lay back on the bed with the leaky leg propped up on my rucksack as high as I could get it. The struggle against gravity helped reduce the flow and eventually it dried up. I suffered no ill effects.

Indeed they may have had a positive effect. Next day we had to take a flight back to Kota Kinabalu, where our group would finally disperse. With all the anticoagulant that the leeches had pumped into me thinning the blood I had no fear of developing deep vein thrombosis during the flight.

You can always find always something positive in a situation, if you look at things the right way.

Chapter 19

Sipadan

The aircraft soared into the clear, early morning sky above Kota Kinabalu. I looked out of the window and there, soaring high above all the jungle-clad surrounding mountains, was the towering rocky bulk of Mount Kinabalu. I gazed in wonder. Did I really climb to the top of that monstrous rock, clambering up those impressively steep, slab-sided flanks in total darkness with only a small head torch and a rope to guide me? Then I was focused only on the few feet ahead or above me as I climbed, gasping for air, unable to see anything of the mountain in the darkness. When you are on a mountain, even in daylight, you rarely get an overall impression of the scale of the thing. Now, I could see this majestic mountain from sea level to summit, all 13435 feet (4095 metres) of green, jungle-clad lower slopes and the sun-scorched, bare grey rock of its lofty summit. Its enormity impressed me. Seeing a mountain from the air is a great way to gauge the scale of it all, and I felt a glow of satisfaction that I had been able to climb it.

My destination now was Pulau Sipadan, a small offshore island acclaimed as one of the world's best dive sites and described by Jacques Cousteau as one of nature's finest works of art. Having crossed the mountainous wilderness of Borneo, my plane touched down at Tawau in the northeastern corner of this huge island.

I was met at the airport by a driver with a minibus to take me to Semporna from where I would embark for the 1-hour voyage by fast boat to Mabul island and Borneo Divers Mabul Resort where I would be staying, about 25 minutes by boat from Sipadan.

Sipadan is justifiably one of the top-rated diving destinations in the world. A tiny tree-clad island perched on top of a pinnacle of rock that rises about 600 metres (over 1800 feet) from the ocean floor, its walls are festooned with corals, sponges, anemones, and an enormous variety of marine creatures make there home there. The drop-off is remarkable. Swim out from the beach about ten metres and you are on the edge of a sub-sea cliff that drops almost sheer to the ocean floor 600 metres below. You look over the edge and all you see is that vertical wall dropping into a dark blue void. You hover above the edge and allow yourself to drop over and down, down, down and level off at around 30 metres depth (about 100 feet) and gaze in wonder at the strange creatures living in this submarine tower block. This is a high density population, with every hole a source of fascination, the residence of fish, shrimps, lobster, octopus, resting sharks sleeping after a night's hunting, or sleeping turtles exhausted after laying several dozen eggs ashore in a hole dug in the sand.

The number of turtles was astonishing. At first the camera was clicking away merrily, but after seeing literally dozens of them it becomes so commonplace you scarcely give them a glance. White-tip reef sharks were also abundant, with a few grey reef sharks cruising along the reef in the deep water. At one site, aptly named Barracuda Point, the barracuda, long torpedo shaped fish, sleek and fast, streamlined like a jet fighter plane for effective hunting and with a vicious set of teeth, schooled in their hundreds above us. We were deep below and it was like a cloud passing overhead, blotting out the light.

The drop off was a favourite place for seeing a huge school of jacks, or big-eyed trevally. They swirled round in a tall circle, like the cloud that forms in a tornado, with a clear hole in the centre where the diver can enter and hover within this dense mass of fish, all circling around him, thousands of them, all packed closely together, going nowhere. Get underneath this living tower of fish and look up and it is like looking up a dark chimney to the light far above on the surface of the sea, an amazing sight. All they do is go round in circles all day long, but at night they split up and hunt; sleek, fast, deadly killers.

A week there passed all too soon and it was time to move on yet again. I had had an unfortunate experience with the agency that booked the diving for me. They had promised me six days at Mabul resort, but it could only accommodate me for two nights. I had to spend two nights at two other resorts nearby, but still had to go back for my food and diving with Borneo Divers. The agency had known of this for over two months, since I booked, had fixed this hotch-potch arrangement, but did not tell me until two days before I arrived. I was not happy.

Well, blazin' mad would be a more accurate description.

However, I had plenty of sympathy from the resort staff and all expressed their regret that I had my stay spoiled by this inconvenience. When I left I was astonished at the farewell I received. It seemed like every one of the employees at the resort came out to say goodbye. The boys came out from the dive centre and the girls from the restaurant. Some who were on the late shift even gave up their free time to come to say goodbye. The manager and reception staff came and shook my hand and even the managing director's wife came out specially to see me off.

They all asked me to come back and I did, next time with "Mr Ray-From-The-USA" - Ray Casavant, a gentleman of similar vintage to myself whom I met in the Philippines on a Tubbataha reef live-aboard, and who has given me no peace ever since.

After the first morning's dive, our heads broke the surface of the sea, glistening wet in the warm, morning sun. I looked around me. It was a heavenly morning, a cloudless sky above and the surface of the sea like silk, smooth and unruffled. To my right the colour was a pale turquoise where the sunlight was reflected back from the white sandy bottom of a shallow lagoon; to my left it was a deep azure where the reef edge dropped in a dramatic, sheer wall almost two thousand feet to the floor of the Celebes Sea. Just a few degrees north of the equator here, the sun was almost directly overhead and even at 9.30 in the morning it was blistering hot.

"How was that, John?" called out Maadil, our dive guide. I spat the regulator out of my mouth.

"Great," I called back.

Ray had more to say. He always does, and waxed eloquently about its wondrous charms. Mind you, he waxes eloquently about everything. He only stops talking when he is underwater or asleep.

"Now I know what the world was like before mankind started to destroy what nature had created. At one point I just squatted on the sandy bottom and looked around me in wonder at the beauty of creation and the sheer density of the fish population, untroubled by our presence. It was like being in an underwater Garden of Eden."

That is the kind of effect Sipadan can have on people. One Italian I met on my previous visit remarked in awed tones, "When you see Sipadan, your life changes."

Our first few minutes underwater were enough to justify its claim to be among the top dive spots in the world. Immediately we had rolled backwards off the dive boat and dropped down into Sipadan's clear waters, we found ourselves mingling with the dense, swirling school of thousands of big-eyed trevally, attracting the photographers and especially the videographers among us.

However, that was immediately upstaged by another of Sipadan's star turns. Behind the swirling mass, Maadil pointed over to the reef. Hovering above it was the biggest school of bumphead parrotfish I have ever seen - dozens of them, all clustered closely together, milling around over the coral. These large, rather grotesque creatures - the Frankenstein Monsters of the sea, with their distorted bumped foreheads - have the most impressive front teeth. With these huge, chisel-like protuberances, ideal for crunching the hard coral which is their diet, they appear to grin evilly at you when you view them head on.

Normally pretty shy, they usually keep their distance. However, like so many other inhabitants of Sipadan's walls and reefs, the bumpheads tolerate the presence of the diving paparazzi and their eagerly clicking cameras. You can get up close and personal and enjoy that rather bizarre smile they appear to offer you.

For those who get a buzz of excitement from seeing sharks, well, there are sharks aplenty. White tip reef sharks and grey reef sharks abound, with the odd hammerhead wandering around too. They are usually resting after a night's hunting, lying on the sandy ledges until the diver gets too close with the camera and then, with a slight flick of the tail, they glide off effortlessly, sleek and streamlined, like a grey torpedo to find solitude once more. They are not aggressive. Timid is a more apt description of most sharks.

The only problem with Sipadan is that it attracts so many divers and now the Malaysian government enforces strict controls over the numbers allowed to dive there in order to preserve this priceless natural environment. A small military presence is maintained on the island to enforce the regulations. No one is allowed to stay on the island now; most dive operators have premises on nearby Mabul or Kapalai, but divers are permitted to take rest breaks ashore between dives. A limited number of permits is allocated each day so you may have to wait for a few days before your turn comes round. That can mean disappointment for those who may only have booked a couple of days there. Better to stay for about five days at least to be sure of one or two days diving at Sipadan, and that usually means four dives per day there.

When we were not diving at Sipadan we explored the waters around Mabul, where we were staying at Borneo Divers' Resort, and Kapalai, a reef and sand bank with a resort built on stilts a few kilometres away. These islands have some reefs on one side, but on the north side they have only sandy bottoms. However, a number of artificial reefs have been created here with sunken bamboo frames, scrap iron, old tyres etc, and these attract an interesting range of creatures. On one frame lives a huge grouper, a cod-like fish of enormous proportions. It has been estimated to weigh 500lbs.

At the other end of the size scale you can find ghost pipefish, pygmy seahorses, frogfish and several varieties of nudibranchs - the slugs of the sea. Much more colourful and attractive than our normal land slugs, they're eagerly sought out by photographers. They don't move much and are usually highly coloured, so they make good - and willing - subjects for photos.

Lying motionless and well camouflaged on the bottom are several large crocodile fish. Members of the sea scorpion family, it is the long crocodile-like snout that gives them their name. But what I find so fascinating about them are their eyes, with what appears to be lace-curtain eyelids, which I imagine offers some camouflage. They are an irresistible attraction for close up photography.

Another star turn was a giant moray eel holed up in a pile of scrap metal and old tyres with its mouth wide open to allow a small cleaner wrasse to come in to clean its teeth: a good example of a symbiotic relationship in which the eel gets its dental care and the wrasse feeds on the scraps of fish clinging to the eel's large teeth.

What the northern shores of these small islands lack in colourful corals, they make up for in interesting creatures, offering the photographer plenty to seek out. The reefs around them lie to the south and west and they offer the usual selection of reef-dwelling marine life. After one particularly interesting dive during which I captured some good images on camera of a blue ribbon eel out swimming freely - a rare sight - I made a major blunder and erased every photo I had taken on the two dives that morning before I had transferred them to the computer. I won't go into details of how (it is too embarrassing!), but I'll just say it was one of the incredibly stupid things I am capable of from time to time.

Adjacent to our resort were two fishing villages. A walk through these simple communities reveals how distant we are in terms of amenities. Water is still pumped out of the ground by hand and in such a low lying, free draining island it is pretty brackish. They do have a limited supply of electricity, powered by a generator. It is switched on at night only. The houses are as simple as it is possible to be. Usually only a single room perched on stilts, the air circulates below and that helps keep them cool. Inside there is nothing in the way of furniture. They sit on the floor, they sleep on the floor, they eat on the floor, with fingers only. Family planning has yet to be heard of here. Hordes of young children swarm around the village playing on what passes for streets, gaps between the houses with nothing more than the sandy beach nature provided. Many of them are of the sea gypsy tribes of South East Asia, though less nomadic than their counterparts in Burma. While the men travel to fish, the women and children stay put, living out their simple lives on the shore.

The occasion also proved to have a pleasant social aspect too. Ray and I had a lot of fun. We were named the Odd Couple, two old farts who constantly argued and insulted each other, and provided entertainment for the others.

One night, the resort organised a barbecue and party on the beach with a few silly games thrown in for fun. We started with musical chairs, and who should be the last two competitors but Ray and I. Now, dive buddies we may be, but when it came to winning a game of musical chairs there was no love lost, no quarter given, no gentlemanly give and take. This was not cricket. This was a ferociously savage struggle for possession of that last chair.

It was war!

I had developed a good technique for getting me to the final, using a seductive Polynesian dance style around the chairs with knees bent and hips swaying sensuously to the music - go on, imagine me in a grass skirt with coconuts covering the boobs. It was a style that mesmerised both the audience and the opposition, and had the added advantage that it kept my backside closer to the chair than the others so when the music stopped I had less distance to travel.

Ray's approach was more brute force and ignorance. He had already bent the legs of one chair in competition with a large Chinese guy, the two of them rolling about on the grass trying to keep on clutching the chair to their backsides.

So that was the two contrasting styles that played out the final and when my cheeks hit that chair first, a fraction of a second before his (though he disputes that, of course), Ray's ice hockey style barging managed to elbow one cheek of mine off by virtue of his weight advantage. The man had no finesse, just brute force, but I clung tenaciously on with the other, my right leg providing an angled strut digging into the ground that buttressed my claim determinedly.

Bum to bum, we fought it out, the only two pensioners in the resort fighting like tigers in a territorial struggle for one small chair, and the audience loved it. The management realised that the only way to restore peace was by awarding us each a prize.

An American lady afterwards laughingly told me, "I loved your dance style, John. It was very entertaining. But I have never seen two grown men getting so competitive over a chair!"

"Grown men?" Ray exploded. "We haven't grown up yet! We are still kids."

The flight from Tawau back to Kota Kinabalu started well enough, with pleasant sunny skies all the way across Borneo offering a superb view of Mount Kinabalu's craggy summit. Its strikingly gaunt, serrated ridges and multiple gnarled summits towered above the clouds that enveloped the surrounding jungle. And that was the problem. The clouds.

Looking out of the window on the port side of the plane the sky was greyish black; a floor-to-ceiling wall of ominous, intensely dark cloud frequently illuminated by flashes of lightning. Underneath that black shroud was Kota Kinabalu, where we were supposed to be touching down and transferring to our flight to Manila.

The plane banked to starboard, veering away from the thunderstorm. We flew out over the sea. Then it banked to port. I was hoping it would be just a matter of circling around for maybe 20 minutes till the storm passed. The intercom crackled into life. "This is the captain speaking.... I am sorry to report that due to bad weather over Kota Kinabalu no planes are being allowed to land or take off so we are being diverted to Brunei until the thunderstorm over Kota Kinabalu passes on and we will get you back to Kota Kinabalu as soon as we can."

"As soon as we can...." My heart sank. That kind of vagueness is not encouraging. Half an hour flying time down the coast to Brunei and the same on the way back up, plus whatever time we would spend on the ground would almost certainly mean we would miss our flight to Manila. However, there was nothing else for it but to sit it out and wait. In the event, we arrived just as our flight for Manila was preparing to depart from its starting gate. Budget airlines don't wait around for latecomers. The plane left without us and we had to buy new tickets for the next flight to Manila the following afternoon. There is no money back or transferring flights with budget carriers. That's the travelling life for you.

It was fun (in a masochistic sort of way) travelling with Ray. He expressed a fascination in everything he saw and always carried a wide-eyed look of curiosity. A great observer, he is a compulsive talker and commentator. I frequently implored him, with my usual diplomatic, rustic, charm, "Ray! Shut up!" However, I actually miss him - well, not a lot - but he is such a compellingly likeable character and, although we argued interminably, we laughed a lot and provided plenty of laughs for the others with whom we mingled. He is not quite as sophisticated a traveller though and I had to teach him a few tricks about flying with budget airlines.

Number one is to travel light. Why do Americans think that they need so much baggage? I had my dive bag with my dive kit as check-in baggage, but all the rest of my personal stuff for six months travelling fits into my carry-on bag, with room to spare. Ray was abroad for a month and appeared with a convoy of bags on wheels, plus a backpack that was almost twice the permitted carry-on weight. This led to some interesting or, more accurately, confusing discussions at check-in desks about excess baggage costs. No two airlines or airports seem to apply the same rules. Ray, quite understandably, had a permanent look of bewilderment about him. Although this is almost home territory to me now and I can almost always predict what will happen at each airport, I still get snared occasionally as one check-in clerk will decide to interpret the rules differently from all the others. Sometimes you can negotiate, other times you just go with the flow and pay up. It is still a cheap flight

Another of the problems with budget airlines is that they don't bother to board the flights according to seat number and simply allow a free-for-all. This is a wee bit inconvenient if you get stuck near the end of the queue as Filipinos tend to carry far more cabin baggage than they should and you may find you can't get space in an overhead locker for your hand luggage. I like to keep my laptop close at hand. However, Air Asia gives priority boarding to adults with young children and the elderly and infirm. Now Ray is very proud of his youthful good looks and excellent physique which make him look more than 20 years younger than he is. Of course, these are his words, not mine! Listen, this is the guy who, when we were enjoying some banter with our waitress and she asked him how old he was, said to her, "How old do you think I am? I will give you a clue by telling you I am nearer to 50, than I am to 40."

The girl thought for a moment. "Mmmm… I think…about 46?"

He beamed a massive smile at her and said, "Oh, you are such a smart girl!"

As she walked off with our order, I gave him a withering look. "You bullshit merchant! Have you no conscience?"

Without a vestige of shame, he held his head erect with the innocent look of a cherub and replied, "Well, it's true - 68 is nearer to 50 than it is to 40!" As you can see, I had to call for a significant change of image when we found ourselves at the end of a very long queue at the departure gate.

I hissed at him: "Ray, do exactly as I tell you. For once, act your age! Droop your head, let your shoulders sag, shuffle your feet and limp, like this, and don't say a word!" And I did a passably good demonstration of the elderly and infirm who would get priority boarding as I shuffled, limping and dragging my left foot across the floor behind me, clutching at his arm for support and gasping my way audibly to the front of the queue. Ray had a look of total bewilderment on his face.

As we approached the girl controlling the crowd at the gate I murmured, in a sickly, hoarse and tremulous voice, "Elderly and infirm?" She waved us through without hesitation along with another elderly and infirm, stooping, drooping and shuffling couple who clutched each other for support. Then, as we exited the terminal to cross the apron to the aircraft, I stepped out briskly towards the plane and muttered, "See, that's all it takes."

Ray finally exploded, "Well, I've seen it all now! You talk about me?" He was spluttering for words. "You are the biggest bullshit merchant ever. You hirpled up to that gate like you would never even make it to the aircraft and look at you now…. stepping out like a teenager. What are all those people in the queue gonna be thinking now?"

"Who cares? We're first on the plane." I said smugly.

He shook his head and chuckled, "Well, this trip has proved to be an education for me." And when we entered the aircraft cabin who did we find smiling a delectably warm welcome to us, but the very same extremely attractive flight attendant who had been on our outward flight to Borneo. Air Asia have the most attractive female flight attendants. It is worth taking a flight just to get a look at them.

Ray beamed at her lustily, "How nice to see you again! You know, I called the chief executive of Air Asia and requested that you should be on our return flight to take care of us once again."

Smooth-talking, bullshit merchant!

"Well, thank you, sir. I look forward to being of service to you again," and she nurtured his unbridled lust with another dazzling smile and a fetching giggle.

He held every inch of his 68 year-old youthful physique erect as he strode up the aisle behind me, smirking and mimicking her sensuous voice, " 'I look forward to being of service to you once again, sir.' D'ya hear that? Yes please, Ma'am! Elderly and infirm? Huh."

As usual, he managed to get the last word.

And the first.

And most of the words in between!

Chapter 20

Thailand

The land of smiles, as well as sights and sounds and smells quite unlike anything
I had ever experienced, Thailand is a charming country. Friendly and fun loving,
the Thai people were always ready to smile and speak with you. For my first
visit I had booked adventure travel tours to both north and south. Having a guide
for a first visit to a country where language may be a problem seemed a good
idea. It was. After that I was able to return and travel independently with ease.
Thailand surprised me. It is much more developed than I had imagined with
bustling, modern cities yet, by way of contrast, the city streets are thronged with
people and market traders selling cooked food, meat, fish, vegetables, spices,
clothes, sculptures, paintings, trinkets and just about everything that can be sold.
In some places, the bicycle powered rickshaw still competes for passengers with
the motor taxi and the ubiquitous tuk-tuk, the poor people's transport.

The smells are distinctive, not only the spices and delicious food, but also
from the drains. Thai drains stink! Everywhere. Eating freshly cooked food
outside is a delight in the evening, but not if you are downwind of an evil
smelling drain. Always have a good sniff around first to check that no offensive
effluvium is likely to drift your way.

Amazing, fantastic, incredible, beautiful, are only some of the words that
can be used to describe the Thai Buddhist temples. They are everywhere,
arresting sights with the burnished golds, whites, reds, blues and greens of the
incredibly detailed decoration of their rather bizarre architecture glinting in the
sunlight. And around them are the Buddhist monks, shaven headed, wearing
saffron robes, adding another distinctive dash of colour.

After a day's sightseeing in Bangkok, we headed north for two weeks. This
adventure tour was aimed at introducing us to some of Thailand's culture, way
of life and outstanding sights, as well as offering the opportunity to trek, live in
primitive villages with hill tribes and explore some of its rivers by kayak and
barge. It was excellent value, a great way to get an introduction to a new country
where language difficulties may be a problem.

First stop after Bangkok was Kanchenaburi on the River Kwai where the
famous Bridge Over The River Kwai was built during World War Two. The
bridge carried the so-called death railway to aid the Japanese imperialist
expansion westwards through Thailand and Burma towards India. Built not only
by allied prisoners of war, but also tens of thousands of Thai and Burmese
civilians, the dreadful conditions, malnutrition and cruelty of the regime under
which they worked resulted in the deaths of over 300 000 people working on its
construction. The famous bridge, immortalised in literature and film, and now a
magnet for tourists, still carries trains over the river and stands as a monument
to those who died there.

A two-day river trip on a former rice barge, now converted to carry passengers, offered many fascinating glimpses of life on the river. All along the banks of the river people live and work, fish and play, do their laundry and even bathe themselves in it, while the river traffic ploughs on incessantly, small craft and large, like the enormous barges dragged by ridiculously small tugs. These barge people live a nomadic life going wherever the cargo is to be taken, living on their barges. I loved it all, the bustle and variety and colour of it. There was also time to explore villages by bicycle and see how rural people lived.

After a visit to Ayutthaya, once the ancient capital of Siam, the trip up north to Chang Mai and Chang Rai proved interesting, the highlight being a steamy trek through jungle, up and over steep mountains, staying with hill tribe people from the Akha and Lisu tribes, people who still live in traditional style in huts made of bamboo and thatch. The huts have no windows and not even a chimney to let the smoke from the cooking fires escape. It simply drifts out through the door or any other space it can find as the structures are only loosely put together. Although these people would be termed poor compared to us they were always smiling, and seemed a contented lot. They work in fields won from forest cleared from steep slopes, growing vegetables and coffee and fruit.

These tribes migrated to Thailand from Tibet and China, staying first in Burma then leaving for Thailand about a hundred years ago. Their dress is distinctive too. The long, warm clothing they wear is more appropriate to the climate of Tibet, and how they can wear clothes like that in this climate amazes me. We were trekking in sweaty temperatures in the mid 30s, although it does get cool at night. In the evenings, children performed traditional songs and dances around a campfire. At one village school we spent some time teaching them English and playing games with them outside.

On the overnight train journey north to Chiang Mai the dining car doubled as a disco, with the staff playing some lively music and dancing their way to the tables with food and drinks. That encouraged a real party atmosphere and when our group leader insisted I get the spoons out, the party really took off. There were smiles everywhere and then the dancing started, with Brits dancing with French, Austrians with Italians, and the charming Thai waitresses dancing with everyone as they served the drinks. Coming back south the waitresses recognised us immediately and we had another party that night too.

Unfortunately, my beloved wooden spoons became a casualty on the night train to Chiang Mai. As usual, people wanted to try them and one of our group who had a bit too much to drink got carried away, banged them down really hard and broke them. My heart sank. I had owned them for many years and they had been round the world five times with me. It was touching to see the looks on everyone else's face. People came over to console me as though a death had occurred, and the young man who broke them was really gutted. However, that forced me to try to make a set when I returned home and I have been making and selling them ever since.

While waiting for the northbound train at the station at Ayutthaya, I looked around the hundreds of faces and my eye rested on two Japanese girls - students, I thought. One of them looked up at me. Her eyes seemed to carry a message, something like 'I'd like you to talk to me' and her eyes lit up with a wee smile.

Left: Bartolomé Island, Galapagos: a very young landscape, volcanic ash cones and lava flows which few plants have yet colonised.

Right:
Marine Iguana.

Left:
Galapagos is
a wildlife photographer's
dream: Brown Pelican
taking off.

Right:
Flamingo

Below:
Male Frigate
bird mating
display.

Left:
Baby Sea Lion

Above: Welcome to Jakarta: the worst floods for 75 years - 350,000 homeless.

Left:
Thailand - transport
in the hills.

Right:
Aka hill tribe
headdress

Left:
Ifugao woman.
My rustic charm
managed to get a
smile on a face
weathered by
labour on the
rice terraces at
Banaue.

Right:
Banaue rice
terraces in the
Philippines,
carved out by
hand by the
Ifugao people
about 3000
years ago,
hundreds of
miles of them!

Left:
He sits and smiles
all day.

Left:
Jeepney -
transport of the
proletariat in
Philippines.

Right:
Life in Manila
slums

Left:
Large families,
small houses,
so many sleep on the
street.

Left: Whale shark - the largest fish in the sea, but like the manta ray, another gentle giant.

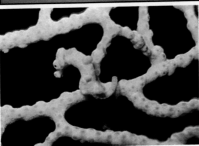

Above: Pygmy Seahorse: only 20 mm from nose to tail, so the body you see is only about half that.

Above: Sea slugs are much more colourful than land slugs with thousands of varieties

Right: Manta Ray dwarfs the diver wth its 5 metre wing span.

Weird landscape of the summit of Mt Kinabalu (4095 m/13435 ft) in the dawn light.

Above: Rocks glowing like coals in a fire   *Above*: As the sun rises above the horizon

Fabulous sand castle. These were built every day.

Above:
The smoking cone and caldera of
Mt Bromo in the dawn light, with
Mt Semeru in the background.

Left:
Mt Bromo: inside the crater.

Below:
Walking along the edge of the
crater of Mt Bromo.

I smiled and said "Hello." She responded warmly and I engaged them both in conversation. Both architecture students, they hoped to come to Europe to study architecture and a visit to Scotland is a must for them now after I let them see some pictures I had on my laptop. What amused me most was that the young men in our group stood back in amazement for a few minutes. Eventually they came over and joined us, asking to be introduced to the girls who were both quite attractive. One of the boys muttered in my ear, "John, how the hell do you do it? You're only in here two minutes and you're already chatting to two beautiful girls." There must be something, like a friendly puppy-dog look, that encourages people to talk.

Two days later in Chiang Mai I was wandering alone along a street heading for an open-air restaurant and I heard a cry, "John!" It was the two Japanese girls again. I was wearing the kilt this time and they had to get pictures taken with me, after which they joined me for dinner. At the next table were four Vietnamese people who had been attending an educational conference. Before long, they too were deep in conversation with us. More pictures had to be taken. As I stood in the middle of the group for a photo, I noticed some of our travel group had arrived at another table, watching all this with interest. "You've done it again, John. Wherever you go you seem to make friends so easily." How? I really don't know, but who cares? It's one of the great pleasures of travel.

And so too was travelling by elephant. It seemed a bit precarious at first, perched up so high on these massive, lumbering beasts, but what amazing creatures they are, and how careful and gentle, delicately placing their feet so diligently on narrow paths along, up and down some fairly steep slopes. They are really loveable.

Following our return to Bangkok, we headed south to experience what southern Thailand had to offer - and it had plenty; beautiful beaches and amazing islands, great food, warm sea and superb diving. The night train from Bangkok to southern Thailand proved to be just as entertaining as the train north had been. Wan, the charming Thai girl who was our tour leader for this southern part of the trip, asked in her delightful accent, "John, you want to go to Pahtee Cah?" Pahtee cah, or Party Car, is the term commonly used for the restaurant car as a result of its frequent use by travellers for some revelry on the overnight train. Having been briefed by our previous guide she knew what to expect from me. We had another lively party, having joined up with other travellers heading the same way.

Alighting at Surat Thani, we moved on by road into the Koh Sok National Park to stay in bamboo raft houses for a couple of days. These were constructed on floating rafts of bamboo poles on a deep lake amidst some stunning scenery. The landscape here is predominantly limestone with towering precipitous cliffs soaring up out of the lake and jungle. Limestone caves abound and we went exploring underground as well as on the lake and in the jungle.

Our local jungle guide demonstrated how to swing on a vine, Tarzan style, and then challenged anyone to try it. I was first in line, but he then started arguing, "No, John. You too old. Need to be stlong to do this. Too dangelous for you." (They have difficulty pronouncing the letter R - it comes out as L). I gave him a withering look and grabbed the vine.

"Havers," I retorted, and before he could drag it back from me I was swinging out over the gully, like Tarzan indeed. It was a long vine - and a long pendulum swings more slowly than a short one - so it was a slow-motion, leisurely glide out over the gully and back again to the cheers of the group and a very relieved smile from the local guide, who now changed his tune.

"Oh John, you vely stlong man," he gushed, feeling my biceps with great admiration.

"Aye, and don't you forget it!" I growled back at him with a grin.

On an evening boat trip on the lake we stopped to watch the sunset. Suddenly, high up on top of a cliff about 300 feet high, erupted a black cloud. Not smoke, bats. Thousands of them. Big fruit bats, about the size of chickens, poured out of the cave that was their home for their nocturnal feed. It was an amazing sight as they surged up and headed east, all in one column about thirty bats wide, like a huge motorway in the sky.

Living on the lake was not without some small pleasures. We had a floating bar. It was accessible by bamboo raft, connected to shore and bar by a rope, which you pulled to take yourself across. The barmaid was a lovely girl from Croatia who had fallen for one of the local lads. She was a real asset to the bar as our young lads were happy to spend all day there, feasting their eyes on her and supping beer to cool their ardour. And at night lying on our backs on the raft we gazed heavenwards at the myriad stars in a sky unpolluted by artificial light, and gazed and wondered and talked about philosophy, the nature of the universe and all the things that star-gazing and a few drinks make you want to talk about.

For more living close to nature, we moved on to some jungle huts. This is a jungle where tigers and elephants still roam wild, where many poisonous snakes slither among the trees, notably the King Cobra, and the monkeys chatter among the tree tops and come down to the river to drink in the evenings. The night noises in the jungle are fascinating, from the incessant screeching of the wings of the cicadas, living among the trees, to the whoops of monkeys and the cat-like screeches of fighting squirrels and strange unidentified rustlings in the bush. It adds a touch of excitement to a walk to the toilet block in the middle of the night. Especially when you confront a lizard the size of a small crocodile occupying the toilet. That cleared a few bowels rapidly. A lot of people would not go to the toilet alone at night.

On our last morning there when we were leaving, Wan, our leader, came down the steps from her hut – they are all on stilts - reached out to grasp the handrail as she was carrying her rucksack and gasped when she almost placed it on top of a 2 metre long green snake which was slithering up the rail. I grabbed my camera and rushed up to photograph it. It had no malicious intent, it was merely making its way up to the roof for a bit of sunbathing, but one of the local boys dislodged it with a long bamboo pole and it meandered off in the bush. Things like that do make you think twice about going to the toilet in the middle of the night.

But it was the latter part of this journey I really loved, when we finally arrived at the coast. Again we spent most of the time in remote places rarely visited, shunning the tourist flesh pots like Phuket and Koh Samui in favour of less well known small idyllic islands like Koh Muk and Koh Rok. But first we had a homestay with a Thai family near Krabi. This is a mostly Moslem area so there were matters of protocol to be observed when staying with this family; long trousers only, no bare shoulders, shoes off before entering the house, no alcohol etc. The owner took us to tap rubber from his plantation and picked some fresh pineapples for us to eat, then we all sat on the floor to eat a huge dinner the women had prepared for us.

The food was good except that in one dish of mixed vegetables, which was moderately spicy, I bit into a red-hot chilli which scorched its way down my throat. My stomach felt like I had swallowed a hot coal and it burned long into the night. It was about 3am before the fire within me had subsided to a glow and I could get to sleep. Since then I have been ultra cautious about what I eat, inspecting every morsel carefully.

Next day I was off to dive around Koh Phi Phi, while the others took a boat trip to the beaches there and snorkelled. The diving was very colourful with huge overhangs of rock where the sheer cliff faces had been eroded by the sea. The islands here are really spectacular.

The following day, a couple of hours drive and a short voyage by long-tailed boat took us to Koh Muk, a small island offshore on the west side of the South Thai Peninsula. It has a superb beach with huts nestling among the rubber trees. These boats use a conventional diesel engine, but like an outboard, balanced neatly on a cradle at the stern of the traditional boat with a long propeller tube trailing astern, hence the name, long tail boat. The boatman can raise or lower the prop out of the water, so finely balanced is the engine, and can swivel it round too. They are handy in shallow waters where they can beach the bow with ease to let people off and ease the propeller out of the water to avoid damage.

Koh Rok where we were to camp for a few days was our next destination. On the way out we stopped just off the sheer 300-foot cliffs of Koh Muk and jumped into the sea. Ahead of us lay the entrance to a large cave about 80 metres long. We swam in, our leader having a powerful waterproof torch. Deep inside, the cave was in total darkness as it swung first one way and then the other, blanking out the light from the entrance. Then, after the second turn we saw light ahead. Rounding a bend we were confronted by the most amazing sight, an emerald glow of light from the water and a beautiful white beach ahead. We stepped out into the sunshine, finding ourselves on the floor of a huge hole in the limestone, about 100 metres across and 100 metres (300 feet) deep, with sheer vertical sides. The only way, short of absailing, that you can get in here is by swimming through that tunnel. It was an astonishing sight. And the only way out, unless you are an expert rock climber, was to swim back through the cave. Fantastic!

Back on board our boat we sailed on for another couple of hours to get to Koh Rok, another paradise island with stunning beaches and great snorkelling, and all the rustlings and mutterings that you hear in a jungle night. I loved it and slept out in the open under the stars in a hammock for three nights in preference to lying on the hard ground in a tent which I found hot, hard and stuffy. I always wore insect repellent and that worked perfectly, keeping the mosquitos at bay, but it did not stop one lizard which fancied sharing the hammock with me. Fortunately it was only a small lizard and I was able to eject it easily.

The snorkelling was good and I skin-dived to observe lobsters, a variety of fish, including some big moray eels, and explored the wreck of a fishing boat. I also managed to teach one of our group, Mike, a fifty year old landlubber from South Dakota, USA, and Wan, our tour leader, to swim. She was so delighted to be able to swim at last so we set off together and explored the bay with mask and snorkel. She was so thrilled and squeezed my hand tightly when we got back, bubbling with joy, "Oh, thank you so much, John." To have success with both my students and introduce them to the delights of snorkelling made my day.

Back on Koh Muk I fitted in another couple of dives. These islands are only rarely dived and have some superb sites with some colourful soft coral gardens and a great variety and density of fish. On one island, a big rock pinnacle about four hundred feet high standing proud of the sea, we went cave diving, dropping off the boat just below the cliffs and descending to about 15 metres depth.

The cliff undersea was perpendicular and presented a colourful wall laden with marine life to explore, but then a large gap opened up and in we went, into the great dark void beneath this huge rock. It was big and dark and teeming with fish, eerily picked out of the gloomy depths in the beam of the torch; a flash of silver here and great school of silver sides glinting there, then a shadowy movement of something big and dark making its way off into the gloom. And all the time I kept thinking this was not far from the earthquake that shook the world and caused the devastating tsunami in 2004, so what would happen if we suddenly had another one while we were in here, deep in the innards of this great lump of rock. Would we be entombed, or crushed to death?

It was quite thrilling, but these thoughts must not be allowed to dominate your thinking. The probability was so slight it was not worth bothering about, so why spoil the day. The cave formed a U shape and we turned the last bend to gaze into the greenish blue light of the second entrance with hundreds of fish silhouetted against the glowing light. It was a great dive.

That was the finale to my trip to South Thailand. We turned about there, to catch the night train to Bangkok again. The "Pahtee Cah" was not so good this time. Neither the train staff nor the other travellers were in much of a party mood. I was in my bunk by 8.30pm. An hour or so later I heard voices raised in concern about two of our group who had stayed on and drank too much. They were arguing with the restaurant car staff about being charged for beer they claimed they hadn't drunk. Wan had gone to try to calm things down, but they were just too drunk to listen to reason and she came back disgusted. This was an unfortunate way to end what had been a very harmonious trip so I got out of my bed and went along. I didn't like what I saw. The atmosphere had become tense, verging on ugly. Voices were raised and language was less than genteel. Five armed railway policemen were standing by watching very carefully as two of our boys still tried to persuade the drinkers to leave and a glance round the other faces in the car revealed a lot of tension, with a few ready to lay some punches was my reckoning.

This was a time for swift action: a touch of diplomacy, with firmness, tact and sensitivity. I waded in and grabbed the loud-mouthed guy and pinned him against the wall. I whispered some sweet nothings in his ear, in a rasping, low voice that carried all the menace I could muster and spelled out rapidly what was in store for him if he did not listen to what Papa John was telling him, but all done in a most loving and caring manner. It worked. I got him turned round and shepherded him back to the sleeping car. With him out of the way the two other boys, who were sober, then managed to persuade the nineteen year old girl who was with him to come quietly too and we got them both back to bed. They both apologised to the group in the morning and the boy went back to apologise to the restaurant car staff too. It was then he noticed one of the policeman on board wearing a big revolver on his belt and realised that there had been some sense in what I had said the night before. He quickly apologised to the policeman too!

That was the final bit of excitement for Papa John, peacemaker and father figure of the group. It had been fun being with them for four weeks and we all got on remarkably well and I still hear the voice of my young, drunk friend offering me the ultimate compliment, "John, I wish you were my Dad."

It had been quite hectic over the four weeks with a lot of travelling to do, but I had seen so much of the country and its culture, much more with this organised adventure tour than I would have seen if I had arrived and tried to arrange things independently. It was good to have all the transport and accommodation arrangements in place and staying in the homes of Thai people was an added bonus. For a first visit it was an ideal way to get to know the country. Having done it once though, I had no fear about returning and doing my own thing. I knew my way about now.

Once again, this trip brought home to me how much I feel a need to be close to the sea. Much as I enjoyed trekking and visiting the hill tribes, I still felt a longing to get near salt water and there was a definite feeling of relief when I got my first sight of the sea again. The Thai people were lovely and friendly in the main, perhaps some a little bit tainted by what mass tourism has done to the country. That is the inevitable price that has to be paid as we travel more and discover unspoiled places. We quickly encourage more people to visit them and so the nature of the place changes, the people change and we destroy that which attracted us there in the first place. I'm glad I found some places in Thailand that are still unspoiled, but I felt a measure of discomfort in others, usually where the tourists throng. In Bangkok it was more than a discomfort, at times a sort of revulsion. It has become a Mecca, not only for youthful backpackers, but also for ageing, swinging, pot-smoking, tattooed, body-pierced hippies swaggering about the streets of Bangkok with rings in their noses, and other places, dressed in a uniform of new-age clothes with long, greying hair tied back in pony tails and wisps of finger thick beards dangling limply from their chins.

I am not a city person.

I could not wait to get out of the place.

Chapter 21

Mantas For Birthday

We were kitting up as the dive boat made passage southwards from Phuket. "How old are you, John?" The dive guide asked.

"Sixty-six today," I told the dive guide.

"Oh, so what would you like to see on your birthday dives?"

"Och, a couple of manta rays will do fine."

Maybe Poseidon, the god of the sea, was listening, for when we did our second dive that day there were two beautiful, big manta rays circling around us, graceful, elegant, magnificent, flapping their wings slowly and gliding effortlessly around and above us. One parted a dense school of trevally and came straight towards me with its mouth wide open giving me the opportunity for a photo looking directly into that huge mouth. Inevitably, our guide claimed all the credit that he had fixed it for my birthday and word got around, so everyone else was gracious and wished me happy birthday, but none more delightfully so than Lina, a charming flight attendant with Singapore Airlines. We had chatted all the way out on the boat from Phuket and on hearing the news that it was my birthday, she held my hand, looked into my eyes and sang Happy Birthday to me, then gave me a wee kiss on the cheek. She then had her friend take a picture of us together and we exchanged email addresses. We have been in regular contact ever since. Now married, she has given birth to her first baby, Sofia, an adorable wee charmer who has been blessed with her mother's good looks. Radin, her husband, is justifiably proud of the beautiful daughter he has created - but he generously concedes that Lina had a part to play in that too.

When we arrived back in port just at dusk, the sky suddenly erupted in a riot of colour and noise as a fireworks display started.

"Hey John, they've fixed up quite a show for your birthday," she joked. It was a nice coincidence that it was timed exactly as we entered port.

The diving in Thailand and Myanmar is mostly around rock pinnacles and small islands that often soar vertically upwards out of the sea. The landscape is often dramatic above sea level and is no less so underwater with sheer cliffs and crevices and caves, in some cases allowing you to swim right under the islands from one side to the other.

Most of the diving in the area south of Phuket is among the small islands around Koh Phi Phi and one or two spots between it and Phuket. The wreck of the car ferry King Cruiser lies not far from a pinnacle of rock called Shark Point. Though still largely intact it is deteriorating, so penetration is limited to only those parts which are safe to enter. It is curious to go exploring deep down and find the lavatory bowls still glowing white after about 20 years in the gloom of around 30 metres of sea water.

The current here runs strongly, so the method of finding the wreck is to haul yourself down a buoy rope attached to the wreck's bow.

There are so many divers visiting this spot that you encounter groups of them clinging to the rope on their way up while having their safety stop at five metres. Let go the rope and you are soon swept off into the gloom. So the only way down is to clamber over their bodies, always hanging on with at least one hand. It is a bit of a nuisance and of course once down on the wreck there were so many other divers thrashing around, many of them inexperienced, stirring up lots of sediment, which makes it only possible to see a couple of metres or so.

The other problem was that as our group made our way around, we mingled with other groups and in the ensuing melee, my buddy got confused and started following the other group who were pounding their way around far too quickly so I had to sprint after him to get hold of his fins and turn him around again.

Shark Point is a beautiful dive consisting of three rock pinnacles, the largest of which just shows above the surface. They are festooned with beautiful corals and anemones and are home to thousands of reef fish. Every crevice seems to have a moray eel's head poking out of it, sharks and stingrays rest on the sandy bottom between the pinnacles after a night's hunting, and lion fish perform their slow-motion submarine ballet, gracefully gliding like a bunch of feathers between rocks.

Anemone reef, not far away, is another beautiful location, aptly named for it is a veritable garden of the most beautiful sea anemones; blues, reds and greens, their fronds swaying gently in the tide, every one harbouring a cute little clown anemone fish, known throughout the world now as Nemo from the Disney film. They peek out at you and then with a flick of the tail disappear among the fronds of the anemone, then show their faces again. Some have families of babies and can get quite aggressively protective if you get close. Cute they may be, but they have teeth and are prepared to bite if you don't heed their warnings.

Koh Doc Mai is one of those dramatic islands with vertical rock walls and a cave or two to explore. Small bamboo sharks can be found resting under rocky ledges, and the walls are a riot of colour, encrusted with beautiful anemones, soft corals and sponges. Appearing to almost cling to the sheer rock faces, are enormous shoals of small fish, swarming together in an opaque mass, for safety, hovering and swirling like clouds along a mountainside.

The small islands around Koh Phi Phi were rich in other interesting species like seahorses, turtles, cuttlefish, octopus and leopard sharks. These are quite nice sites and, although the visibility was not as good as I had hoped it would be, there was plenty of colour and variety of marine life to be seen close up. These were all enjoyable dives, but the sites were generally overcrowded. That is always the drawback when diving from Phuket. There are literally hundreds of divers going out every morning on the boats that depart daily from Chalong pier. Live-aboard boats offer the best value when diving from Phuket and it was on one such boat that I celebrated my 69th birthday.

Now what could a diver ask for on his birthday as he prepares for the first of five dives planned for that day? How about a great display by giant manta rays again? With maybe a whale shark thrown in as the icing on the cake? No problem, sir. Wish granted.

And so it came to pass that on the first four dives on my birthday I saw the most delightful display by manta rays ever, close up and personal, intimate almost, as it would have been possible to reach out and stroke these sleek and beautiful monsters of the deep. Huge, yet elegant and graceful as they performed their aquatic ballet, they were there to greet me on all four daytime dives, swooping and soaring and wheeling around the pinnacles of Hin Daeng and Hi Muang, two memorable dive sites in southern Thai waters.

On my first visit to Thailand I had dived some of the islands in the far south, but closer inshore, and had been impressed. Subsequent visits took me to all of the dive sites accessible daily from Phuket and on four live-aboard cruises northwards to the Similan Islands and two into Burmese waters. On one of these trips I had heard that Hin Daeng was worth diving. It was a delight.

The trip didn't start all that well though. Scheduled to leave at 5pm, we had to wait for one diver's baggage. It had not arrived on the same flight as he had, but it was due to arrive at the airport at 5pm. A driver was there to rush it through to us. His "rush" took until 9.30pm. At 4.30 pm some of the streets of Patong had been closed to traffic as a parade to celebrate the start of the "high" season was due at 5pm and this caused utter chaos. It took our truck with the dive gear and ourselves crammed into it three hours to detour the two kilometres to the jetty at Patong from where we embarked. We then had to wait till another truck with tanks of nitrox and petrol for the outboard engine on the dinghy fought its way through the grid-locked of traffic. We were scheduled to make a stop at the island of Racha Yai for a night dive on the way south at around 8pm. We were still sitting immobile in traffic at that time. It was almost 10pm before we got underway, so that ruled out the night dive. However, we then planned on fitting in five dives the following day. If we started early, with only five divers on board, the compressors would be able to cope with re-fills of air to accommodate that programme.

Waking up at 6am, after a quick cup of tea and a dive briefing, we dropped off the stern of the boat in quick succession to explore Hin Daeng. All that showed above the surface of the sea were four black, fang-toothed rocks, many miles offshore, without any navigation warning light on them as they were not in a recognised commercial shipping lane. About 300 metres away was Hin Muang, another pinnacle. It does not even break the surface of the ocean, but lurks just underneath. Our skipper had brought us safely to a mooring buoy close by these menacing rocks in the darkness. Nice work.

Dropping down to around 30 metres and working our way slowly back up we meandered among the gullies and pinnacles of what is like a small mountain range. Scenically very attractive, these rocks are covered in bright soft corals, marine algae, sponges and anemones and are teeming with fish. Even without the mantas it would have been a good dive, but the mantas made their appearance and mesmerised us from then on, soaring around the pinnacles in a majestic display of effortless power and gracefulness.

It is an awesome sight to see a monster fish weighing around 1100 kilos (5000 lbs) with a wing span of around 5 metres and jaws a metre wide banking in a steep turn and coming straight towards you. At any distance their size looks impressive and awe-inspiring, but when you get a sea monster of those dimensions approaching you closely, so closely that you could touch them, then they are simply overwhelming. They seemed to slow down on the approach to have a good look, then when it seemed a collision was inevitable, a flick of the wing tip took them soaring overhead, blanking out the sunlight, as if a large tarpaulin had been thrown over you. These were timeless moments and it took some discipline to check the gauges to make sure we had enough air to see us safely to the surface.

Breakfast on board was dominated by animated conversation after that display. And it was matched on the second dive at Hin Muang and on subsequent dives as we alternated between the two rocks. The mantas continued to delight and dominate the dives. Having seen it all before, I wandered off on my own to take photos of other things around the pinnacles. I enjoyed exploring colourful canyons on my own, gliding silently up to fish and capturing them on camera. The dive guides were unperturbed about this, knowing my experience and let me roam around unfettered, taking pictures.

Just as we were having lunch a call came through on the ship's radio from another boat that had arrived, telling us that a whale shark was cruising around Hin Muang. As we had just finished the second of two long dives we could not safely dive again so soon, but we did get masks and snorkels on and the ship's dinghy took us over and dropped us off. And there was the other giant of the deep, the largest fish in the ocean, which may grow up to 12 metres long. This one was about 7 metres I would guess, cruising at around 6 metres depth, just too far away to get a decent photo.

I was thrilled about getting all this on my birthday, but Olivier, a young Frenchman who had just completed his open water dive course with only 8 dives behind him at the start of the cruise, was witnessing a fantastic display by mantas and a whale shark, something few people see in a lifetime, and all before he had even completed 10 dives. Spoiled brat!

The best moments of all came the following morning when we did one more early dive on Hin Daeng and again we were treated to another amazing display by the mantas. As soon as we were out of the water the ship was on the move again, heading back northwards to Koh Haa, a lofty pinnacle of limestone rising sheer from the seabed. As is common with limestone pinnacles, it was riddled with tunnels offering some interesting cave exploration. Honeycombed with inter-connecting chambers and passageways, I can imagine it would not be too difficult to get lost in there. Those of us prepared to venture in followed our guide, but I have to admit that I would have liked to explore a bit further into these dark recesses than he took us.

Making passage back towards Phuket again we dived Koh Bida Nok and Koh Bida Nai, two "brother" limestone rocks with dramatic sides dropping vertically into the ocean; then on to Shark Point, after which we returned to Phuket. This cruise was well worth the money. Hin Daeng and Hin Muang in particular were excellent; scenically attractive, colourful, rugged, with as much marine life as you could wish for and the other sites all had their merits.

There are other things you can depend on in Thailand. The food is delicious and inexpensive. You can depend getting a good massage, and you can depend on having your ego massaged as well. "You handsome man, velly stlong. You got powah, good body. You no old man, you young man." It makes you feel good. Except that they do it to everyone else and when you see what some of the others look like... well, it devalues the compliment a bit.

However, my own doctor back home agreed that I was still in pretty good shape for a young man of 69.

Chapter 22

Imagine

Imagine you are having a dream. One of those dreams in which you can fly and you are soaring around a mountain top. A mountain with several pinnacles towering from its summit, its steep slopes scattered with blue and yellow flowers. It is like the kind of picture you may find in a child's fairy-tale storybook. The sky is not the bright, light blue of summer, but is of a more opaque, ethereal shade of blue, like the half-light of dawn just before the sun has risen on a clear day. The stars are there too, brilliant sapphires, gleaming; not just above, but all around you, giving you the feeling you are not in a place of this world, but are suspended in some surreal world, like floating in space.

You soar up to the highest pinnacle and hold on, resting a while, for here the winds roar over the top of the mountain making flight directly into the wind well nigh impossible. You hold on grimly, fingers straining, your body stretched taught, streaming out horizontally by the force of the wind.

As you hang on there, enjoying the view of this magical looking peak, a dark movement to your left catches your eye. From the gloom soars a huge bird, enormous, like something out of a fable. It flies towards you, its huge black back and white underside now clearly visible as the gigantic wings flap slowly, and at the last moment it flips its wings and effortlessly glides past you, so near you could almost reach out and touch it. You let go your perch and follow, entranced by this huge creature.

But it is not a bird, and you are not flying around a mountain-top. You are not in some dream-like trance, though it feels like it. You are a diver, clinging to the top of a sub-sea pinnacle in the Andaman Sea, and the great bird is not a bird at all but a giant manta ray with a five-metre wing-span. The stars that glow like the brightest of sapphires are light emitting plankton; creatures so tiny yet with the capability to outshine even the brightest of precious stones with a breathtakingly beautiful, bluish tint as they flash their light when pressure waves excite them. The flowers that adorn the mountain sides are delicate soft corals in primrose yellow, cornflower blue and pink; and all around this majestic peak swim the smaller fish in their thousands, like birds trying to hold their position in a wind that threatens to blow them away. It is not a wind of course, but a powerful ocean current.

This was the scene on at 7am on the first dive of the day. We had dropped off the stern of Jonathan Cruiser in quick succession and went straight down to Koh Bon Pinnacle. The currents here are strong and any delay could mean being swept away without even seeing this spectacular pinnacle hidden below the sea a few hundred metres west of Koh Bon Island.

Dropping down its sides into the shelter of the rock to escape the force of the full-moon tide, you become mesmerised by the variety in colour, shape and form of life around you with marine plants, algae, sponges, corals all taking their place, each secured at a level in an environment that suits it. All around you are countless numbers of fish, darting tunas flashing in like bullets to feed on the small fry that school in vast numbers like clouds hugging the sides of the rock.

However fascinating all this was, it was the mantas that stole the show that day. They kept coming back, gliding around the peak as we clung to it, fingers straining against the ferocious current. It seemed that they were as interested in observing us as we were in them as they flew past, swung round in a graceful glide and came back for another look from those strange, large eyes set so far apart on the side of the wide head. It was a breathtakingly beautiful experience.

On our second dive that day, over a ridge stretching out from the island of Koh Bon there were more. Every diver loves a manta and I separated myself from the others in order to try to escape the air bubbles as divers exhaled in order to get better photographs.

I was rewarded. A huge manta swam past, a little below me, and then it turned. It banked steeply, like an aircraft coming into the attack and made straight for me. I hovered, mesmerised, as this monster soared up towards me. I looked into its massive, wide jaws. It was only a couple of metres away now and a collision seemed inevitable. At the last moment it flipped its left wing up and over my head - I could have stroked it - and then brought it down again as it passed me.

Wow!

That was really neat. I had a close up view of its underside, a beautiful, white expanse of silky smooth skin, comme le gigot d'une jeune femme as the French might say. Fantastic. It was like a dream.

This is typical of life undersea in the Similan Islands. A string of small rocky islands, uninhabited, apart from one or two with small holiday resorts on them and the occasional nomadic sea gypsies, they are a mecca for divers. The first day was a day of kind currents and excellent visibility, long underwater views with all the usual colourful small reef fish and a few octopus around; very pretty and colourful and a nice way to start the cruise.

Then came Koh Bon Pinnacle and Ridge with their mantas and powerful currents, majestic underwater scenery and density of marine life, followed by Koh Tachai and Richeleiu Rock, Surin, and Elephant Rock and Boulder City on the way back south again with their fearsome currents and huge boulder landscapes; impressive, powerful, awesome to view and great to dive among.

It is an amazing underwater landscape, a great jumble of enormous boulders that dwarf the diver. The spaces between are like canyons, hanging with large fan corals. Rocks pile one on top of the other with spaces underneath to swim through where large, spiny lobsters secrete themselves away in dark crevices among the huge boulders, their presence betrayed by their amazingly long, white feelers and in one dark cave no fewer than five white-tipped reef sharks rested in the shade.

Having been on Jonathan Cruiser before I knew what to expect and coming aboard on the first day, I looked into the galley. Mama Lek, our 63 year-old Thai cook, was busy preparing dinner.

"Hello again, Mama Lek!" I cried.

"Mistah John! You come back!" she squealed with delight. "How are you?"
"Och, I'm fine, but a year older now."
"No! You same-same last year. You still young man!"
I laughed. "Oh, you are a charmer."
Her eyes narrowed, with a mischievous glint. "You still single?"
"Yes, of course."
"OK, I go wit' you," and she threw back her head and laughed. I laughed too, but I wonder just how serious she was.....mmmm.... she is a marvellous cook. Her cooking was one of the attractions that drew me back again and again to this vessel, altogether four times, and each trip managed to offer new experiences.

Being eaten alive at the bottom of the sea may not be everyone's idea of fun. No, you can forget all the baloney about sharks as portrayed by Hollywood and storytellers with more imagination than experience. It is the small fish that are hungry for human flesh. I was at the bottom of the Indian Ocean around the Similan Islands. Visibility was very good and the bright sunlight filtered down all of 26 metres clearly illuminating the scene; a white, sandy floor dotted with lumps of brightly coloured coral with many beautifully coloured fish flitting around in a seemingly carefree manner. I felt that way too. It was a delight to be back in such clear, warm water with a temperature of 30 degrees Celsius and I was soon taking photos.

It was then I became an item on the menu for some hungry fish. My neck, face, ears and lips were being being attacked and bitten. Like a scene from a horror movie, a host of remoras, otherwise known as cleaner wrasse, were swarming around my head like a plague of locusts, devouring me bit by bit. Incessantly and voraciously they nibbled away, tearing off dead skin cells from my lips, cheeks, forehead and scraping out the debris that had gathered in my ears. Cleaning me up, in fact.

OK, I confess I hadn't bothered to wash my face before the early morning dive. It hadn't seemed worth it, for it wasn't long after sleepily crawling out of my bunk on the dive boat that I was underwater so I might as well let the sea do the job for me. And it did, with a vengeance. I have been nibbled at before by one or two of these small fish, but this time was different. They were attacking me in hordes, like piranhas. It wasn't painful, just a series of wee sharp nips, more amusing than alarming, so I got on with my photography. Then before they had all eaten their fill of me I hit on the idea of turning my camera round and tried to point it to where I felt the nips and sure enough I got a nice picture of the last remora still nibbling away at my lips, proof of my being eaten alive on the seabed. Well, not exactly all of me, just some of me, skin cells that were redundant and would have fallen off anyway for the dust mites to eat, but it was an interesting and amusing experience.

Now this is not as bizarre as it may seem. If you go into a Thai massage parlour you may see a bath-sized fish tank with dozens of small black fish in it. The clients for a foot massage sit around the fish tank dipping their feet in the water. The fish make a dive for the feet and do just what the remoras did to me, they devour the dead skin cells and bacteria, a nice, natural way of cleaning up the skin of the feet. They are only about 3 inches long and the bites are simply ticklish, but it is a strange sensation to see your skin being devoured by a black mass of tiny fish, if you have the mental discipline to sit and watch yourself being eaten alive. However, they only seem to eat up the dead skin cells and leave the nice, clean, pink skin cells underneath intact.

Richelieu Rock was one of the places 'discovered' by Jacques Cousteau (Thai fishermen led him to it of course, but they hadn't dived on it). He reputedly described it as one of the top dive sites in the world. I would agree. Only visible as an unremarkable, tiny rock above sea level at low tide, underwater this spikey multi-summit pinnacle rises steeply from the sea floor and is ablaze with colour. The corals are simply glowing and among its caves and gullies and around its precipitous walls dwell an enormous variety of marine life forms: octopus, seahorses, harlequin shrimps, cleaner shrimps, boxer shrimps, hinge beak shrimps, ghost pipefish, banded pipefish, sting rays, spotted rays, snappers, fusiliers, trevally, spanish mackerel, tuna, long-nosed filefish, porcupine fish, boxfish, pufferfish, butterflyfish, angelfish, basslets, cardinalfish sea slugs and those beautifully coloured sea slugs, the nudibranchs. Whale sharks occasionally cruise around it too. Everything in the ocean seems to gather here. You see every colour in the artist's palette, and a few more that haven't been invented. It really is a fantastic dive site whose visual impact is so enormous and stunning that the camera cannot really do it justice.

All sorts of other delights lie in wait for you if you take your time - and look carefully - for they do not advertise their presence boldly. I was gliding alongside Yay, our dive guide, exchanging signals as we had to change direction to go with the flow of the current. My head was turned towards him as I signalled my acknowledgement of his message. He suddenly grabbed my arm and pulled me towards him. He had noticed that the current was pushing me toward a rock shelf and there, sitting boldly on top of the shelf was a large octopus. I was only about 18 inches away from experiencing an intimate embrace with it.

It sat quite still, curling its long tentacles around it, much as a naked photographic model may do with her legs and arms in order to conceal all her private parts. Its colour was that of the rock it sat upon; its skin texture, rough and horny-looking to match the texture of the rock, made it virtually indistinguishable from its background. Yay had done well to notice it at all. We stopped and raised our cameras. It posed beautifully for us, quite unconcerned by our close proximity. That is unusual. If you get too near they begin to flash like a warning light at you, their skin emitting different colours in an amazing, threatening display. This one was a real poser. It sat confidently secure on its perch until we had enough pictures and moved on. It never moved.

Then it was time to turn back and head for home and, after having completed our last dives at Elephant Rock and Boulder City on the way south again, the boat got underway for the overnight journey back to port. The ocean was burnished gold in the light of the setting sun, then streaked with silver in the light of the full moon. We dined well again and stood out on deck where we could see the approaching mainland in the soft moonlight, savouring the last few hours in the warm tropical night, dropping into our bunks around midnight. Shortly after that the engine note changed to a gentle throb as we approached and picked up our mooring just off the pier at Chalong, and then fell silent. Another wonderful voyage to the Similan Islands was over.

Jonathan Cruiser can sleep 14 divers, but on this trip there were just the four of us, Mike, Ray, Tony, all from the USA and me. Buddies I had met on my Tubbataha reef trip in the Philippines, they had all asked me to keep in touch and let me know where I would be going and then they joined in for this trip. Having the boat to ourselves, it felt as though we had chartered the entire vessel, and it was a joy to dive again with my three very experienced buddies.

I love the pattern of life on a live-aboard dive boat: wake up and have a dive before breakfast. Eat breakfast and rest, with another dive before lunch. Eat again, rest for an hour or so and have an afternoon dive. Enjoy a snack around 4pm, rest and go down in the dark for a night dive around 7pm, followed by dinner, relaxing and swapping yarns around the table, and then sleep. Dive, eat, sleep: it is a great way of life and all in the most glorious weather with calm seas and mostly good visibility.

It reminded me of those excellent TV programmes that were broadcast in many countries for several years back in the 1960s and 70s: The Undersea World of Jacques Cousteau. I remember looking with envy as Cousteau and his colleagues got geared up for diving on their converted ex-British minesweeper Calypso in glorious sunshine on a silky, smooth sea and then went exploring some of the same locations I was diving now. Never did I imagine that one day I would be able to do exactly that, visiting so many of the locations explored and filmed by Cousteau's team.

I was indeed living the dream.

No need to imagine it.

Chapter 23

In Bed With Two Nurses

You never know what kind of people you will encounter on a live-aboard dive boat. If you are lucky, a great camaraderie can develop and form a basis for lasting friendships. On the other hand, if the dynamics of the group don't work favourably, it can be a bit of a pain having to endure the company of people you cannot stand for a whole week or more in the limited confines of a boat. Usually it works out well. My first trip into Burmese waters was aboard, Gaea, a ketch-rigged trimaran which can carry up to eight guests, but on this occasion there were only three of us.

Simon was a tall Californian, the same age as me, but there the resemblance ended. A long-haired ex-hippy, ex-pot smoker, with the obligatory Californian ex-wife and a typically dysfunctional Californian family of ex-delinquents who had graduated to being grown-up pot smokers, and in some cases ex-pot smokers, with ex-wives themselves, as seems to be the habit there. A product of the 1960s Flower-Power age, Simon had a permanently vague, distant expression on his face. When asked even a simple question, it seemed to take a long time for the message to get through to his brain and then he took an awful long time to formulate an answer. Conversation was therefore challenging and invariably convoluted as you waited for an answer, which was often enigmatic and so late in coming you had moved on and forgotten what the question was. He had spent a few years on a cruiser in the US Navy during the Vietnam War.

"Did you enjoy life in the navy?" I enquired. Silence. His blue eyes stared distantly towards the horizon. He showed no obvious signs of having heard the question. I waited patiently. Then he shook his head. I probed further, "Oh? Why not?" More silence. Maybe he did not like talking about it. Perhaps I had touched on a sensitive area. He did not answer. I decided to move on, leave him to his thoughts and started talking to someone else.

A moment or two later in the middle of my conversation he suddenly said, "I am from California." We all knew that already and that bore no relation to what I had been talking about for the past minute or two, or so I thought. He thought otherwise. I looked at him in puzzlement. Another long pause. He explained. "They are always telling you to do things in the navy. In California we don't like to be told what to do." Ah.... Now I understood. Eventually.

He could be amusing, though. He brought with him a laconic sense of humour and a determined bowel-plugging dose of constipation, which required some severely drastic medication from the ship's first aid kit to get his tubes cleared.

Melissa was a fifty-year old nurse from the USA, a single mother of a thirty-three year old heroin addict, herself an ex-pot smoker who was now deeply into Zen Buddhism and meditation. Having paranoias was her hobby.

She dosed up on antibiotics before she arrived, just in case there might be some nasty bug waiting to attack her when she stepped off the plane in Thailand. If it did, it would soon find out that she had the stuff within her to annihilate it, whatever it might be. One night at around 2am she was aroused by the sound of a Burmese fishing boat anchoring nearby. She then went into paranoid mode, imagined that they were pirates coming to kill us all and steal our boat, so she locked herself in her cabin and sat on her meditation cushion for two hours until she was able to convince herself that they were not intent on murder and mayhem. She also had the notion that these islands (nearly all uninhabited) may be infested with ruthless drug producers who may take exception to our vessel anchoring in their sheltered waters and shoot us. Maybe she had read Alex Garland's novel, The Beach, or had seen the film that was based on the book. Every fishing boat was regarded with the deepest suspicion as she was convinced that they were all rogues intent on serious mischief. She was almost begging our captain not to go near them as we eased alongside one to buy some fish. "They all look so dark and sinister," she protested. "Maybe they just want us to think they're fishermen to lull us into a false sense of security." They were all actually very friendly and gave us some squid to feast on. "Maybe it has been poisoned," she cautioned. You can only take so much of this and I suggested to her that her mind had been been corrupted by Hollywood movies, or writers with lurid imaginations. As with Simon's constipation, she could have benefited from a dose of some purgative of the mind to cleanse her of all these paranoias.

In spite of her incessant fears she was very well travelled and had recently decided to try diving, had completed the theory part of the course, but had never been in the water so it was arranged that she could do the practical part of the course during this cruise and that would enable her to become certified by the end of the week.

Josh, aged 36, our guide, divemaster and a certified dive instructor, was from San Francisco. He had rebelled against just about everything as he grew up (well, that seems quite normal, especially in California), established his own trucking business, made a heap of money and then sold out before the government suspected he may not be paying enough in taxes. He then elected to travel and work abroad as a snowboard instructor in Japan and a dive instructor in many places. He had also taught English in Japan and the United Arab Emirates, and is now based permanently in Japan, but works for six months in the year as a dive guide in South East Asia. Another ex pot-smoker (well what do you expect? He was from California after all) he was a thoughtful guy who hated so much of the hypocrisy of American politics and lifestyle today. I liked him.

And there was me, the real oddball of the group, who has never smoked pot, doesn't have an ex-wife (but a deceased one after 29 years of marriage), never had delinquent children (their behavior was invariably a cause for positive comment), never drifted around from one job to another, never got in trouble with the police, or the government for tax evasion, never got into meditation and Buddhism, nor any other fashionable "ism". I seemed so dull. The others looked at me in shocked disbelief. "But how did you manage to avoid getting into all these things? Everybody does it."

"I don't come from California!" I retorted. "Let's just say I am a bit of a rebel, but I rebelled against all the self-destructive things that the self-styled rebels did to let it be known that they were rebels. It just seemed plain stupid to me to poison a healthy body with drugs. Why? Because everyone else was doing it? Well, I can assure you, all the rest of the world is not the same as California, and as long as I am not doing it, it is fallacious to claim that everyone else is doing it." Despite the disparities, we all got on very well.

My foray into Burmese waters began with a four-hour journey by road from Phuket to Ranong, a town on the river estuary that is the border between Thailand and Burma (I use Burma rather than Myanmar, its current name, as Burmese is easier as a descriptive word rather than Myanmarese, or whatever the term might be). A forty-minute boat ride took us across the estuary to Kawthaung on the Burmese side where we had to deposit our passports with the immigration office, presumably to make sure we returned, and take on board a government official for the duration of our voyage. Every foreign boat seeking permission to sail in these waters must have a government official on board, feed him and pay his wages. It is claimed that this is to ensure our safety in these waters, but from what or whom, no one is prepared to say. It seems like a good job creation scheme for Burmese officials.

Jojo, our guy, was a really nice bloke. A graduate in physics, his wife was a teacher, but he was making a better living doing this job which basically meant every week he was cruising on one of the few dive boats that work this area. He worked on board helping us kitting up for our dives, hauling the anchor, washing dishes, making tea. He was a real asset.

Having completed all the formalities, the immigration officers left our boat and we were able to leave the bustling harbour of Kawthaung where long-tailed boats clattered noisily to and fro, incessantly bringing home fishermen, transporting catches of squid, taking people across the border to Thailand or returning them to Burma. It was almost like the bustling canals of Venice, a scene of continuous clatter with men shouting as boats jostled in and out of berths and dodged around each other.

We made passage northwesterly towards the islands as the sun set in a golden haze. Delicious smells wafted up from the galley where the captain's young Thai wife, an excellent cook, prepared our dinner. With only two gas burners on her stove she prepared the most delicious and varied dishes for every meal, both western style and Thai food. The crew consisted of the captain, his wife and one deckhand. Jojo helped out cheerfully turning his hand to any task required. They were all very friendly and helpful with a great sense of humour. As soon as my sleepy head appeared from my cabin in the morning, one of them was by my side with a big smile, thrusting a mug of tea into my hand.

This cruise, a mixture of diving, sailing, kayaking and scrambling through dense jungle was great fun - well, most of the time. The jungle was difficult, to say the least. Traversing an island from one side to the other meant forcing a way through dense entangled undergrowth, scrambling up steep, rocky, overgrown slopes on one side and down steep, rocky, overgrown slopes on the other. Plants here conspire to trap you. Creepers and vines get you ensnared in their tendrils and have an almost animal-like tendency to wrap themselves around your legs and ankles. They are so damnably insistent, defying you to escape from their grip. Like wrestling with an octopus, you just free yourself from one tendril only to discover that, while you were unraveling it, the others have you in their most intimate embrace.

Other plants have long curving leaves armoured with stinging barbs, like a row of fish hooks along each edge, which lock into your skin as you pass, hooking you up in dozens of places. Bushes sport long, penetrating thorns that rip your legs to shreds. Large spiders' webs shimmer in the dappled sunlight, sometimes. At other times you just blindly stumble into them and then claw frantically to get their sticky webs off your face and look around frantically for the spider. But where were the large spiders? Nowhere to be seen. Had they jumped on to your shoulder and scuttled round to the back of your neck? Were they lurking behind a branch of the tree waiting to leap on you and sink their poisonous fangs into the back of your neck? Maybe Melissa's paranoias were justified here. The mosquitoes whined and pined for you in the forest and the sand flies danced a merry greeting for you on the beach: "Hey guys, we have some visitors for dinner tonight!" And at the end of this skin-ripping, shirt-tearing, ankle-biting, neck-slapping experience you arrive at another pristine, white, sandy beach identical to the one you left; and then you have to endure the return journey with more scraping and tearing and ripping as you hack and curse your way back through the jungle. It's easy to understand why no one lives on most of these islands. The Moken people have the right idea: they stay on their boats.

No, the jungle here wasn't much fun.

Kayaking was very pleasant, quietly cruising along the rocky shores of islands overhung with jungles, exploring inlets and caves and silently slipping into idyllically beautiful, turquoise-coloured bays fringed with white sand and the dense backcloth of the jungle. Always fun, it induces a sense of real exploration as you can get into nooks and crannies that only a small craft like a kayak can ever get into, where the only sound is the gentle lap of the waves and the tense scuttling sound of the crabs as they scurry along the rock faces. The landscape was pleasant and interesting, but it was the sea, and in particular under the sea, that was endlessly fascinating, exciting, adrenalin pumping, thrilling.

As in the Similan Islands, the underwater landscapes of the Mergui Archipelago are strikingly beautiful. Rock pinnacles soar straight up out of the sea, their vertical walls plunging down a hundred feet or more to the sea bed, offering a sort of high-rise tower block environment for marine life. These walls are colourfully decorated with waving soft corals of delicate hues and large white and orange fan corals which in turn are festooned with beautiful feather starfish in brilliant yellows, whites and black, looking more like ferns or flowers than animals. The dark fissures and tunnels in the rock provide refuge for a variety fish, lobsters and shrimps.

Some islands are just a jumble of huge boulders, the gaps between them providing arches and tunnels, swim-throughs with many cavities for fish to hide in or rest. Rising from the sandy floor of the sea, these islands are great places to see giant stingrays, sometimes four of five all resting together on the sandy bottom, like a family. There are reef sharks, schools of snappers, trevally and barracuda and enormous schools of small juvenile fish so dense they look like dark clouds above you. Frequently under attack from predators, these little fish school densely for protection. One bullet-like dart from a swift moving tuna or mackerel will instantly turn the school in a flash of silver as the tiny fish panic, desperate to escape the jaws of the predator, sometimes engulfing the diver in a cloud so thick you can't see a hand's length in front of you. On one occasion they came pouring downwards over a rocky ledge above us like a waterfall composed entirely of millions of small finger sized fish and we were engulfed in this swirling mass of tiny bodies desperate to escape being eaten. Although packed so close together, they never seem to collide.

Every hole seemed to be occupied by moray eels of various kinds, some brown and dark eyed, some white eyed, some yellow with spots, their mean looking jaws sticking out and gulping water. Lionfish floated lazily up and down the rock walls, their highly coloured feathery spines spread out in a blaze of red, black and white. And everywhere danced the brilliantly coloured small fish; flashy bright fusiliers, yellow and blue striped sweetlips, emperorfish, butterflyfish, angelfish, red and blue spotted wrasse, tiny, tubby boxfish, canary yellow with black spots and the soft green and blue tints of the parrotfish. These were densely populated fish communities, breathtakingly bright and colourful in every aspect from the coral encrusted rocks to the dazzling hues of the small fish. It was a joy to be down there, to explore this magnificent wonderland with its gardens of anemones swaying in the tidal currents, like wild flowers in a meadow dancing in a breeze.

Almost every dive had its excitement; the sight of giant stingrays up to 2 metres across demonstrating the beautiful sinusoidal movement of their wings in their elegant flight, comical looking cuttlefish with their big, dopey, sleepy-looking eyes, the sinister movement of sleek, cold-eyed sharks and of course the caves, with who knows what lurking in their dark shadows.

Hordes of small dancer shrimps populated the narrowest fissures, like ballet dancers dancing around on tip-toe. Cleaner shrimps waved their white feelers at you from tight holes. Lay a hand on the rock and they will come out and pick away at your fingernails, cleaning them of the accumulation of dead cells that grows around the line where finger nail and skin meet. Many of the larger fish use them for cleaning and can often be seen lying there having their bodies picked clean of parasites in the 'cleaning stations.' Oozing ponderously across rock faces were strikingly coloured nudibranchs, the slugs of the sea, but amazingly beautiful. For every environment there was a creature with a purpose suited to it.

At night, parts of the sea flashed like diamonds imbued with an almost preternatural energy. This bioluminescence was caused by tiny planktonic creatures called dinoflagellates, being agitated by any movement such as a passing fish or the anchor chain of the boat. One night it was particularly spectacular and Josh suggested we put on the masks and snorkels and try a swim. It was amazing to watch our hands stir up a glow, like a million diamonds sparkling, as we thrust ourselves through the water. Watching another body swimming in this was like watching some ghostly creature glowing in the blackness of the sea. You couldn't see any of the features of the body, only the glow of the bioluminescence as it passed by, strange, ghost-like and eerie.

Simon of course had to take time to ponder whether he would take the plunge and after a few moments of silent deliberation he murmured, "OK," stood up, took a step backwards, and did just that, falling off the stern into the sea, fully clothed. He'd just forgotten the boat ended there. We were doubled over with laughter.

One small rocky island, shaped like a bun, provided the most memorable moments. On one side its walls dropped sheer to the sea bed, on the other there was a jumble of rocks and a large fissure as though some giant had cleft the rock with a massive axe. Open to the north it offers a narrow V-shaped canyon to explore. That was good, but better was yet to come. At the closed end of the canyon there were two features of interest; one a dark hole like a mineshaft dropping vertically downwards into the rock, the other a large swim-through where one huge boulder had toppled against the main wall of the island. Josh stopped us here and dropped his head down the dark hole, shone his torch around, but came up again shaking his head. Melissa, being a novice, was neither ready nor willing to try such an exploration so Josh took us through the swim-through instead. That was OK, but I was a bit disappointed. I wanted to see inside that big, black hole. Despite that minor disappointment it was a really good dive with lots of big and small fish and plenty of colour so we were all delighted when we surfaced at the end of the dive.

"I'd love to do that dive again," I muttered to Josh as we bobbed about in the sea waiting for the boat to pick us up.

"No problem. So would I," he muttered. "We'll go down again before lunch, but without Melissa this time. She's not ready for this yet, and we can explore the cave." She had found it all a bit overwhelming anyway so that was OK with her. Josh, Simon and I dropped into the water again shortly before mid-day. We approached the cave from the opposite end, entering by its southern entrance. Josh handed me the torch and indicated for me to lead as he wanted to take photos and needed two hands to operate the camera. The entrance was steep, a 45 degree slope and quite narrow at first, as I kicked down into the gloom. A hefty pillar of rock loomed up ahead splitting the entrance tunnel into two channels. The left side looked lower so I took the right hand route and shone the torch up ahead. The roof of the cave was low, offering little more than a metre of headroom.

I was close to the right-hand wall and then the thick pillar ended and revealed a much wider chamber to my left side. As I swung the torch round, slowly examining walls and roof for life I suddenly became aware of a large fin, in the eleven o'clock position, about a metre in length and touching the roof. "That's a shark's tail fin," I thought at once. "A big tail fin. And there must be a big shark attached to it." I let the torch beam follow the line of the fin to its meeting with the body of the shark and then traversed the length of the monster. And it wasn't a shark. It was two sharks, four metres in length, lying side by side, resting on the floor of the cave, just about a metre and a half away from me.

The adrenalin surged through my body, demanding an intake of air. As I gulped in air, my buoyancy increased and I rose from the floor of the cave, clunking my air tank against its the low roof. I scolded myself, "Shush, you'll wake up the sharks". I flashed the torch back to the others and then pointed the beam on the sharks to let them see this amazing sight. Josh wasted no time and took some photos. The sharks were quite unimpressed by us and just lay there, the only sign of life being the movement of their gills. I moved on into the darkness of the cave and eventually saw a welcoming bluish hue up ahead. This was the light coming down the mineshaft-like hole at the north end. I powered my way towards it and inhaled to increase buoyancy. This elevated me up the shaft and out into the open sea once more. I heaved a sigh, not so much of relief, more of exultation, as the others followed out in line astern and we all exchanged animated signs to express our delight at what we had seen.

Back on board for lunch at the end of the dive Josh said, "The plan for the afternoon is to go to another island for kayaking among the mangroves." He looked at me quizzically. I could swear he was reading my mind. "Unless you want to dive here again."

"Definitely!" I spat out. Josh smiled.

"I thought you might feel that way, John." He then asked how the others felt, offering to take Melissa on an easier dive to let Simon and I explore the depths again. As usual, Simon looked vague, pondered awhile and then murmured softly, "Yeah, that's cool."

So that afternoon we went down for a third time. This time we rolled off the boat at the north end of the island. As the more experienced diver, I was leading, heading for the cave once more to its north entrance, the one like a mineshaft. Just as we approached the opening a great blotchy black sheet appeared out of the hole, a giant stingray. I veered off to the side and watched it glide away from me. I then approached the entrance to the cave. Just as I was about to descend head first Simon grabbed my fins and tugged. I looked round and he gave me the "something's wrong" sign with his hand and pointed. The giant stingray was coming back towards the cave. Now if the two sharks were still in there and we joined them and then a giant stingray almost two metres across tried to squeeze in there as well, that might become a wee bit too intimate. And we did not know if there were other stingrays in there already. We had seen four of them all resting together that morning just outside the south entrance and the cave had a nice sandy bottom, which they like.

I came back up, but when it saw me emerge it sheered off and glided on down to rest on the sandy bottom of the gully. That was good enough for me and I plunged into the darkness to check things out. Simon was not so keen and hovered outside, but I had a look around and then flashed the light up and gave him the OK signal so he dropped in behind me.

The sharks were still there, but were more restless this time. The current was stronger and they were having to move those massive bodies and tail fins to maintain their positions, making them even more awesome looking. Think of two big-bodied sharks almost twice the length of your bed writhing sideways in a snake-like motion, which meant there was less room for us to pass by. If they panicked and that tail lashed out sideways it would give me the kind of slap that my mother would have been delighted to administer to 'that boy' of hers, who continually worried her sick. With less than a metre of headroom in some places there was no chance of floating overhead, but it seemed after watching their massive bodies oscillating to and fro for a few moments that they were unlikely to encroach on our passageway so I kicked forward gently and glided past them, on through the darkness to the south entrance. Simon didn't hang about either; this was no place for a laid-back Californian ex-hippy to linger.

After that we circled the complete island, observing the life on its walls and rocks, and kicked away from its rocky wall at the north end, breaking the surface just a few yards from the boat. "Well done. Your navigation is spot on," cried Josh as he reached down to help us get back aboard. I beamed with delight, not just because I'd managed to navigate all the way round the island to surface at exactly the right spot, but because I'd had such a thrilling dive, revelling in another close encounter with two monsters of the deep.

Now just in case you think I am crazy having sharks as bed-fellows, these were nurse sharks, large but benign bottom feeders that eat small shrimps and crab, and I don't look much like either so they were not likely to be tempted to taste me. Of course, I didn't know what they were until I was right in bed beside them. Nurse sharks have been reported as seeming to enjoy the company of divers and have been known to sit still and let divers caress them.

I read that in a book. But that was after I got back ashore.

Chapter 24

A Real Man

Leaving Burma's most southerly outpost, Kawthung, for my second exploration of Burmese waters in just over a year, Colona II sailed westwards as the sun set over the Andaman Sea. Freddy Storhiel, our Norwegian skipper, had given me the helm for the first watch. A fresh offshore breeze filled her sails and I felt that indescribable longing being fulfilled again, a longing for the sea and sailing, calling me onwards to explore once again the Mergui Archipelago, that scattering of hundreds of small, mostly uninhabited, islands and rocks that stretch from the coast of Burma out over the Burma Banks, where the continental shelf then drops into the depths of the Indian Ocean. There is something magical about going west. It's hard to explain. Maybe it goes back to my childhood when the sea lay to the west, the horizon to the west, adventure and the unknown all seemed to lie to the west, so I tingled with anticipation of what was to come on my second voyage to these remote islands.

It always brings a feeling of relief to a mariner on getting away from the land, a feeling of oneness with the sea and the boat. Colona II was a 67-foot ketch. She had sailed round the world in 1979 and had been on charter for diving in the Red Sea for a time before coming to Thailand in the 1990s. Her skipper and owner, Freddy Storheil, had eventually settled in Thailand after an adventurous life of sailing and diving in various parts of the world. Like many other European ex-pats he had no wish to return to live in his homeland and the chill of a European winter.

His crew consisted of two local deckhands who did the cooking and everything else, the obligatory Burmese government official who helped out with on board duties, and his old friend and guest for this voyage, Haakon Hellner, a former Norwegian jet fighter pilot who later became a commercial airline pilot flying Jumbo jets until he had retired a year previously. Haak and I were the same age, Freddy a couple of years younger. Roger Talbot, 46, from Newcastle, England was our dive guide.

Colona II can carry six divers. On this trip there were only three: myself, a 61 year-old English lady called Sue, and Tom, her 64 year-old American boyfriend. She was a very competent and experienced diver; he had not dived for many years, was a bit overweight and sucked twice as much air as the rest of us. That was a pity as all his dives were relatively short and he missed out on some great sights on these pristine dive sites. Roger always had to surface with Tom to ensure his safety, so Sue and I were dive buddies and we stayed on below. She was good, keeping an eye open for photo opportunities for me. I was focusing on taking pictures or, as she eloquently put it, always had my head stuck in some hole, but we made a good buddy team. The others crawled off to their bunks most nights at around 8.30 or 9pm, but Haak and I sat up on deck most nights swapping yarns long after the others had gone to sleep. He was a really interesting shipmate, having flown to most parts of the world.

The fact that this area is largely uninhabited and relatively remote (there is not even a road connecting Kawthung to the rest of Burma) means that only a few dive boats come here from Thailand, none at all from Burma, so the dive sites are generally in excellent condition, unlike the places near to Phuket which are overcrowded with divers. I had heard claims that this area had been spoiled by dynamite fishing, but on my two trips in these waters I saw only one bay in which there had been any reef damage, and that was not one of the usual dive sites, but a bay we decided to explore one day when rough weather prevented us from diving an exposed rock site. All the other dive sites were in excellent condition. We only encountered one island with a small holiday resort on it, just a cluster of bungalows on a nice sandy beach; nice if you want a really quiet holiday, lazing around doing nothing, but that is not my scene. Fishermen from Burma and Thailand, are frequently encountered, lighting up the night sky with powerful lanterns that attract squid to the surface, and to their doom, every night.

The Mergui Archipelago is a cluster of hundreds of small rocky islands in the Andaman Sea in the southwest territorial waters of the Republic of Myanmar, formerly known as Burma when it was under British rule. Nearly all uninhabited, these islands are however home to the Moken people, a tribe of sea gypsies who meander among the islands in crude boats with only a simple roof slung across the boat for shelter, living on their boats as their ancestors have lived for hundreds of years. They're born on the sea, live on the sea, die on the sea. They know its moods and motions. They're nomads, constantly moving from island to island, living more than six months a year on their boats, coming ashore to live in crude shelters during the monsoon season. At low tide, they collect sea cucumbers and catch eels. At high tide, they dive for shellfish. They've been living this way for so many generations that they've become virtually amphibious. Their children learn to swim before they can walk. Underwater, they can see twice as clearly as the rest of us, and by lowering their heart rate, can stay underwater twice as long. They are truly sea urchins. They do a little hand-line fishing, taking just enough to feed the family and a little to trade for fuel for their boat's engines. Despite their traditional way of life they recognise the advantages of having a reliable diesel engine.

I felt privileged to be invited on board one of their boats, which had anchored for the night nearby. About 26 feet long, it was simply an open boat with a primitive roof slung over the mid-section to provide shelter from the heat of the sun and the rain. Fish were laid out on the roof to dry in the baking heat of the sun, a simple way of preserving them. Inside this crude open-ended shelter a few pots and cooking utensils lined the narrow shelves of the boat and that seemed to be the family's only household possessions. We took over some fresh fruit as a gift and this was well received. Our Burmese official knew a few words of their language and, in return for our offering, we were accepted as friends and allowed to take photographs.

At the forward end of the boat the eldest son, a boy of about 15, chopped a fish into chunks for some sort of stew while his younger brother fished with a handline from the bow. Another young brother and sister sat watching mother and grandmother go about their tasks. Grandmother sat cross-legged on the hard boards, pounding something to a fine powder with mortar and pestle while mother squatted on one side, tending a pot on a cooking fire contained within a metal bucket pierced with holes on the side which sat on a flat stone. The smoke simply made its exit through the open ends of the crude shelter. While the women worked, preparing dinner, the father greeted the visitors cordially.

They speak no English. Many of them don't even speak Burmese, but our Burmese official was able to converse with them in their own language. In common with other vagrant peoples of the world, the Moken are regarded as of lower status by the rest of Burmese society. They are mainly unschooled, but they learn how to survive in this wilderness, how to build and maintain boats, to find food on land, in the sea and on the shores, what herbs to gather for their medicinal properties.

They seem happy to continue to live this very basic lifestyle which is so remote from the technology-based existence of the western world, and it was their intimacy with the sea that saved many of the Moken people from the devastation that affected other coastal communities when the massive tsunami of 26 Dec 2004 brought death and destruction. Long before the tidal wave bore down on them some of the Moken people had read the signs of the sea correctly and moved to higher ground, avoiding loss of life, even though their communities were smashed to pieces.

They don't ask for handouts from the government. They have no need for governing. Some attempts by both the Thai and Burmese governments to encourage them to adopt a more conventional lifestyle have met with only partial success. However, as in most other places, the traditional way of life is slowly being eroded and their numbers are reported to be dwindling, though how anyone can tell is a mystery as these people are literally here today, gone tomorrow. Registering births and deaths is not part of their lifestyle.

It is a peaceful, idyllic area with rocky islands covered in dense jungle and many pristine, white beaches. The downside, of course, is that if there is an accident you are a long way from any assistance. There is no coastguard here, no lifeboat service on call, no rescue helicopters to whisk a casualty off to hospital within the hour. For divers with decompression sickness, the nearest hyperbaric chamber is at Phuket. That means a lengthy sea passage to mainland Burma, check through immigration, followed by a short cross-border boat ride to Thailand, more immigration procedures and then a five hour car drive to Phuket - not ideal if you have a life-threatening condition. This scenario, which was spelled out in our briefing at the start of the voyage, had to be enacted on the last but one afternoon when, after our third dive that day, Tom became ill. His body began to tingle and became blotchy with blue marble-like streaks all over it. Tom thought he was having a heart attack, but Freddy took one look and said, "Decompression sickness. We have to go back and get him to hospital."

He was sent to his bunk and given oxygen. The remaining day's diving was cancelled and we set course for the mainland. By mid-night we had him in Thailand again, in a car being driven to Phuket, arriving there around 5am. That would get him to the decompression chamber about 12 hours after he first felt ill. Not ideal, but there was no other choice. There was no clearly obvious reason for his sickness, but the doctor at the hyperbaric chamber remarked that most of his cases tended to be divers who were overweight. That brought the voyage to a premature end on a rather sad note as we had all been enjoying it immensely until then.

It wasn't the only problem we'd encountered though. The masthead navigation light, a tri-coloured light showing green and red forward to indicate starboard and port sides of the vessel and a white light showing aft, had come adrift in rough weather. The fitting had been corroded over the years by the salt-laden air and the light had toppled off the masthead and was dangling by the wires. This meant that the white light, which should only be visible from astern, was now showing forward and the port and starboard lights were the wrong way round and showing aft. This created some consternation among the fishing boats at night as they could see what appeared to be a vessel bearing down on them in reverse, but with the whole assembly hanging loose, the lights swung and turned according to the motion of the vessel making the lights change from one moment to the next. It must have been very perplexing for them to interpret.

It simply had to be fixed, but it was at the top of the mast, 75 feet above the deck. Freddy now had a mutiny to deal with. The two deckhands and the Burmese official refused point blank to climb the mast. Freddy was not prepared to do it himself, telling me that the last time he had done it was about ten years previously and when he came down he was shaking all over and had to go to bed for the rest of the day to recover. Haak, who was there as Freddy's guest, sat on deck drinking beer most days so it was out of the question for him to attempt it. Roger, the dive guide, was a big fellow, six feet three, and would go up if it was absolutely necessary, but he had never been up a mast before and was not at all happy about it. Tom? Completely out of the question. He was overweight, bulky and even climbing the steps out of the cabin was a gasping effort for him. Sue? She was in reasonable shape, but climbing 75 feet up a mast can be a stern test physically as well as mentally and it simply did not seem an altogether appropriate task for an imperious, sixty-one year-old English lady with a plummy accent when there were seven men aboard. Anyway, she hadn't a clue about what was likely to be involved in fixing the lights, nor was she at all keen on the idea. And how could the men have held up their heads if she had been the only one willing to do it? There was only one solution. I offered to go up. Freddy's eyes lit up. A volunteer at last! "But John, are you sure you are fit enough to do it?"

I glowered and growled at him. "Freddy, I've been up and down my own mast dozens of times. And I've been up other people's masts fixing things as well. It'll be no problem." We dropped anchor in a sheltered bay and I shot up the mask to assess the situation, came back down and told Freddy what I needed for repairs, went back up and within ten minutes the lights were fixed. Freddy was delighted and pumped my hand. "John, after that your drinks are free."

Haak was there already with a glass in his hand. He beamed at me, "John, I really admire you. You went up that mast like a monkey, not once, but twice, and so effortlessly! Sit down and let me pour you a rum and coke. You deserve it."

I enjoyed being useful and had a great view of the boat from 75 feet above the deck. And it was good to show the young guys on board, the two deckhands who always seemed to assume that at my age I needed their help to get in and out of the water, that the "old man" could still do a few things they couldn't. 'Mr John' had their respect after that.

As always, the deliciously caustic, imperious Sue had the last word. "Thank goodness there is at least one real man on board this vessel."

Chapter 25

The Paradise Islands

For many tourists it is the ideal tropical island paradise: two parallel lines of
coral atolls (circular or oval reefs enclosing a lagoon in the centre, the remnants
of extinct undersea volcanoes) lying north to south in the ocean below India. It
is the Maldive Islands. Each atoll has several small sandy islands around its rim,
some so small you could walk round them in 15 minutes, with resorts offering a
relaxing tropical island holiday. You can fly in by seaplane from Male
International Airport and have your luggage carried from the plane to your
room. Then you can eat, sleep, lounge around the pool or swim in the lagoon till
your holiday is over. Idyllic - if you like that kind of thing.

Male, the capital, is not idyllic. An unattractive, congested, small city, it has
no merit whatsoever, as far as I could see. It is worth avoiding. There were few
tourists to be seen; they tend to head straight to the luxury island resorts. A
small, island-city, it occupies the entire island, about 3 km long and maybe 2 km
wide with narrow congested streets. Male International Airport is situated on a
neighbouring island, occupying virtually the entire island and small ferries
shuttle back and forth between the airport and Male, a 15-minute trip, day and
night. Walking around its streets on my overnight stay before embarking on the
MV Stingray, I was not impressed. Cafes and restaurants were filled with men,
only men. Their wives or girlfriends were nowhere to be seen. In this Moslem
state, the women seem to be confined at home while the men go out to relax,
drink coffee (alcohol is forbidden) and socialise. It is an expensive place too and
it was a relief to get off the island next morning to board Stingray.

A very comfortable live-aboard dive boat, Stingray can accommodate 18
divers in shared cabins, but with only 14 aboard I had a cabin to myself. A
friendly, helpful crew and a good sociable bunch of divers from Austria,
Denmark, France, Italy and USA, provided the ingredients for a very pleasant
social and diving experience. Their friendship and sociability created a good
on-board atmosphere and we had a rollicking New Year's Eve party.

The Maldives claims to be a great place to see manta rays and whale sharks.
Well, the mantas were pretty shy, only making an appearance at one site. After
clinging to the rocks on the bottom for the whole dive, waiting for them in a
strong current until we had run out of bottom time, we did get a brief glimpse of
a couple on the way up, just two fleeting shadows in the gloom below. And that
was all the mantas we saw. The first dive of the year on Jan 1 did provide a thrill,
a passing whale shark, looming like a submarine out of the gloom.
Unfortunately it was just too far off to get a decent photo, and it did not hang
around to pose for us.

Many of the dives were scenically attractive, with large pinnacles to swim
around, often festooned with brightly coloured corals and sponges, vertical

walls with lots of colourful fish which offered good photo opportunities, large overhangs, caves and swim-throughs. All the usual reef fish were there, offering plenty of colour on a sunny, early morning dive, a great way to start a day.

Sharks abound here; grey reef sharks, white-tips, silver tips, hammerheads too. As I was flying out at 1.30 a.m, I had to skip the dive on the last day to fit in my 24 hours no-fly time after diving, and inevitably that was when the hammerheads made their appearance. You'll see plenty of turtles too, a few napoleon wrasse, tuna, trevally, lots of reef fish, schools of snappers, some free-swimming large moray eels etc. On one dive a school of mobula rays, came flying past like aircraft in tight formation. Beautiful and elegant, they resemble mantas in appearance, but are very much smaller. This is a location to suit those who like the big scene with the large fish to be found in places with strong currents. Overall it was pleasant and colourful with lots to see.

However, what the Maldives lacked for me was the unusual, the intriguing, the bizarre; the smaller stuff that I find absorbing. There must be plenty of it around, but the dives guides seemed only interested finding the big fish. It is easy enough to find a shark on your own, but to find a pygmy seahorse or a hairy frogfish requires a guide who knows where to look and has the patience to do it. I saw nothing new until the last day when, as we waited for the group to gather to surface at the end of a strong current dive, the guide noticed something odd in a hole in the reef, a strange kind of shrimp I had never seen before, nor had anyone else on board, including the guides. It was probably a marble shrimp, of the saron genus.

Although it was a very enjoyable dive trip, taking all things into consideration, especially cost, the Maldives would not entice me back. I am surprised that some people go back there year after year when they could see so much more in Indonesia and the Philippines for less money. But the lure of the big fish is a powerful attraction and that is what many divers want to see and there is no doubt you can see them there. While the mantas are always so impressive and thrilling to see, and a whale shark is so overwhelming because of its size, sharks generally do not excite me greatly: grey, lacking in colour, distant, timorous, they seldom let you get close enough to offer great photo opportunities. However, I do appreciate the sensuous grace with which they glide effortlessly through the water; these are sleek, efficient machines that have been designed with such perfection they have hardly evolved at all in millions of years.

I prefer more variety, a range of colourful, interesting and unusual creatures to photograph, the intriguing small creatures of the oceans. I have found more satisfaction diving in the Philippines (much cheaper too) and Indonesia, which has everything; spectacular underwater scenery, big fish, interesting small things with an extensive biodiversity.

The Maldives I felt was overpriced, more orientated towards the high-spending tourist market. It suits the honeymoon couples who want pampering on a tropical island, and the European divers with a two week holiday who don't mind paying two or three hundred US dollars per night for an overnight stay before embarking on a live-aboard, but it is not so attractive to the budget-conscious, six-month traveller/diver such as me. I may not be unique, but I haven't found anyone else who does what I do. I have to budget carefully to travel and dive for six months and 300 dollar rooms are definitely not on my agenda. That equates to a lot of dives. The problem in Male was that even at the scruff end of the market you still pay 80 dollars per night for a bed, with breakfast extra. My in-bound flight time left me no alternative.

The diving while good, many would say very good, did not match what I saw a few days earlier in Thailand at a fraction of the cost, or in Indonesia, Papua, and the Philippines. But that is my view based on experience of other places and the photo opportunities the diving presents. As a photographer, your feelings about a dive are based on what you capture on camera, not just the big scene and the big fish, which are often too far away and lacking in colour to get a really good photo. That was where I felt a slight disappointment in the Maldives. There is more to diving than sharks and mantas. If I put aside my grouse about not seeing so many small things, it was a very enjoyable experience, especially socially. I enjoyed the company on board

These atolls certainly do have that romantic, tropical look about them, but the weather can change pretty rapidly too and, with strong tides ripping through the channels between the islands or reefs, that can lead to some uncomfortable and worrying sea conditions. Even paradise can throw up some unpleasant surprises. And it did.

It was the end of a pleasant drift dive between two submerged reefs. My buddy, a French lady called Magali, and I surfaced together and looked around in amazement. The sea, that had been flat calm on entering for an afternoon dive just over an hour previously, had been whipped into a frenzy of menacing, foaming, white breakers by a strong northerly wind howling in from under a dark leaden sky. Worse than that, we could not see any sign of the dive boat! Now, when you are all alone on the surface of a turbulent sea with a strong tide sweeping you out to the depths of the Indian Ocean, under a darkening sky without an island or even a solitary palm tree in sight, you may feel entitled to a wee bit of panic.

"Oh My God. They have gone away and left us!" cried out Magali.

"No. They must be around somewhere." I muttered as we were tossed around in the turbulent tide race.

The dhoni, the small dive boat that took us from the live-aboard vessel Stingray, had dropped us off about half a mile away at the entrance to a channel between two submerged reefs. All we had to do was keep the reef on our left side and we would drift along to the pick up area. I had been taking photos and Magali hovered around looking for things for me and keeping an eye on which direction the others had gone. However the reef, which had started as a fairly steep slope eventually flattened out. We had found some interesting photo opportunities over this plateau and had drifted a bit away from the others. The dive time had been set at around 60 minutes, so when our time was up we surfaced.

The perfect conditions earlier had changed so dramatically while we were underwater, blissfully unaware of the rapidly approaching weather front. The wind was blowing against the tide that ran strongly through the channel and was now whipping up steep, breaking seas. The waves were at least a metre and a half high and that was the problem. If we were in a trough, or the dhoni was in a trough some way off, neither could see the other.

I had experienced this situation once before in the Coral Sea and quickly realised that I must crest the waves at the same time as the dive boat, and sure enough there it was, about three hundred metres away, wallowing beam-on to the seas as she hauled the last of the other divers aboard.

"There it is," I roared. "She'll soon come and pick us up."

While still below, I had inflated my surface marker buoy, a long, red and yellow sausage-like balloon to show the boat where we were. However, once the other divers were aboard the boat, it understandably turned head into the breaking seas and began to look for us where it thought we might be, coming down the current behind the others. But we had stayed down longer and travelled further in the strong current and the boat was now heading away from us. We were about 300 metres behind it and getting further behind with every passing second. What was disconcerting was that no one seemed to think of looking astern for us. And there was no sign of Stingray. It had moved on to our next anchorage.

"Oh John, they are leaving us behind!" cried out Magali as the boat headed away from us.

"No. Don't worry. They know we are not aboard. They will do a square search pattern and see us when they turn." I hoped my confident assurance would ease her fears. I was hoping my assessment would be correct. Dive boats have been known to leave behind and lose divers. It has happened in Australia and Indonesia and Philipp, my German buddy, with whom I had dived at Palau, Indonesia and the Philippines, once had a nightmare experience in the Philippines when a group he was with spent 26 hours in the sea before being found by a fisherman.

I could see the headlines now in the newspapers: Divers Missing in Shark Infested Waters! They love to dramatise it.

But it was not an appealing thought, no matter how the tabloid hacks would phrase it. I thought it best to dispel such negativity and maintain a positive outlook and action. I grabbed for my whistle and blew with all my might to attract their attention. Magali cried out as loud as she could.

But it was futile.

The strengthening wind carried all sound away behind us. The boat receded into the distance, often remaining hidden in the troughs for what seemed an eternity before reappearing as we crested the waves simultaneously. It seemed so far away now. It did indeed look alarming,

Then, as I had predicted, it turned broadside on to the waves and started the second leg of its search pattern.

"They'll surely see us now," I cried out, imagining the lookouts peering right and left as well as ahead, but why never astern? I pumped more air into my surface marker buoy to make it as tall and erect as I could get it and then as I crested a wave I saw her turn back towards us. "She's coming for us now," I called to Magali. She looked at me, ashen faced.

"Oh, John, I was so afraid they were leaving us. I will never dive again."

"Och, don't be daft. You love diving. You can't give all that up. It was only a matter of time till they turned and saw us. Besides, what would I do if my buddy gave up? I need you with me down there to keep watch for me and let me know which way the others have gone. You are not giving up! We do the next dive together!"

It's great what a wee bit of manly assertiveness can do. She smiled. The boat drew alongside, leaping and bucking in the waves. We struggled out of our fins, passed them to the deckhand and climbed the short ladder, not the easiest task with the boat bouncing up and down like a cork. I saw Magali up the ladder first and then clambered aboard.

"Are you OK, John?" asked the deckhand cheerily, helping us with a steady hand as he always did. I grinned. "Sure." Then I growled at him, "But I would have swallowed a lot less sea water shouting at you if you had kept a lookout astern!"

I wriggled out of my gear as he clipped my air tank securely to the side of the vessel. He patted me on the shoulder and gave me a dazzling smile. "Aaaah…. You're OK, John. You strong man."

As the dhoni punched through the waves and into a sheltered lagoon where Stingray lay with twin anchors out to hold her steady against the fresh wind, I reflected on how the crew had changed their attitude over the past few days. I was by far the oldest aboard and on the first day or two I had been aware of an attitude of concern to help the old man along with steadying hand, "Careful now, John," as I stepped from Stingray on to the dhoni. However, after a couple of days they seemed to realise the old man was really a boy at heart, was as fit as anyone else on board, was usually one of the last to emerge from the depths and had more air left than most. I had earned some respect

And to prove to you that that positive mental attitude works - Magali did come again with me on the next dive.

Chapter 26

Beauty and Chaos

An archipelago of over 7000 islands at the western extremity of the Pacific ocean, the Philippines is an intoxicating mixture of beauty and chaos. The beauty is in the landscape, the beaches, the submarine world, and in the people; not just physical beauty, but often an inner beauty that shines through their smiles despite the fact that so many of them live in poverty. It is a country of contrasts. Long hours of hard work for very little pay and widespread idleness; kindness and begging; squalor and elegant living, adaptability and intransigence. It is a country you can love one moment and hate the next. It has a peculiar magnetism.

The chaos is evident in the traffic. Traffic lights? Och, don't bother too much about them. Only stop for red if you really have to. Just drive through if there is a gap in the line of traffic. Road signs? Ha ha ha…. My taxi driver totally ignored a Give Way sign at an intersection and steamed on into the crossing traffic. Everyone else was doing the same. That is normal, and somehow he carved out a channel for us to cross the continuous flow of traffic. It was like fairground dodgem cars, but for real. My amazed reaction to the blatant disregard for road signs elicited a reassuring response from the driver.

"Filipinos are very good drivers. We don't need road signs. They're only for the foreigners."

Aye, right! Anarchy rules on the roads here. If you actually obey the instructions of the road signs, or hesitate, you are likely to cause an accident; for then it will be such a surprise to the guy following you that he is likely to shunt your rear end. Yet maybe there is some truth in what the driver said about Filipino drivers. They may drive in what appears to be a heart-stopping manner, but they do so with such skill, seizing opportunities to squeeze into gaps with only millimetres to spare. There seem to be relatively few accidents in Manila. Mind you, that is probably because the traffic is usually moving so slowly, often grid locked, going nowhere with horns blaring in frustration. I could never understand why a driver approaching the tail end of a stationary line of traffic of infinite length should ever imagine that blasting his horn would miraculously, like Moses parting the waters of the Red Sea, clear away the hundreds of vehicles blocking the road for miles ahead. Despite the lack of evidence of such miracles, they still do it. They just like using their horns.

Then there are the ubiquitous motorcycle trikes, Japanese motorbikes with a third wheel to the side and a little cab built over the whole contraption, the poor man's taxi. The cab is usually big enough to seat two people with luggage behind, as well as the driver and a pillion passenger, or maybe even two on the pillion, sometimes with more clinging on the outside of the cab. I sat in one that carried 9 adults and three children. It had a bigger cab than most. As well as the usual forward facing front seat for two, it had another seat in the front cab facing backwards. Three adults and three children had squeezed in there. This cab also had a rear compartment that could accommodate four. The driver and another adult on the pillion made a total of twelve people on that trike. Filipinos are designed to fit into small spaces. (Male: Filipino, Female: Filipina) They are generally small compared to westerners, but are beautifully proportioned. I squeezed in there beside three attractive Filipinas wearing brief shorts or miniskirts. I wondered about the smiles on the faces of the two young ladies opposite me as our knees and thighs interlocked in intimate embrace. I was smiling too. As the cab rocked and rolled over the rough roads, knees caressed thighs. I am not sure whether every caress was as a result of the cab rocking, but I have to confess, the cramped conditions did not detract in the slightest from my enjoyment of the journey!

And there are tricycles of the pedal variety too, small Filipino legs powering tricycles often laden with overweight tourists, along dirt roads on some of the smaller islands. The conventional two-wheeled motorcycle is a machine of amazing versatility. It is not unusual to see a whole family of five, mother and father with three children sandwiched between, all on one motorbike. Filipinos are also extremely creative when it comes to adapting their motorbikes to carry cargo: mountains of fruit and vegetables, building materials, pigs, crates of chickens. I saw one motorcyclist happily chugging alone with a bull strapped into his sidecar. With a little ingenuity they will carry almost anything. Imagine a wee man on a motorbike with six, 24-foot long, 4-inch diameter bamboo poles lashed on to it somehow. The forward end protrudes about 10 feet in front of the handlebars and is neatly raised to about decapitating height and the after end is almost scraping the road 10 feet behind and, like a knight of olden times jousting with his lance, he forces his way into the middle of a dense traffic jam.

Jeepneys (derived from Jeep and Hackney Cab) are charming wee buses, unique to the Philippines. Well, charming if you have a warped sense of humour and lust for adventure. Bald tyres are almost standard. Wheel nuts? Why bother with four when three is perfectly adequate. Originally built over the bodies of World War 2 jeeps left behind by the Americans, they are everywhere, often packed with a ridiculous number of people. Usually painted in vivid colours, they are often customised with radiator grills in the style of a Rolls Royce or Cadillac. It's crazy, but delightful, and they are part of the charm of the Philippines.

Manila is a driver's nightmare; a vast, sprawling conurbation of around 15 million people so heavily polluted with exhaust fumes that many people walk the streets wearing masks or holding cloths over their mouths and noses. The pavements are so cracked and uneven it often looks like there might have been a recent earthquake, which is always a possibility. Street lights are few, drains emit foul smells and so too does the greyish-green, very sickly looking river that runs through the city, its surface covered with floating rubbish, and who knows what may lie underneath the surface. Falling into that would be a nightmare. Elegant, modern, high-rise apartment and office blocks and hotels sit cheek by jowl with crumbling slums and shanty dwellings that are simply crawling with people.

It is colourful, dirty, rundown, chaotic, yet it has a peculiar vibrancy about it. It would be difficult to like the place, but I admit to a fascination with it, a feeling that I would love to spend more time to go around with the camera to try to capture the essence of life in this shambles of a city.

And through it all the people still smile and greet you cheerfully in the street. Taking a stroll along the street at night after dinner (I usually only stay overnight between flights), all the gun-toting security guards spoke to me. Every bank, hotel, restaurant and shop appears to be protected by uniformed security men with revolvers in holsters strapped to their waist. It is an incredibly boring job just standing there all day, or all night, and the rare diversion of a pale-faced kilted Scotsman walking by - they don't get many of them here - was enough to elicit cheerful smiles and friendly greetings.

"Good evening sir, where are you from?" How could they tell I was not a local? Not that telling them was enlightening. Very few Filipinos have ever heard of Scotland. OK, try the UK? No. Great Britain?

"Oh yes.... that is in Australia!"

"Noooo.... that's on the opposite side of the world. Ever heard of England?" Vague look.... "You are speaking English. Do you know which country that language comes from?"

Big smile: "Ah, yes.... America!" This is going to be a long night.... Try again.

"Ever heard of Johnnie Walker?" The eyes light up.

"Ah, Johnnie Walker whisky! Very good!"

"Aye, well, that is made in Scotland. That's where I come from." And that was as near as I got to educating them about Scotland. Who cares? The Johnnie Walker brand is recognised the world over. There are five words you can say in almost any language in the world and be understood immediately: "Johnnie Walker, Coca Cola, McDonalds."

I wandered through slum areas taking photos of living conditions that astonished me. People bathed from barrels of rainwater on the pavements and in over-crowded alleyways. Give them credit, they are fastidious about their personal cleanliness. Others did their laundry sitting on the ground confronted by huge basins of soapy water and mountains of family clothing. The laundry was hung to dry on lines strung above the narrow alleyways. A man and his wife lived in a ramshackle hut constructed on the pavement. Made of corrugated iron, bits of wood and plastic, it was just big enough to cover a double bed. The roof was not nailed down, but tied and weighted down with old tyres and broken bits of concrete. The street was his workshop, where he sat and repaired broken umbrellas. Their kitchen was a rough wooden shelf nailed on to the outside of their home with a bucket of charcoal on the pavement for cooking on.

At least they had a home. One of the saddest sights was the number of homeless people sleeping on the streets, a sheet of cardboard to lie on their only luxury. Permanently dirty with the dust and grime of the city ingrained in their skins, whole families slept under bridges, in doorways or simply out in the open. Pathetic, haggard mothers sat cross-legged, with a begging bowl, while tiny babies sucked their thin, sagging breasts for whatever meagre nourishment they could provide. It is not uncommon to see babies, not yet able to crawl, left to lie sleeping on a dirty sheet of cardboard as though abandoned, flies crawling over their tired, malnourished bodies while their mothers wander off to scratch around in rubbish bins and beg for a few pesos to buy some scraps of food. It is horrific. Beauty and intense poverty live cheek by jowl here.

Travelling in the Philippines is never anything less than a fascinating experience. There are good air links and dubious looking ferries to most of the major islands. On land there are buses, many of which should have been condemned to the scrap heap years ago. Open-sided to let the wind blow through - it would be unbearable otherwise - they are very cheap; a few pesos takes you a long way in the Philippines.

And they carry a lot more than people. Don't be surprised to find yourself sitting on a bus with a goat standing in the aisle beside you, or a hog-tied pig lying on the floor, a crate of chickens on the seat opposite, bundles of fruit and vegetables heaped in the aisle, to be climbed over when you want to get out. Anything goes.

A slightly more comfortable alternative is the 'van.' Usually an air-conditioned minibus with no timetable to adhere to, it waits at the terminus until it fills up, or nearly so, and then heads off towards its destination a few hours drive away, picking up more passengers at villages along the route. Now an air-conditioned minibus may sound luxurious compared with some of the buses you see, but wait. It may start feeling comfortable, but these drivers make their money by carrying passengers, right? That means the more passengers they carry, the more money they make, right? And that usually means cramming as many people as possible into the minibus and ignoring all considerations of health and safety, as well as comfort. You pay to be transported, not to expect comfort as well, right? Thankfully, I shared the front seat with the driver and one other passenger, but in the back I could only gaze in wonder at each stop when yet more people piled in on top of the bodies that were already there. On the plus side, that may be a good way to get some interesting introductions. Imagine having two attractive Filipinas sitting on your lap for a two or three hour journey. Maybe next time I should go for a seat in the back! They are a gregarious lot and don't seem to have any concept of personal space, but this was incredible; they were writhing about like maggots in there and nobody seemed to mind in the least. It was only slightly more expensive than the bus, but worth every peso for the entertainment value.

Driving along in the provinces is an endless source of wonder. Maniacal bus drivers, forever blasting their horns, threaten to bulldoze anything travelling in the same direction out of the way and are seemingly intent on mounting a kamikaze attack on everything that comes in the opposite direction while they are overtaking. He who dares wins! It looks suicidal, but as Admiral Nelson is reported to have once said, "To be daring offers the least risk."

A bus ride is a great way to see life in the provinces, an endless pastiche of people and places, with every village apparently having a tiny store attached to almost every house, all selling the same wares. I am baffled by the economics of this. If they are all selling the same things who needs to buy? However, the ladies sit there all day and have an untroubled look on their faces. What else is there to do? Men sit in the shade in groups, talk, gamble with cards or other board games, and smoke. Nobody seems to do much work.

But this is the middle of the day when it is daft to work under a scorching sun. Work may have been done earlier. The evidence is already there in the tarpaulins spread out on the roadside covered with rice drying in the sun, heaps of vegetables and fruit that had been harvested in the early morning, piles of coconuts waiting a cooler hour of the day to be husked and the flesh dried as copra for making coconut oil. Chickens and swine, of many colours and configurations wander in groups along the road sides, meandering in their search for food among children who are often stark naked, playing in the drainage ditches, or having a pee as nature intended, just wherever they happen to be at the time. The men are just as bad. Even in the cities they will stop on a busy city street and pee against a wall. The smell of stale urine is one of the many aromas that assault the olfactory organs in the cities.

In the cool of the morning, women will sit in a ditch washing clothes. That is one thing that impresses me. Despite the poverty and lack of plumbing, their clothes are clean and they change regularly. Dogs, scrawny and mangy looking, whose pedigree defies description, fornicate with gay abandon, producing yet more complex-looking mongrel pups. Every bitch seems to be heavily pregnant. The people often do the same; young mothers in their mid-teens are often to be seen suckling babies instead of attending school. They never seem happier than when they have a baby in their arms, and a child never seems to want for love. The sad part is that so often the fathers abandon the girls when they get pregnant with the result that many of these young girls are destined to migrate to the cities, or abroad, to work for a pittance in factories, hotels, restaurants, bars and often go into prostitution in order to earn enough money which they send home to support their children. The fathers just disappear and find another girl to get pregnant. The babies are often left with the grandmothers who seem content to have yet another baby to love, and so the cycle of exploitation goes on. It is accepted as normal. One unmarried waitress, pregnant for the second time, just smiled, shrugged her shoulders and said, "It is the way in the Philippines."

Wherever I went, away from the normal tourist trails, the people I met seemed pleased to see me. Maybe because I was accepting them and the environment they lived in, city or village, enjoying the sights, sounds and smells - well, maybe not all of the smells! One woman walking along a street smiled at me as she approached, planted a kiss on the tip of her index finger and then placed it on my arm as she passed. She said nothing, just smiled and walked on.

Everywhere the streets were a hive of commerce. And I mean on the streets, not just the shops and offices. Fruit sellers set up their barrows, caterers cooked skewers of barbecued chicken and pork on barbecues on wheels, others sold second hand clothing and shoes, repaired watches, made keys, repaired shoes, patched clothing, took in laundry. Flower sellers set up stalls outside funeral parlours - where better to secure a good trade? Candle sellers were a permanent feature outside churches. The Catholic custom of lighting candles while praying for someone ensures thriving business for candle makers and vendors. Whatever service society required it was available on the streets, and the opportunists were never far away.

Everyone seemingly knows of a good "money-saving" deal for you: renting a car, a motorbike, accommodation, diving, tours of the city or island's highlights, which restaurants to go to, massage, souvenirs, a girlfriend. They are all trying to earn a little commission by bringing customers to the business to supplement the poor pay they get. Everyone… taxi driver, hotel receptionist, shop assistant, man in the street, they all know someone who can offer what you want. It gets a wee bit annoying, but it is understandable given their appallingly low incomes. A refusal does not deter them from enjoying your company and they will ask all sorts of personal questions. "Are you married? Family? Living alone?" (Unheard of in the Philippines where they pack in like sardines and often sleep 3 or 4 to a bed, with more on the floor). They are incredulous. "You live alone? No, that it is not good. You should have a woman to look after you! Come. I introduce you to my cousin. She will take good care of you." And off they go again, trying to arrange a meeting and get you to part with a tip.

Marrying a foreigner, or at least having one for a boyfriend, is the dream of many Filipinas. It is synonymous with financial security, not only for her, but also for her family, and is actively encouraged by many parents. The term 'boyfriend' is pretty flexible. Talking to a twenty year-old waitress, I learned that she had no time for younger men. They could not be trusted and were always playing around with other girls, she told me. An older man was more likely to be faithful. How old? Well, she already had ended a three-year relationship with an Australian in his fifties, who, in spite of her devotion to him, was "messing about with other chicks" (her words). He was too young and immature for her. She was now hoping to meet a loving, caring man in his sixties as she believed that he would be more likely to be faithful to her. What a pity I had to leave in a couple of days!

There are certainly plenty of beautiful young Filipinas, apparently adored and supported by much older white men, predominantly Europeans, Australians and Americans. The physical beauty and inherent charm of the Filipina is a very marketable commodity and these girls enjoy a lifestyle far superior to that they could expect with most Filipinos. The fact that their male escorts may be of significantly less than average looks and physique doesn't seem to matter, nor does age. In many cases what matters is not so much age or the size of his waistline, but the waistline of his wallet! There are plenty of the gold-diggers around, many of whom simultaneously 'manage' several supportive boyfriends in different countries. That can be quite chaotic for them, especially if two boyfriends decide to come at the same time, but they are never short of excuses… "Sorry I can't see you this time, honeyko. My cousin in the province (a far-off rural province with no attraction for a tourist) is in hospital and needs me to look after her children" etc.

They are creative and adaptable people - if not always honest. It is how they survive.

Chapter 27

Island Hopping

You have to be a bit of a masochist, or simply mad, to stay in the mayhem of Manila for more than a couple of days. On my first visit I had nothing planned in advance and spent the first two days there finding out where to go, arranging flights, diving and accommodation. The lure of the islands was strong. With over 7000 islands, transport between them depends heavily on a multitude of ferries. However, don't rush enthusiastically to book a berth on them as these are often geriatric vessels, poorly maintained, frequently overloaded and have a habit of going to the bottom with remarkable regularity. The statistics for ferry disasters in the Philippines make sobering reading. Flying is a far better option with most islands little more than an hour's flying time from Manila and with Philippine Airlines, Cebu Pacific and more recently Air Asia in competition on many routes, there are some really cheap fares if you book early.

Flying at around 28000 feet also offers a perspective on life in the Philippines, enabling the observer to gain a sense of the remoteness of many communities, the extensive agriculture on the plains, the difficult mountainous terrain and dense jungles, the paucity of roads on many islands and the scars created by earthquakes, landslides and volcanic eruptions.

Lying just to the north of Mindanao, the most southerly of the major islands of the Philippines, Camiguin is a gem. In an archipelago of more than 7000 islands, Camiguin manages to be different. Very scenic, it claims to have more volcanoes per square kilometre than any other place on earth. Just over a hundred years ago during a major eruption the lava flow buried several villages, killing hundreds of people. As if that wasn't bad enough, at the same time there was an earthquake (catastrophes often come in twos and threes here), which caused a part of the island to sink below the sea, the part with the village cemetery on it. It is a bizarre experience to encounter an entire cemetery with headstones when diving there.

The lava flow that poured down the mountain and into the sea cooled rapidly and now the hard, black rock is covered with coral growths and is riven with canyons and gullies to swim through. At another spot, I dived in what can best be described as a huge underwater garden with some of the loveliest soft corals imaginable, like the shrubs in a garden, soft branches waving gently in the current, tiny brilliantly coloured fish flitting among the branches, like the birds do in a garden.

Many people ask me if I am not afraid of attacks by sharks. The answer is no; the risk of attack comes not from the big things, but from the ferociously territorial small fish like triggerfish. At Camiguin, I met a most determined little terrier. Having gone down to the sea floor to look at an interesting nudibranch, a kind of sea snail, I felt an astonishingly sharp pain on my heel, as though I had cracked it against some razor-sharp coral. I gasped and looked round. It wasn't a collision with coral, it was a determined attack by a triggerfish on the one-inch strip of white skin that was showing between the bottom of my wet suit and my fins.

The wee devil had drawn blood!

Not satisfied with that, it came in for the attack again like a dive-bomber and had another bite at me. I roared through my breathing apparatus and recoiled in pain, pulled up my legs, and when it attacked again I lashed out with my feet. That sent it back, but it was still game to mount yet another attack. That's enough, I thought, no sea snail is worth all this hassle, and finned my way out of danger. I had unwittingly entered its territory and it came out of its lair like a torpedo and sent me on my way. I couldn't believe how sore it was and it required some first aid when I got back. So, forget the big things, the wee ones are the devils of the deep.

Hiring a motorbike for a couple of days I set off to explore the island, driving up some really rough, rocky tracks to see some waterfalls. The people who live in the forest were very friendly, nearly always calling out to me, "Hello, my friend," as I passed their simple houses, bouncing my way up over the boulders on what they laughingly call a road. It was more like a dried-up riverbed. Which it was in reality, for when the tropical rains fall here the steep mountain roads become rivers. Their houses, built on stilts, are not much bigger than a garden shed, made of woven leaves tied to some bamboo frames and thatched on the roof. They cook outside on a fire and take their water from the streams. In such an island community it was perhaps unsurprising to see the results of inbreeding with a significant number of deformed and mentally handicapped people gazing vacantly at you from the roadside.

The children coming home from school were a delight. As they walked up several miles of rough track to their homes away up in the mountains, they all called out too and waved to me. It felt good being here. This was the legendary friendliness of the Philippines at its simple, innocent best.

Bohol is a large island, one of a group of islands known as the Visayas, in the central Philippines. Its airport is at Tagbilaran, a city of about 100000 people, another shambles of narrow streets with ramshackle stores and crazy traffic - is there any other kind here? The rest of the island is pleasantly rural in character with plenty of cottage industries, rice farming and fishing along the coasts. They are very proud of their Chocolate Hills on Bohol, a must-see for visitors, the eighth wonder of the world, they say. Conical in shape and ranging from about 100 feet to almost 400 feet in height, these hills have been created by a combination of the dissolution of limestone by rainfall, surface water, groundwater and erosion by rivers and streams after they had been uplifted above sea level and fractured by tectonic processes. They consist of sandy to rubbly marine limestones and contain abundant fossils. In the light of the setting sun they take on a chocolate-coloured appearance, hence the name. They are a unique and intriguing curiosity, but to describe them as magnificent spectacle, eighth wonder of the world is stretching it a bit, in my opinion.

Mind you, the Philippines' tourist industry claims to have at least *three* eighth wonders of the world. I have heard the truly remarkable rice terraces at Banuae and the underground river in Palawan similarly described by enthusiastic promoters of tourism. My sojourn through rural Bohol was enjoyable, but it was the beautiful white sands and the diving sites of Panglao, a small island connected by a bridge to Bohol and only half an hour's taxi ride from the airport, that was the primary attraction for me.

The diving was good in general. The reef walls along the coast of Panglao offered some fairly interesting sites, but the best diving was among the coral-rich reefs of Balicasag island, a 45-minute boat ride offshore. Here were very colourful and interesting walls teeming with fish, and nearby in the channel in the early morning it was possible to see dolphins playing.

"Good morning, Sir John," was the daily greeting from the smiling girls who cleaned the rooms at the resort and the waitresses in the restaurant. They are well trained to greet you as 'sir' or 'ma'am', but when I told them to call me John they could not drop the 'sir' and I got the 'Sir John' greeting, same as I got from the Filipino crew on the ship I was on in Antarctica a year previously. Most of the visitors here were in couples or in groups so I was endowed with some curiosity value in being solo - well, maybe wearing the kilt also aroused some interest. Whatever the reason, the room maids, the waitresses, the boys who tended the gardens and the security guards all wanted to stop and chat. However, when the spoons came out to join the band that played in the restaurant each evening, well, that really rocketed me up the popularity ratings. The receptionist abandoned the reception desk and the kitchen staff bailed out to come through to the restaurant to listen. Waiters and waitresses smiled and danced among the tables as they served the guests who gazed in wonder and dug out cameras to take photographs.

Mehmet and Kim, a Canadian couple, showed a lot of interest and enjoyment while I was playing and invited me to join them at their table afterwards, an invitation they repeated every night after that. Being solo does not mean you are always on your own. It is the best way to travel if you want to make friends.

Malapascua, a small island to the north of Cebu Island is a nice wee island of palm trees and white sandy beaches, with maybe a thousand or so friendly inhabitants. Sadly the main attraction eluded me, the thresher sharks, large sharks with one tail fin exceptionally longer than the other. Timid creatures (most sharks are!) that feed in the depths at night, they come up to a shelf at about 20 metres at dawn to be cleaned by the cleaner wrasse, fish which feed on the parasites that cling to the shark's skin. So, early each morning at about 6am, I was in my diving gear and down into the depths to watch this sight.

Huh! Not once did I see a shark of any description.

The annoying thing was that other groups who dived from the same boat, on the same day in the same general location always seemed to see at least one. We were scattered around several so-called cleaning stations where the sharks have their morning ablutions performed by the cleaner wrasse, but when they did appear it was never at one where I lay in wait. Otherwise the diving at

Malapascua was pleasant with some colourful corals and a Japanese wreck. On my last night I offered to take my dive guide and boat crew out for a drink.

"Where is the best place to go?" I asked in all innocence.

My guide smiled. "Karaoke Bar. It is the only place to go."

I hoped he wasn't being literal - but he was! So that was Malapascua nightlife: sitting in a rough wooden shack, measuring about 4 metres square, with a bare earth floor, drinking bottles of beer and slaughtering songs in true Filipino fashion. The locals seemed to be enjoying themselves - and after a couple of beers, miraculously, so did I.

In fact, the more beers I drank, the better it sounded.

Boracay is the premier holiday destination in the Philippines and can justifiably claim to have one of the best beaches in the world, a 4-mile long sweep of fine, white sand fringed with coconut palms. It is idyllic. Viewed from the sea, it is surprising how effectively they obscure the proliferation of resorts and restaurants. This white crescent of sand is washed gently by a vivid, blue sea, which sparkles in the almost ever-present sunlight and is liberally sprinkled with dozens of boats. Daily it presents a dazzling scene, packed with activity.

The boats are nearly all traditional-style outriggers; the double outrigger is favoured here in the Philippines, with booms stretching out on both sides of the hull to offer stability, whereas in the South Pacific the single outrigger is the norm. Some are powered by sail and are very fast, their sleek hulls slicing through the water like a knife. Others, powered by growling, smoking diesel engines, continuously ferry passengers to and from the airport at Caticlan on the nearby large island of Panay, or carry scuba divers to the scattering of diving sites around the island.

There are a few reasonable dive sites around Boracay, some colourful and rich with corals like Crocodile Island, some spectacular and deep like Yapak where the current can be powerful, sweeping up from the depths and over the reef so that it feels like you are clinging on in a gale. Most other sites are mediocre, yet it the most expensive diving in the Philippines.

However, it is a lovely place to relax. Every day a team of professional sandcastle builders earn their living by building the most amazing sandcastles; tourists get their photos taken beside them for a fee. Swimmers and sunbathers proliferate daily on the beach and, to ease away the stresses of life, you can lie on a mat on the sand, or in one of the beach side parlours, and have a whole body massage, a deliciously relaxing way to spend an hour.

A team of masseuses worked at one resort with a good restaurant where I nearly always dined at night. At busy times they also doubled as waitresses and were always ready to chat with me at my table. Sometimes, if customers were thin on the ground I had two of them working on me, one above the waist, one on the legs.

Well, you have to be fair, after all, don't you? And it was the only way I could share myself out to satisfy their desires to get their hands on my body. They also shared the fee so they both had some income.

They were always such pleasant company, teasing me, complimenting me on my blue eyes and fair skin, telling me that I was very handsome and had a good body. Impressed by their impeccable judgement of my aesthetic qualities, I never felt so good about myself.

OK, I know, I know... but massaging my ego as well as my body worked wonders for my morale and, of course, it was just impossible not to give them a tip after that.

They had become my friends on Boracay and Agnes, one of the waitresses, insisted that I come to her 20th birthday party. Her friends, mostly the other waitresses and waiters and the chefs from the resort, gathered on the beach after closing time that night. Sitting in a circle on the sand were these young people from the Philippines, all in their early twenties, and the only foreigner present, a Scotsman wearing a kilt who had been his twenties, well.... maybe a year or two ago. It was a delightful experience. They were respectful, interested in me and learning about my country, and when we parted company around 1am the 'goodnights' and handshakes were repeated several times. I felt honoured to have been asked to join them.

Having developed a wee bit of a cold towards the end of the week I was unable to go diving for the last couple of days, but Sheila, one of the waitresses, had a day off to see her family and offered to guide me on a tour to her home province, Aklan, where I could spend a day visiting a butterfly farm and a coastal conservation area and to visit her family. I really enjoyed that glimpse of Philippines life, meeting people away from the tourist places. We used various forms of transport, travelling by ferry, minibus and then motorcycle tricycle. For the European accustomed to traffic discipline, even out here in the provinces this was quite an experience as you become engulfed in a kind of motorised mayhem. In Kalibo, the main city in this province, the streets are filled with exhaust fumes, mainly from hordes of motorbikes and the ubiquitous trikes, the cheap cabs so beloved by the Filipinos. Engines roar, horns are always being blown, and people and machines mingle in an utterly chaotic fashion. It is pandemonium. Yet somehow, miraculously, it all seems to happen without accident.

Sheila's father made bamboo furniture - and babies in his spare time, twelve of them! Well, OK, her mother helped out a wee bit with that activity. I wondered how they could cram twelve children into one wee house. Sheila laughed and told me he had to build four houses to accommodate them all as they grew up, although with the older girls now working away from home he plans to sell off two of the houses. Her mother, now looking after her grandchildren, had the serene look of someone who loves children - just as well with twelve of them, four girls followed by eight boys and who knows how many grandchildren. After a lunch of fresh fish and rice, we went off sightseeing, to the butterfly farm and a conservation area of coastal marshland with a mangrove forest. An important breeding ground for fish and mud crabs, this interesting environment was so unlike anything in Scotland. Sheila's neighbours were fishermen who seemed pleased by my interest and were happy to pose for me while taking photos of their catch, tiny finger-sized fish, which are tossed into the frying pan and eaten whole. It was an interesting day trip, offering some rare insights into how people live in the provinces.

Also on Boracay, I met up again with Kim and Mehmet, the charming

Canadian couple I'd met at Panglao the week before. Teachers working in Taiwan for a year, they were now coming to the end of their holiday in the Philippines and were about to return to Taiwan to continue their work. We swapped email addresses before we parted and have been in touch ever since.

My flight to Coron, part of Palawan province in the southwest of the Philippines, was on a small plane which landed at an airstrip on the island of Busuanga. Transport into Coron town itself was by jeepney, a dusty, bumpy ride over 'provincial' roads. Oddly, Coron town is not on Coron Island, where I was to stay, but on Busuanga. The coastal scenery in this area is attractive and the diving offers one of the best wreck sites.

It was in September 1944 that US bombers, launched from aircraft carriers at Leyte on the extreme east of the Philippines, crossed to this most western province and attacked a fleet of Japanese supply ships anchored among the small islands, to the west of Coron. The planes, sweeping in low around the hills of the neighbouring islands mounted a surprise, low-level attack and achieved such accuracy with their the bombing that they destroyed the ship's bridges and engine rooms, leaving the rest of the hulls mostly intact, ideal for divers to enjoy, decades later.

Visibility is often not good here and currents can be very strong in this most westerly province where the South China Sea forces its way between islands closely packed together. However, on this occasion my timing coincided with neap tides, so there was less of a current, and visibility was fairly good, allowing panoramic views of the ships as we descended. This was my first experience of serious wreck diving with considerable penetration, exploring the ships' interiors; the cargo holds, engine rooms and various deck levels.

Entering the dark void of the cargo holds, the eyes slowly became accustomed to the gloom and dark shapes began to become recognisable: bags of cement, rolls of steel mesh for making aircraft runways, a bulldozer. The engine rooms, torn apart by the bombs, proved fascinating. Bomb holes allowed light to enter so everything could be seen clearly: huge steel boilers still intact, the propeller tubes, tangled and fractured pipework and cabling, ladders and girders twisted by the searing heat of explosion, steel plate ripped apart, fragmented and scattered randomly around. The bridges of each ship I dived on were totally demolished, a chaotic tangle of shattered metal, testimony to the devastating effect of high explosive and I wondered what kind of hell the men who crewed these ships had gone through in that sudden onslaught of explosion and fire and how many must have died a horrible death there.

Unlike a bombed building, which collapses into an amorphous mass of rubble, a ship may often be still largely intact. The holes in the side or deck where the torpedo or bomb struck, shows metal plating ripped apart like paper wrapping and inside, where the full explosive force wreaked havoc, there is one hellish mess of destruction, with engine rooms now a tangled and twisted morass of tortured metal. Such intimacy with the devastation caused by the bombing of a ship like this always leaves a deep impression. This was more than a dive; it was a lesson in history and the folly of man's wanton lust for power.

It was also a lesson on the power of nature to overcome the destruction we cause. These stricken ships are now thriving communities of marine life. Big fish loomed out of the gloomy darkness of the cargo holds; lionfish, festooned with feathery spines, danced spectacularly in the shadows of the wheelhouse and through the gaps in the shattered wreckage on deck. An octopus timidly backed itself into a dark cavity near the stern, a large cuttlefish gazed at us through dopey eyes and showed little concern about our presence. Wreck diving is fascinating.

This is very much a frontier area and no one knows how many people live in its remote jungles. There are still indigenous tribes on Palawan and Coron who are shy of outsiders, even other Filipinos, and disappear silently into the bush if outsiders approach. I saw a couple of remote settlements from the dive boat. Living a traditional way of life, as their ancestors have done for hundreds of years before them, they inhabit remote coastal bays and jungle clad hills and have little concept of 'civilisation' as we conceitedly call it. Amongst all the people of the Philippines, they must have been the ones for whom the Japanese invasion of World War Two had negligible effect. If a Japanese patrol boat ever approached a coastal village they would simply melt away into the dense jungle until it had gone. Living in a remote area of dense jungle with no towns or cities, no natural harbours, factories, transport routes, nothing of interest to an invading force, these people could live quietly and peacefully as they had always done, while the 'civilised' world tore itself apart with bombs and terror.

The town of Coron has a frontier feel to it. Unsophisticated, with many small crude homes built on stilts out over the murky waters of the harbour, it is a place for fisherman to spend their money in the multitude of noisy karaoke bars that line the jetty, all side by side, each one belting out murderously tortured songs at full volume, all different, all equally terrible to listen to in a hideous cacophony of noise that bears little resemblance to music. And they love it, and do it every night. So typically Filipino, it has the kind of inelegant lack of charm that inevitably attracts me.

I had been ambivalent about my first visit to the Philippines, hopeful that it would live up to its reputation for friendliness and excellent diving, but concerned about the overcrowded cities and the social problems that can create; a potential breeding ground for various forms of crime. Happily, I had no problems. Poverty is endemic and many live in the most desperate squalor in the poorest housing conditions I have seen anywhere, particularly in Manila. It is little wonder that some turn to crime and prostitution, but millions of Filipinos seek work abroad where the pay is better and they can support their families financially. Some Filipino families have been reported in the press as living on as little as 10 pesos per day (about UK £0.15 or 24 cents US), yet I found so many happy, laughing and handsome people. It exceeded my expectations. It had a kind of magnetism that lured me back again and again.

Sitting on the stairs of the resort on my last day there, I enjoyed talking with the girls who cleaned the rooms as they rested between spells of work. Brown skin, black hair and brown eyes are standard in the Philippines, so my fair skin, blue eyes and fair hair had always attracted comment wherever I had gone. It was quite enchanting to have these pleasant girls sitting beside me on the stairs, looking into my blue eyes, stroking my fair hair and telling me, "You are so handsome, Sir John, much better looking than the Filipino men."

And do you know, I was told this so often... honestly... I even began to believe it myself! Is it any wonder that I resolved to return as soon as possible?

Chapter 28

The Tide Of Fortune

My next visit to Coron was on a former Japanese fishing trawler, Oceanic
Explorer, which had been converted for diving expeditions under the house flag
of the Philippines based Expedition Fleet who run dive live-aboard vessels in
various parts of the Western Pacific. A very substantial vessel, it was my home
for a week while combining diving at Apo Reef with the wrecks of the Japanese
fleet of supply vessels at Coron Bay. I have always enjoyed being on live-aboard
diving trips: the way of life afloat, the excellent food (and plenty of it), the
chance to do four, sometimes five, dives per day in exciting diving environments
and the social aspect. Life on board can be great for the camaraderie that
develops among divers.

Sadly this trip did not live up to expectations. Although I enjoyed most of
the diving, there were serious shortcomings in other ways. The engineers could
neither control the icy blast of air that masqueraded under the title air-
conditioning in some cabins, nor could they manage to provide hot water in all
the cabins. I was moved from my blast-freezer style cabin with hot water, to one
in which the air-conditioning was working normally, but the hot water system
had failed completely. Even in tropical waters you lose much body heat with
repetitive diving and that hot shower is very important in the evening to warm
your innards and restore a feeling of wellbeing. On this ship all they could
muster was a kettle of water giving me two inches of boiling water in the bottom
of a bucket. That made three inches for washing after some cold water was
added to get it to a tolerable temperature, not quite the standard expected from
the advertising for a trip that boasted air-conditioned cabins and hot showers.

The initial briefing on board left much to be desired. No safety procedures
were mentioned. Dive times were seldom adhered to: a group of Russians
seemed incapable of moving themselves to get ready in time for each dive
(seemingly a common trait among Russians, I have noticed) and the divemasters
sat around lazily waiting for them instead of hurrying them on until I got fed up
with this nonsense and took matters into my own hands and started hounding the
divemasters to get moving and chase up the rest. There were two small fast boats
to take the divers to precise locations over the wrecks. Our guide was new to the
area and did not know exactly where to go so we were dependent on the guide
in the other boat (the one with the Russians) to find the wrecks, but 30 minutes
after we should have left one afternoon they were still sitting smoking and
making no effort to get ready for the dive. I lost my cool and got them stirred up.

The boats left from opposite sides of the ship. When the Russians finally got
going from the starboard side no one came to tell us, still tied up along the port
side. They left with the one guide who knew where to go and when I eventually
went round to check and discovered they had gone ten minutes previously and

had disappeared round the headland, we were left in the state we were in before, with a boat waiting full of divers and neither dive guide nor boatman knew where to go. We set off, almost an hour after the scheduled time for the dive, following another boat a long way off heading out to the open sea. That was clearly not right. I had to tell them they were headed completely in the opposite direction. By the time it took them to realise that I was right they could not find the location of the wreck among the many inlets in the area, but almost added to the list of wrecks by hitting a reef while at full speed.

Luckily it was the skeg of the outboard engine that struck and took the blow, not the hull of the boat. We had to return to the ship to get the cruise director to come and locate the wreck for us, arriving just as the Russians were finishing their dive. What should have been an afternoon dive had now become a twilight dive and ended up as a short-time dive because light was going fast and we were not equipped with torches for a night dive. It was a farce. It just went on and on; incompetence, bad management, changing plans at the past moment, always to suit the Russians, with never any consultation with the four other non-Russian divers.

Poor visibility and strong currents are not uncommon there. I could tolerate that, but the Russians wouldn't, so to please them the diving on wrecks was aborted (and this was advertised as a wreck diving trip) and the ship took off to let us dive some reefs instead. That did not please me. The reefs were in very poor health and harboured little of interest. The only memorable sight there was at the end of a night dive when we came up under a flock of small marine worms swimming on the surface. They generate their own light and glow in the dark; little luminous worms, wriggling their way along the surface of the sea, leaving a trail of luminescence in their wake. Looking up at that from below when diving at about 5 metres was an amazing sight, like looking up at the night sky and seeing dozens of tiny, randomly moving, luminous comet trails.

I like wreck diving, and despite the fearsome currents at times and the poor visibility, it still excited me. A ship is still an object of fascination to me even when it is a wreck, maybe even more so then. The sights of the bomb holes in the ships, metal peeled apart like torn paper and engine rooms devastated by the searing heat and blast of explosion was very much in evidence here. Massive boilers still stood erect, having boldly defied the inferno that had blazed there in 1944. Cavernous cargo holds lay open, cathedral like, inviting exploration of their dark and gloomy interiors: passageways, dark and eerie, are now traversed only by the resident population of fish, and the occasional adventurous diver. I love it all, even when you can only see a couple of metres ahead of you. It adds to the sense of mystery.

The exterior surfaces of the ships now host a myriad of corals, sponges, anemones among which flit the many fish that live in this city below the waves; big dopey-looking, flat-faced batfish, and the cleaner wrasse that groom them daily; large moray eels lurking in shadowy holes among the wreckage; lionfish, festooned with 'feathers' performing their slow-motion marine ballet, scorpionfish, stealthily lying in wait for their prey, so well camouflaged as to be almost impossible to detect.

Although there was some enjoyment in that voyage, it was sadly spoiled by too many irritations and it was a relief to step ashore. It may not have been a total disaster, but it got close to it, and I wrote to the company pointing out their failings in a 3500 word report. To make matters worse, I had also booked a trip with the same company to Tubbataha Reef, a world heritage site and reputedly not only the best dive site in the Philippines, but one of the best in the world, which can only be dived between March and June. However, this trip had never been confirmed by the company, and within three days of the date of departure I had cancelled due to the lack of communication. I decided to take a flight from Manila to Dumaguete for a few days diving there instead.

On arriving at the Cebu Pacific check-in desk I was informed that my flight to Dumaguete had been cancelled due to technical problems with the aircraft. My heart sank. However, the airline would put me up in a hotel, bring me back in the morning for an extra flight and give me a free flight on any of their routes at anytime within the next year. That was not so bad, although I had to have a 3.30am wake-up call, which was not so good, but I got to Dumaguete at 7.45am and found accommodation, contacted my friend, Paul Allen, and he took me to a dive shop to fix up some diving.

Unfortunately, our plan to dive together had to be aborted as he had had a motorcycle accident and had lumps of skin scraped off his arms and legs so he was beached for a while. However I got some diving arranged for next day. Then the weather took a turn for the worse, a storm blew up and diving was cancelled. Every plan I made now seemed to be doomed to failure.

I then received an email from the Explorer Fleet agent, very apologetic about the lack of communication and explaining that they had to change the dates for the Tubbataha Reef trip to accommodate a group booking, but they had never bothered to tell me! They did offer an alternative on a smaller boat, either on the same dates or on the transition cruise starting 9 March when the boat leaves its base at Anilao in the north and sails south to its base at Puerto Princessa for the Tubbataha cruises. This transition cruise also offered diving at Apo Reef and Cuyo Island on the way south, plus four days at Tubbataha reef with five dives per day there and then back to base at Puerto Princessa.

Now that sounded very attractive, but I was then at Dumaguete about 500 miles away, having been at Sabang, only a stone's throw from Anilao just a couple of days previously, and there were only two days left before the boat was due to sail. I was fuming. I was only in Dumaguete due to their failure to run the boat trip on the advertised dates. On receipt of my complaints about the shortcomings of the Coron Trip the previous week they had suggested some recompense, but had only offered a $200 gift voucher which I could only use on their boats for gifts (who needs another T shirt or mug?), nitrox, food or drink. Not much good if I wasn't going to be on their boats again.

I decided to take the initiative and made my own suggestion for recompense. They could fly me back, at their expense, from Dumaguete to Manila, arrange a taxi to meet me at the airport and take me to Anilao (a two-hour drive), give me the transition cruise free to make up for all the inconvenience and discomfort I had suffered as a result of their bungling and lack of communication, put me up overnight in a hotel in Puerto Princessa at the end of the cruise, and then fly me back to Dumaguete.

In return I would write a full report on the cruise for them and, if the experience proved to be a good one, I would promote the company among the diving fraternity and in my lectures when I come home. As they had stated that they wanted to use my previous critical report in their boat operator's manual, I would accept the free cruise, flights etc instead of demanding a management consultant's fee for the use of my report.

My demands went all the way up to the owner of the company, Mr John Wee. He issued orders to his staff that my demands should be met in full, but instead of the smaller, more basic boat, Apo Explorer, I should be accommodated in a de-luxe cabin on board the Stella Maris, the flagship of the fleet. Furthermore, I should be given two nights in a hotel at Puerto Princesa because the flights from there were only operating three days per week. Now, that was not so bad. The tide of fortune seemed to be flowing in my favour at last.

My arrival on board Stella Maris at Anilao for the transition cruise as a non-paying guest proved interesting. John Wee had come down in person to meet me at the dock, and to brief the crew as a result of my lengthy feedback from the previous fiasco. He had gone over my report in detail with the crew and spelled out exactly what was expected of them on this cruise. Axelle, one of the dive guides told me later my report had had quite an impact on the company, really shaking things up. She said they had all been living in dread of this "character who had made so many complaints," but, as she so sweetly put it, "It was such a surprise to actually meet you. You're not like that at all. You are really quite nice." I did notice that they were all very keen to make sure everything was OK. Even the captain came down from the bridge in full dress uniform, brilliant whites with gold-braided cap and epaulettes, to welcome me on board.

The ship left Anilao that evening. It was a moonless night, the sea black. Our bow waves thrust themselves away from the ship, tumbled creamy white and speckled the surface of the sea with foam. The gentle north-easterly breeze was neutralised by our south-westerly course and speed, giving us virtually still air on deck; warm tropical air, as close to a perfect comfort level as you could imagine.

Above was a brilliant, star-spangled sky, the kind you only ever see when you are far from any source of artificial light; unspoiled, a black backcloth hung with diamonds and the great, glowing band of the Milky Way. We stood on the upper deck looking in wonder at the sky above, with that awe and sense of infinity that comes from seeing the universe reveal itself in all its glory. Constellations were identified: astern of us lay Ursa Major, the Great Bear, otherwise known as the Plough or Big Dipper, lining up its leading edge with Ursa Minor, the Little Bear, and within it, Polaris, the Pole Star, invaluable to navigators, always indicating the direction of North. The stellar signpost for South, the Southern Cross, was also visible, close to the horizon off our port bow, and high off our starboard bow stood Orion with his studded belt standing out clearly against the glow of the Milky Way. A meteor plummeted downwards at breakneck speed, glowing brightly as it burned itself out on entering the earth's atmosphere, its glow dying as suddenly as it had had been born, its short life lasting perhaps only two or three seconds. The only earthly light visible was that of our sister ship Apo Explorer, several miles ahead of us, her white aft steaming light showing a few points off our port bow. It was the kind of night when sleep seemed superfluous; you felt you could stay up till dawn, enjoying the beauty of the night sky.

The guests on board this time were five wise-cracking American divers travelling as a group, a great bunch with whom I have formed lasting friendships, meeting them somewhere for diving every year since, and another American, from California, who had been everywhere, done everything and found everything "really interesting." A married couple from Denmark and myself were the only Europeans. Two of the dive guides were girls, Axelle from France and Emi from Japan, plus Danny, a Filipino and Paul the cruise manager, a very experienced diver from Wales. They were a good team and we all got on very well together. The food was excellent: they even had oatmeal porridge for breakfast.

Tubbataha Reef looked beautiful in the sunshine when we arrived; a thin strip of white sand fringed by the palest turquoise blue giving way to the deep aquamarine of the ocean where the reef drops off dramatically in a sheer, underwater wall to the seabed over 1000 feet below. Dropping off the boat and into the water, it was a delight to see that visibility was as near perfect as it could be. Beautiful white sand lay between the corals on the ledge, then that fantastic wall, encrusted with growth, dropped into the blue void. Sharks patrolled like grey gunboats along the edge of the wall and loads of brightly coloured small fish danced among the corals. Several turtles cruised around in leisurely fashion and you could see for miles along the reef, or so it seemed. It was a breathtaking introduction to this spectacular reef.

There were sharks galore, large stingrays, huge napoleon wrasse, large groupers lurking silently in caves, or resting on ledges under overhangs, blue-finned trevally, brilliantly coloured sweetlips, both the oriental and spotted varieties, sea snakes, turtles, and all the usual smaller vividly coloured reef dwellers, large schools of thousands of spiralling trevally and brilliantly coloured blue and yellow fusiliers racing along in lines like cars in a formula one motor race. The star of the show was a large manta ray that cruised, quite unconcerned by our presence, right through the middle of the group. The Americans were gob-smacked by it all. They raved about it.

"I've seen more varieties of fish on that one dive than I've seen in all the dives I've done in the Caribbean," gasped one of them when we surfaced.

Maybe I have been spoiled, having dived so many of the world's top spots now, but when asked for my impression, I replied with typical Scottish understatement, "Och, it was no' bad."

"*Naaat Baaad!*" drawled one of them in astonishment. "How could anything be better than that?"

Joking apart, it was really spectacular with fantastic visibility. The reefs here consist of two atolls, about five miles apart, elongated coral reefs encrusting the tops of ancient undersea volcanoes which drop steeply to the ocean floor. There is little to be seen above the surface; on each atoll only one small hump of sand with a handful of palm trees on it, a few lumps of coral showing at low tide and a long white strip of sand washed by the sea. A ranger station manned by a few armed guards is perched on stilts. They are there to protect the reef from the predations of illegal fishing. Sadly there is evidence of dynamite fishing from a few years ago; in one place the reef had been totally devastated, leaving a barren desert almost devoid of any life forms. It will take many years before it will return to its natural state.

They still practice this invidious method of fishing in many locations in South East Asia. Dynamite is not selective. It does not kill only fish with commercial value, but destroys thousands of the small immature fish that inhabit such reefs: and it kills the coral, the source of food for so many of the fish and the provider of shelter for millions of small and immature fish. Corals may be hard, but they are brittle; or they may be soft, tender, plant-like growths. Either way, they cannot stand up to the shock of a dynamite explosion. And once the coral has been killed the shelter and food source has also been destroyed.

Maze-like coral structures become heaps of rubble. The reef lies forlorn, its skeleton shattered into millions of pieces; it becomes a desert where there was once a Garden of Eden, a grey wasteland offering no food, no shelter, and no more fish. The easy catch for the fisherman is a one-off event. His fishing method has effectively killed off his source of food and income for at least a generation. No living coral means no fish. No fish, no livelihood. It is crass stupidity.

Of course nature has a wonderful way of regenerating. But a coral reef is a living growing structure that has taken thousands, or even millions, of years to construct, yet it can be destroyed in seconds. It will take a long time for nature to re-build what was so callously destroyed. Growth is recovering, but to get back to the colourful state it was in before will require many decades, probably hundreds of years.

The wall, honeycombed by caves and tunnels, is a great refuge for fish. I found one cave at a low level and had a look in. Dark at first, a bluish light ahead signified that it had another opening higher up. I pushed on in, fish darted away into darker recesses, and I looked up what was like a chimney to the blue light. It was clear ahead so I drew in some air and slowly floated upwards through this vertical passage to the daylight, eventually emerging at a smallish opening just large enough for one diver to pass through quite easily. Axelle had been taking the role of tail-end-charlie to mop up any strays who may have been left behind the group. She hadn't noticed that I had slipped into the cave about five metres below and she timed it to perfection to turn and look towards the hole just as my head appeared, framed in the opening in the wall. She literally jumped with fright! "How did you get in there?" she demanded when we surfaced, "I thought you were way ahead of me."

"Och, I just slipped in down below when you weren't watching. It looked like an interesting cave so I carried on in and upwards. It was so funny to see the shock on your face when my head appeared in the wall."

"I couldn't believe it at first, seeing this apparition appearing in the hole in the wall. It was like I was having a dream, no.... more like a nightmare!" she retorted. Huh. Girls really know how to put a guy down.

So my encounters with the explorer fleet did have a happy ending and I was happy to submit a very positive report to Mr Wee. I didn't have to pay anything, not for drinks on board, or nitrox, or national park fees to make amends for my previous bad experience. They deserve credit for that. My luck had changed at last... or was it luck?

It reminded me of a book I read while trekking in the Patagonian mountains, given to me by an American. It was discussing why some people seem to be lucky while others appear to be unlucky in life. He thought I should read it as he felt my life seemed to be just such a case study. Basically, the thesis was that so-called lucky people make their own good fortune by the decisions they make, how they live, and in particular by how they react to situations: keep cool, stay positive and always look for a win-win outcome.

It seemed to apply in this case.

Chapter 29

Palau

"Palau? Where is that?" Other than among the diving fraternity, no one I met in the Philippines, Palau's closest neighbour, seemed to have heard of the place. I doubt if many people in other parts of the world will have much knowledge of Palau either. A small independent island republic with a population of about 18 000 people it lies about 600 miles east of the Philippines, away out in the Pacific, so it is not surprising that few people know it exists. Ask any serious diver, however, and you will be met with envious looks, for it is widely regarded as one of the top dive spots in the world. A flight from Manila, lasting about about an hour and a half, makes it accessible if you are already in the Philippines, as I was. I also resolved to visit Yap and Truk Lagoon, both in the neighbouring Federated States of Micronesia while there.

The indigenous people are very laid back; some call them lazy. They are apparently quite stubborn in their attitude towards work; it is something to be done only when necessary. I have been told the reason why a third of the population is Filipino is that they will work, whereas many of the locals will work for a couple of weeks till they get paid and then take time off to enjoy life being idle. Survival is not a problem. Food can easily be found: just go fishing, or pick fruits and coconuts. There certainly are few Palauans to be seen working in the hotels, shops and restaurants. They are nearly all staffed by Filipinos. It was the same at the dive shop.

Koror, the main island, is a pleasant place with a wide, main thoroughfare and modern buildings. Tourism, the mainstay of the economy, is booming. Large new hotels cater for mainly Japanese, Korean and American customers, but a fair number of Europeans endure the long flights to get here for diving.

In spite of its remoteness, I met two people who recognised me within the first three days. On my first day, an Italian diver approached me and smiled. "You were at Malapascua, in the Philippines, last year in October." Correct. Maximo was formerly the technical director of Lamborghini, the prestigious Italian sports car company. He is now self-employed as an engineering design consultant so he can have more time off for diving.

On my third day here, in the Internet café, a familiar face looked up from its computer and the eyes opened wide. It was Jason Shaw, a lawyer from the USA who had recently landed a nice job here as district prosecutor, with plenty of time for diving. We had been on the same live-aboard cruise to Tubbataha Reef in the Philippines nine months earlier.

Who would have believed I would meet two people who knew me on such a tiny, remote island in the vastness of the Pacific Ocean? In fact, there were actually three - as Jason told me that Paul, our cruise director on the Tubbataha trip, was now working on one of the live-aboard boats that cruise around Palau.

It is a small world, that of the diving fraternity.

The few inhabited islands are so close together that they are connected by bridges. The others, hundreds of them, are the remnants of ancient reefs formed millions of years ago. Mostly limestone pinnacles which have been thrust up above the surface of the ocean, they are now thickly clad with trees. These rocky outcrops are scattered to the southwest of the main islands, a maze of islets covered in dense green foliage with the sea in between offering every shade of blue imaginable, from almost white over the shallow sandy reefs, through pale turquoise and deep green to dark blue in the deep channels. It is a striking landscape.

Currents run strongly here bringing a rich supply of nutrients from deep in the ocean and that attracts the fish. Sharks are everywhere and one of the things you do when diving here is just find the right spot in one of the channels, such as Blue Corner, where the tide runs briskly and that is where you'll find the big fish. Drop your reef hook and hover in the current and the sharks come to you, gliding out of the blue, prowling around silently, their sleek, streamlined forms easing through the water effortlessly; lean, mean-looking machines so perfectly designed for what they do that they are one of the oldest life forms on the planet, remaining virtually unchanged for millions of years. They have become accustomed to divers, mingling easily among us, as we hovered motionless. They were swimming in front of us, on each side and behind us, paying no more attention to us than they would do to a lump of coral. They had nothing to fear, nor had we. Cameras clicked and video cameras followed their graceful movements.

Some large bumphead parrotfish gnawed at the reef below us; some large Napoleon Wrasse also mingled freely, showing no concern, just curious to have a close look at us. They have such warm friendly faces. One in particular was as playful as a puppy and seemed to enjoy being stroked. I don't approve of that. Touching anything underwater can be a risky business either for the diver, who may suffer stings, cuts and abrasions, or for the fish, which may suffer skin disease through contact with us.

There were mantas too, coming in for their daily cleaning, hovering around the cleaning stations where the small cleaner wrasse poked their heads into the gills and cleaned out the remnants of the mantas dinner, scouring their enormous bodies for parasites and dead skin cells, cleaning and keeping the giants of the sea in good condition, while at the same time earning a good feed for themselves.

A Japanese wartime shipwreck provided some poignant images. A freighter with its stern blasted open, depth charges lying around in an untidy pile inside, having been tossed around in the explosion, motor vehicle engines still lying deep in its hold. Around the stern-mounted gun, ripped off its mountings and now lying askew and useless, lay canisters loaded with shells that it never had time to fire. A rifle, heavily encrusted with growths and a large saucepan with a gas mask inside, had been placed in an open spot so that divers could see them without having to penetrate the dark chambers that once were occupied by men. It was a vessel full of images, some moving, a poignant reminder of the horrors of war.

The Blue Hole, one of the world's best-known dive sites is literally that, a big blue hole. You drop off the boat and locate a dark hole in the reef. You descend into it, slowly, dropping down an enormous funnel until you reach a cathedral-like chamber at 20 to 30 metres depth. There are various openings on the sides allowing light inside, each one offering a blue neon-like glow, which illuminates the cavern. The walls are clothed in marine growths and in crevices you can find those remarkable electric clams and, when you approach, their open jaws flash lightning across from one end to the other. It never fails to thrill to see that electric-blue lightning flash across this bi-valve shellfish's open mouth. It seems to say "Keep Off."

At the bottom of the Blue Hole a small, dark tunnel leads you deep into the reef, into a cavern called the Temple of Doom. Its narrow entrance allows only one diver at a time to go through and, once inside, the chamber is enormous and totally dark. A rope has been stretched across this huge black cavern as a guide. Follow that and eventually your torch light reveals the skeletons of some turtles that had wandered in here and could not find the way out, hence the Temple of Doom moniker. It is not surprising.

Total blackness can be very disorienting. I usually find I have a good sense of direction, but in there with absolutely no terms of reference to give hints as to which way I had come or should go, it had me confused completely after I had stopped to try to photograph some interesting little shrimps I found on the pure white limestone floor of the cave.

Unfortunately, just as I was about to press the shutter, the female half of our pair of divers from hell (a Russian couple) came barging blindly into me with her enormous camera, scared the shrimps which took off like rockets into the blackness and, as she passed, her fins stirred up clouds of white dust. She was an absolute disaster. Her partner was not much better. They had no sense of awareness of their surroundings and blindly barged into other divers, they finned like they were in a sprint and crashed into so much coral they left a trail of broken pieces along the seabed, and as for buoyancy control... she left me speechless.

I had watched in amusement when she had been raised by a strong current while we were hooking on to watch the sharks at Blue Corner. She dumped air to get back down, but never thought to re-inflate with air to stop her descent. She came down like a bomb, landing on a group of divers who were hooked on to the reef watching some sharks. She, and her huge camera and its gantry with lights, became entangled in the divers below and then it got amusing to see them trying to extricate themselves from this mess of arms and legs and photographic paraphernalia and air hoses. One turned on to his back to try to see what he had to get hold of and there she was sitting astride him with her crotch in his face, her legs tangled in his air hose as they wrestled with each other to free themselves. It was like an obscene movie.

I don't understand what it is about Russians, poor training, or just a devil-may-care, selfish attitude, but from my experience they have no idea how to behave as divers. In Komodo, the dive boat I was on refused ever to take bookings again from Russians. In Sipadan I heard some horror stories about their dangerously lunatic behaviour, when two lives were lost through sheer stupidity, going deep.

Chandelier cave is an impressive limestone cave, mostly underwater, with a chamber in it known as the Crocodile's Bedroom. The only way in and out is by diving. And how do the crocodiles get in and out of their bedroom? That's right, they have to dive too, using the same exit and entrance as we did. That's a sobering thought! Once we were all in there our guide showed us the ledge in a small cave off to the side of one chamber where the crocodile liked to sleep. However, it hasn't been seen for some time and no one had ever been attacked. The Palauan crocodiles are tourist friendly it seems.

This cave was quite spectacular, a large, dark cavern with four chambers, each with an air pocket where you can surface into the chamber and gaze in wonder at the sight revealed by your torchlight. It is almost like being in the middle of a huge cathedral with ornately carved walls. It is really quite ethereal and provided an interesting change from the usual dives.

Jellyfish lake is another peculiarity. One of several inland lakes on the small limestone islands, it was formed around 15000 years ago. The islands at that time began to slip back into the sea, and what had been a valley above sea level in the middle of the island became flooded as the sea made its way in through the many fissures in the limestone. The result was a salt water lake, fed by the sea as the tides rise and fall and home to a couple of species of jellyfish which have remained there ever since, some anemones and a few species of fish. It became a major tourist attraction after being featured in National Geographic Magazine in 1982. Now the tourists come to swim in the lake among the millions of jellyfish. Like the Palau crocodiles, the jellyfish are tourist friendly and do not sting you. Diving is not allowed as toxic hydrogen sulphide gas is produced in the deep silt on the lake bottom as organic matter decays. Stirring this layer up with fins would release the gases and kill the jellyfish. Snorkelling is all that is required to enjoy what is a truly remarkable experience.

These jellyfish are gorgeous creatures, their mushroom shape pulsating slowly, rhythmically, the short tendrils trailing below, or behind the dome-shaped head depending on whether the jellyfish is swimming upright or horizontally. When you hover there in that warm water in the soft light of the afternoon sun watching thousands of these beautiful creatures pulsate before you at their sedate pace it is impossible not to feel an intense tranquility. They are stunningly beautiful and so soft as they brush gently against your body, sensuously caressing you.

It is like a dream, inducing a sense of euphoria and is incredibly relaxing. It would be great therapy for people suffering from stress.

Chapter 30

Yap

Only about half a dozen passengers got off the plane at Yap, my next destination after Palau, the rest going on to Guam so this made baggage collection and immigration clearance quick and easy. The immigration officer was polite and friendly and wished me a happy stay on Yap. A Yapanese warrior in traditional dress waited to greet us with a friendly welcome and draped flowery garlands over our shoulders, a nice touch, which alleviated the pain of arrival at 3.15am and getting to bed at 4am. I began to think this was a place that might rival the friendliness of the Cook Islands, but it went downhill from then on.

The people I met here are even more laid back than any other island group I have encountered in the Pacific. How long does it take to cook a fried egg and a couple of strips of bacon? Five minutes maybe? Not on Yap. They need half an hour. There is no point in getting flustered. Action is anathema to them. It is easier just to shrug your shoulders and accept their way of life. Relax. Of course, but...

Then the frustrations build up. I had booked a dive and accommodation package several months earlier and supplied my credit card details for payment. However, it seems the owner of the dive business had since died in a diving incident and no one else knew what business he had completed; he was the only signatory to the bank account, which had been frozen since his death so the dive business could not use the credit card machine and they wanted me to pay in cash. I didn't have enough cash, so I went to the Bank of the Federated States of Micronesia, the only bank on the island, to draw some from my UK account using my bank card. Simple. Not so.

First, there is no cash machine in this entire state. Second, this is a bank that is not even able to do business with either credit or debit cards over the counter. If you don't have a bank account in this actual bank you can't get any money from it. You get the feeling that Yap still hasn't quite found its way into the 20th century, let alone the 21st.

After some negotiations, the hotel allowed me to pay by credit card and include the cost of the diving and they would then give the cash for diving to the dive shop. However, they charged me 7% extra for this service. Add to that the 2.5% service charge my own bank levied for a foreign currency transaction and I was paying nearly 10% more. All because the owner of the dive shop who arranged the package had not completed the business at his end and then gone and done some silly things on a deep dive to please some stupid American woman who wanted to go deep, 87 metres (284 feet) according to their computers, on a single tank of air. That's more than twice the depth limit for air diving. They both ended up with the bends; she survived in a hyperbaric chamber, he did not. I had been offered a 10 % discount for making the booking four months early and agreeing to pay by credit card up front. Now I was being charged the full rate and asked to stump up 10% extra as a result of his negligence and stupidity.

As it was the owner's negligence that led to this situation I saw no reason why I should be penalised by having to pay more. I was only prepared to pay the agreed price. But I had fitted in extra diving, for which I would be charged extra. Fair enough. I suggested a compromise. I would pay the hotel the package price by credit card and they could give the cash for diving to the dive shop for which I would be charged 7% extra, but the dive shop could compensate me for that extra cost by allowing me to have the extra diving I had done for free. The stalemate was resolved. Travelling to remote places can be challenging.

Yap was a massive disappointment. The diving did not live up to all the hype I had read about it. In what claims to be the number one location for seeing manta rays in the world, only one manta ray was sighted in very murky waters. Visibility had been very poor throughout my stay. OK, that was just my bad luck; you can never guarantee these things and on another day it could be clear with maybe a dozen mantas. You take your chance. But what really disappointed me was the state of the coral. So much of it was dead with very little colour and very few fish around. On the last day, the weather improved. The wind dropped and we were able to dive around the exposed outer reefs to the south of the island, which the guide said had the best dive sites. One wall dive was moderately good with a fair bit of life on it, but the rest was a sad picture of what is happening in so many parts of the world with over 60% of our coral reefs dead.

Global warning has raised sea temperatures and that is enough to kill a lot of the coral. Is it our fault, creating global warming by our lifestyle? Or is it a natural phenomenon? The debate goes on. Whatever the reason, Yap presented a depressing picture compared to some of the excellent dive sites I had seen in South East Asia with pristine reefs teeming with fish.

The cost of everything was high. That is to be expected on a remote island, but the cost/quality relationship did not quite balance out. You pay very high prices for very mediocre food and extremely poor service. In a place like this they should be able to serve fresh vegetables. In equally remote islands in Indonesia for example they were prepared to cook the food rather than just tip it out of a tin and heat it up. Compared with neighbouring Palau where you can have good quality, freshly prepared Thai, Indian, Chinese, Korean, Japanese or western style food, this place fell far short in the catering sphere. You pay high prices for low quality food and service.

The waitresses in general were sullen, overweight, with their jaws so stuffed with betel nut and tobacco they could hardly speak. Periodically they spat out a large mouthful of foul scarlet juice into a bin in a corner of the restaurant. What does that do for ambience in a restaurant? Never once did I get a smile from them, nor did I see them ever smile at anyone else. They had no interest in their work. What a difference from the charming Filipinas who worked in the restaurants at Palau.

Everywhere you go you have to watch where you tread as the islanders here are forever chewing betel nuts and tobacco and spitting out mouthfuls of blood-red juice on the streets. Their teeth are stained so ugly with the red and brown dyes of the nuts and the tobacco, with the teeth slowly rotting away under the attack of the chemicals in the juice. It looks hideous.

Yap. Yeuch! This is one place I will not be returning to.

However, on my arrival at the airport on my way out of Yap, I was greeted with the utmost courtesy by the staff who were all very pleasant, as they had been on my arrival. They were so different from those dull, dumpy, betel nut chewing waitresses who served in the restaurants. The immigration officer told me he hoped I would come back. I hadn't the heart to tell him, "No way."

After checking in my baggage, I had time to kill as I waited for the incoming flight. Two guys sitting on a verandah at a café beside the terminal were playing guitars and singing. I wandered over. They were good. I pulled out the spoons and joined them.

"Hey, that's cool, man! You're really good on them things. We should have had you join us at the hotel when we were playing there last night," said one. Later in the departure lounge, an American who'd also been listening opened up a conversation on the subject as well. He too had been fascinated. Play spoons and make friends quickly.

That was the best part of my stay on Yap.

Chapter 31

Truck Lagoon: Chuuk

Chuuk, one of the Federated States of Micronesia, is a group of 15 small islands surrounded by a near-circular 140-mile barrier reef forming one of the largest atolls in the Pacific Ocean. Within the shelter of the reef, which has five passages large enough to allow shipping to enter, lies a deep-water haven for shipping. Beyond the reef there are also nearly 200 smaller atolls. Most of the 50,000 inhabitants live on the five largest islands, all close together in the centre of the lagoon, the remnants of an extinct volcano. The outer reef marks the edge of the caldera of this vast volcano. Beyond the reef its slopes tumble dramatically down for around 3000 metres (almost 10 000 feet) to the cold, dark floor of the Pacific Ocean.

Linguistic and archaeological evidence suggests that the first settlers of the islands of Micronesia arrived over 2000 years ago, migrating across the Pacific Ocean from South East Asia. It is believed the first settlers arrived at Chuuk around 1400 AD from neighbouring Kosrae. The first Europeans arrived in 1526 when the Spanish claimed sovereignty and ruled the islands until 1899 when it sold its holdings to Germany. The Germans allegedly had difficulty pronouncing Chuuk and it became known to them as Truk Lagoon. They were not popular overlords and after a rebellious uprising in 1910-11, control of the islands passed to Japan in 1914. The Japanese brought development and some prosperity to the islands, and the most terrifying event in its history.

Truk Lagoon's extensive sheltered waters became the Japanese Imperial Fleet's most important central Pacific forward base in World War Two. This was where its supplies were marshalled and distributed to the warships and submarines operating so far from their home bases. However, that same shelter, with its few navigable channels that protected the fleet in rough weather, also made it difficult to escape when under attack.

Just before dawn on 17th February 1944 the drone of American bombers alerted the Japanese to the attack that was to prove such a devastating blow to the Japanese war effort in the Pacific. A total of 450 American bombers attacked in wave after wave, bringing terror and destruction on a vast scale. Japanese aircraft were scrambled to its defence, but 37 were destroyed before leaving the ground. The attack continued on 18th February and met with little resistance as the islands' anti-aircraft defences had been badly damaged by bombing the previous day and the airfield runway had been left full of bomb craters. With air defences and communication centres immobilised, the American bombers picked off ship after ship, sinking them with bombs and torpedoes launched from low flying aircraft.

In two days, over 400 Japanese aircraft were rendered useless, and more than 50 ships sunk. Japanese casualties numbered over 600, Americans less than

30. Only 22 US aircraft were lost and 28 US airmen were picked up from the sea by a patrolling submarine. The attack was a resounding success, disabling to a large extent the Japanese naval forces operating in the Pacific. With their supplies cut off they were left without food, fuel, medical supplies, ammunition; even the largest Japanese warships had to head home, unable to operate in distant waters.

Having dealt this killer blow, the US forces then left Chuuk alone and cut off from Japan as they pressed on westwards towards the Philippines and eventually Japan itself. Chuuk was ignored for almost two years until after the war ended. Its people and the Japanese forces left there, starved of supplies from the outside world, had to revert to subsistence living. Fortunately, the sea was always a good provider of food and coconuts and fruits were available in abundance on land.

Operation Hailstorm, as this attack was code-named, ultimately brought Chuuk to the attention of the diving world in the 1960s. It was then that exploration began of the sunken ships of the Japanese supply fleet, many almost intact, still with cargoes in their holds. Under the tranquil waters of this famous lagoon lies the evidence of such a violent chapter in Chuuk's, and the world's, history, when fire and explosion brought death to so many.

It is this actual museum of World War 2 naval war history that draws divers to this lonely outpost in the middle of the Pacific. Arguably the best wreck diving location in the world, it offers so many delights to the diver exploring the decks, holds and dark chambers of these wrecks. Unlike other major wreck dive sites like Scapa Flow in Scotland, where the ships of the impounded German High Seas Fleet from World War 1 were scuttled by their crews rather than allow them to be taken over by their captors, the ships here at Chuuk have not been stripped of so many of their valuable assets like their huge bronze propellers. Engine rooms are often intact with machinery clearly visible in the light of the diver's torch, dark passageways can be navigated to visit toilets, galleys, cabins. Cavernous holds still contain artillery shells, depth charges, tanks, trucks, fighter aircraft and spare parts. A submarine supply ship carries torpedoes and spare warheads, extra periscopes to replace those damaged by depth charge attack, bottles of wine and cases of beer. It is an impressive display of the logistics of war.

To gaze in wonder at a bomb hole that has been blasted in the steel plate of a ship's decking or to swim through the enormous gap in her side created by the explosive force of a torpedo, to see how something as strong as steel has been ripped apart like a hole punched in the side of a cardboard box, the entire hull of the ship around that gaping hole bent inwards and to view the shattered destruction inside the ship as a result of these explosions is an awesome testament to the destructive forces unleashed here. This was home to the men who served on these ships, homes ripped apart by horrific explosive force, terrifying noise and fire. So many went to a watery grave.

The dark passageways, often littered with the debris of the blast of explosion, and the cargo holds of these dead ships still serve a purpose. After so much death, they now offer protection from large predators to vast numbers of juvenile fish, giving them a secure start to life.

The external surfaces, especially those presented to direct sunlight, are now richly encrusted with marine algae, corals, anemones, sponges, tube-worms. All the growths that you would expect to find on a natural reef are here on these artificial reefs, providing a new structure, an external skeleton, that will engulf the steel on which it is based, as the ever-expanding coral swallows up each ship. Already the masts, guns and derricks are thickly encrusted in growths, their details now obscured, only their general outline informing the observer of their original function. Built by man, destroyed by man with the aid of explosive force, these ships have now been recreated by nature into something of wondrous beauty.

Truk lagoon is a powerful magnet for divers, but it is not an easy place to get to, being so far away from everywhere. Continental Airlines seems to have a virtual monopoly on flights from the outside world with links to Hawaii and the Philippines. It is also an expensive place to live as so much upon which modern existence and business depends has to be imported from abroad, usually Japan, China or the United States. It is an expensive place to dive, but that unique historical record of a chapter in the violence of a war that shook the world when I was a child was irresistible. I had to see it for myself.

As a place to live, Chuuk leaves an awful lot to be desired. Its "capital city" on the island of Weno is little more than a collection of rough huts, a bit like the gold rush towns as portrayed in old western movies. This is real wild-west territory too. The indigenous people have developed a liking for beer, often go crazy when drunk, and old tribal feuds erupt. Violence is a common way of settling old disputes. A year or two back one local guy, driven by some alcohol-fuelled rage was reported as chasing cars with a machete in hand. Now it may seem that a machete wielding lunatic, in terms of speed, is no match for a car, but this is Chuuk, where the roads are so deeply potholed they look like they have never been patched up since the American bombs dropped in 1944. No car is seen moving at much more than 5 miles per hour; any faster would shake the car to pieces. A machete madman with a dislike for cars then becomes a formidable foe.

Visitors to this island are advised not to go out at night. "Why would anyone want to go out at night anyway? There is nothing to see or do. There is nothing here but shacks and shit," as one of my American dive buddies graphically described the place. I went walkabout during daytime after diving and was greeted with warm smiles and friendly hellos. I never felt threatened at any time, except by the enormous potholes in the road filled with grey water of unknown depth. There are no pavements either and walking along a grass verge - and remember this is in the downtown area of the "capital city" of Chuuk - my feet suddenly became engulfed in soft grey mud, an evil-looking slurry that literally sucked the shoes off my feet. No drainage. No one seems to have thought of digging a small channel to let the water drain off the roads into the sea which is only a few feet way. But that would be work - and work is a concept alien to the culture of Chuuk.

An American development aid worker told me, "Nothing works here. The roads are unspeakable, piles of rubbish lie rotting by the roadside or in heaps in back yards, very few homes even have electricity and the power supply is forever cutting out, the water system is a mess, telecommunications are unreliable, there is no TV, not even radio!"

Now just think of that, no TV or radio! That is like going back to the early days of the 20th century in most other parts of the world. The hotel has a TV set in each room, but to see anything on it you have to hire DVD's - and even then you are at the mercy of Chuuk's temperamental power supply.

He went on: "There is no economy as such. The place is dependent on foreign aid. Most people work for the government, which is a bit of a joke; basically it is just a glorified welfare system. They get paid for doing little or nothing, and doing it badly too! Many of those who do work disappear for several days after pay-day, taking time off to relax and enjoy the money they have earned: that usually means drinking beer, getting drunk and beating up your neighbour, if you don't like him.

"Corruption is rife. One of the local supreme court judges was imprisoned after being found guilty of what was described as 'only a white-collar crime' or, to put it simply, misappropriation of funds. He had the temerity to demand that he be released from prison on the days when court was sitting in order to preside over the trials of other criminals and so continue to earn his salary."

Our hotel had an impressive looking menu with a wide range of dishes including several kinds of steaks. But when one of my American dive buddies ordered a steak he was told, "We have no steaks. The ship has not arrived yet."

I ordered fish. "We have no fish. The ship has not arrived yet." And this is an island in the middle of the Pacific Ocean! Of course to catch a fish means actually doing something, but the Chuukies seem to be averse to doing anything, except drinking beer. Strangely enough, there never seemed to be any shortage of beer. No doubt that formed the bulk of the cargo of 'The Ship.'

At breakfast there was no jam with the toast. "We have no jam. The ship has not arrived yet," explained the waitress. "Would you like a drink sir?"

"Yes, cola please."

"We have no cola." OK you've guessed it…. "The ship has not arrived yet." The steaks, like the fish, the jam, the cola and the fuel and most other supplies, are delivered from the mainland. That is the USA, several thousand miles across the ocean. Of course, a ship will only come this way if it has sufficient cargo to deliver, so you wait until it builds up enough freight to make a stop here worthwhile. Then you can have steak, fish, jam with your toast, or a drink of cola. I didn't want to wait that long.

The diving on Chuuk was good.

But life there is a mixture of comedy and tragedy.

Chapter 32

Incredible Journey

Back in the Philippines and seeking a change from diving, I decided to visit Banaue and the amazing rice terraces carved out of the steep-sided Cordillera Mountains, the rocky backbone of Luzon, largest of the Philippine islands. I hadn't realised how big this island was, but after seemingly interminable hours in a variety of clapped-out buses and rickety jeepneys, well, both me and my aching backside now know better.

The journey began in Manila in an air-conditioned bus, not luxurious, but moderately comfortable by Philippine standards. Six hours later I had exchanged the sweaty mayhem of Manila traffic, and the sultry heat of the patchwork of rice fields on the plains as we headed north, for the refreshingly cool mountain breezes in the city of Baguio at around 5000 feet altitude. A quick glance at the map in my guide book gave the illusion that Banaue was only a short hop from here. That's the trouble with small-scale guidebook maps; they can be deceptive, even more so when what appears to be a fairly straight road actually has to snake its way over a series of very steep mountain ridges increasing the distance ten-fold, but the guide-book ignores such minor details. The only way is over the top of some of these mountains, and the scale of the map prohibits those kind of details which would reveal that the short hop of 2 hours or so which I had envisaged from Baguio, was to prove to be a tortuous ride along perilous, snaking roads, lasting nine hours.

Despite the agony it was a fascinating journey. Who needs to pay for budget-busting extreme sports for thrill seekers like bungy-jumping and sky-diving when you can have (for only a few pesos) a nine-hour, white-knuckle, throat constricting, bowel clearing, terrifying ride in a ramshackle bus or jeepney along roads like this - where they existed at all - for this is landslide country. Now just to set all this in context, the Philippines is the most catastrophe prone country in the world. If the world can do the dirty on you it is most likely to happen in the Philippines which has it all; killer typhoons, earthquakes, volcanic eruptions, torrential rains, floods, landslides, and where I was heading was the place to get them.

A super-typhoon had just swept across north Luzon as I was flying into Manila and I caught the tail end of its torrential rain. The result, floods on the plains and landslides scattered randomly around the mountains. In places the road simply disappeared under a lake where water buffalo wallowed as though in paradise, with only their dopey, horny heads showing above water. However, our driver cheerily drove unhesitatingly onwards and, without navigational aids like radar or GPS, managed to navigate through the lake without ever straying from the submerged road, unerringly locating the road even around an underwater bend. You have to admire these guys. They may drive like maniacs, but you've got to give them credit for skill, maniacal skill maybe, but they do get you there in one piece.... well, usually.

The road - I mean proper road, as we would recognise one in our developed countries - didn't last long after Baguio. I had spent a couple of nights there, a pleasant city with a climate like Scotland in summer, cool and wet. Even the beds had blankets and duvets on them - so unlike the rest of the Philippines, where usually you seek air conditioning to maintain a reasonable temperature to sleep in.

After only a few miles of concrete surface, we hit the first landslide. That had taken care of a large section of the concrete surface. It was now way down the mountain. Shortly after that we hit a rough, so-called dirt road, but with most of the dirt washed away by the torrential rains it was left in skeletal form - bare rock, some hard and unyielding, some loose. It was a bit like driving along a river-bed. Except that on one side there was a very steep mountain towering above you and threatening to throw more of itself down upon you with every drop of rain that fell to loosen its grip on the world and on the other side (there was no barrier of any sort), a sheer drop into a terrifying void. This started with a vertical drop of maybe 200 feet or so and then a steep rocky slope down a further 1500 feet to a raging, foaming river which would be the destination of all your bits and pieces if another landslide did occur, for survival was unimaginable if you did go over the edge.

One section was carved into a sheer rock face. It was like driving through half a tunnel with the rock wall almost scraping one side of the bus and allowing just a few inches above the roof and, on the open side, a sheer drop down hundreds of feet. The edge of the road was so close that it was impossible to see it when you looked out of the bus window. How close the bus wheels were to that horrifying drop, I can only imagine, but it is more comfortable not to. And to add to the pleasure for thrill seekers - I loved this! - the world had thrown part of itself away at both ends of this half-tunnel in a couple of majestic landslides which had taken away at least half of the road. Undeterred by this, our driver unhesitatingly swept his bus through the torrent of water that still rushed over what was left of the road and past the water-swept gully where our side of the road had once been, and was still being eroded away by the water.

It was an incredible journey. Our driver showed not a single vestige of fear, nor the slightest hesitation in executing any manoeuvre, and there were plenty to be executed. He had a fiendish grin on his face as he hurled his bus round hairpin bends and took us to the very brink of extinction on precipitous cliffs where no bus should ever have been, or so we would think in our safety conscious world. But this is the Philippines, where life is fun despite the hardships and catastrophes and endemic poverty. And it was infectious. Marvelling at the skill which took you so close to extinction yet always brought you back just short of having cardiac arrest, it was impossible not to find an overwhelming confidence growing in your driver, a confidence that grew almost to the point of hero-worship. And, like him, you began to enjoy the ride and grinned fiendishly with him, revelling in the thrill of it all.

The nightmares came later - as you lay in bed in the darkness, re-playing the action in your mind, and oozing cold sweat at what *may* have happened!

And that was only the first six hours of the trip north from Baguio to Sagada. Another three hours of buttock-crushing, knuckle-clenching, lip-biting, heart-arresting travel by jeepney was in store to get to Banaue after that. But that was for the next day. Why cram all the fun into one day? Spread it about a bit!

Drained with all the excitement, it was a relief to step out on to terra firma once more and explore the sleepy village of Sagada, a place noted for its limestone caves and cliffs with hanging coffins. Tradition is still strong among the Igorot people who inhabit these mountains and it is not unusual to see elderly men wandering along the road wearing just a G-string and loincloth. The women wear colourful garments and head-dress. You are in the frontier territory now.

This is head-hunter country and inter-tribal wars are not uncommon. The government rarely bother to intervene in these disputes, allowing the tribes to settle their grievances in the traditional ways. They don't involve outsiders so they don't harm anyone but themselves, but if you are trekking in these mountains it is best to have a local guide to ease things along for you. Hotels? Camp sites? Toilets? Forget all that. Trekking up here means you go native; squat in the bush, and leave a feast for the pigs which may well accompany you in eager anticipation as you seek some privacy. There is a kind of primitive satisfaction in reverting to nature.

More rough and tumble, slithering and scrambling over landslides that had piled earth and rubble over the roads and engaged the imagination in all sorts of horror scenarios in a three-hour jeepney ride finally got me to Banaue and what has been called the eighth wonder of the world (one of the three eighth wonders in the Philippines!), the astonishing rice terraces. Think of a forty-five degree mountain slope - and that is steep - and imagine cutting a series of ledges out of it to give you some flat land to grow rice and other vegetables. To support these ledges you need to build retaining walls, some as high as ten feet, and pack the stone work with clay to retain water. The rice fields require irrigation so water has to be ducted in and out as required. Multiply this by the effort required to build thousands of such terraces up thousands of feet of mountainside following its contours for mile after mile, and I travelled a lot of miles in my nine hours from Baguio and saw an awful lot of such terraces. You cannot fail to admire the vision and industry of the small Igorot people who built these terraces two thousand years ago or more with only the most basic hand tools. And even today, those who maintain them, growing most of the fresh vegetables for the big cities, and all the rice they can use and more. It is a remarkable feat of labour, the scale of which dwarfs that required to build the pyramids of Egypt, and it presents an astonishing sight.

Banaue is a grim looking, grey town clinging precariously to the steep sides of the mountain. The front door of a house may be at road level, but if you look out the back window you could be looking down a drop of fifty feet, so steep are the slopes upon which they are built. As always, it is fascinating to wander around such places with a camera for it is in places like this that you find people living and working in a style to which we in the so-called developed countries can hardly imagine. It is a town of craftsmen, wood carvers in particular. Their carvings are sometimes immense, often statues of human figure and animals, but those I liked best were the ones made from tree roots, which inspired the artist to create all sorts of interesting semi-abstract creations. Betel nut and tobacco chewing is a common custom here. The problem with that is that it generates a bright red juice that is spat out on to the streets, which were liberally sprinkled with these great gobs of spittle. It looked like someone had been running around bleeding to death.

The trip back to Manila was also eventful. Is ever a trip in the Philippines not eventful, I began to wonder? The air-conditioned bus direct from Banaue was fully booked for two days ahead so I travelled native again. The first leg, from Banaue down to the plains to the east, was another rough, bum-aching mountain ride in a packed jeepney. These guys never refuse a fare. Several passengers were sitting on the roof and others clung on to the sides with not a care in the world.

Three hours later, down on the main road, I caught another bus heading towards Manila. It wasn't any more comfortable than the jeepney. Its tired seats, having supported more bums than they were ever designed for, had long since ceased to offer any cushioning effect. They were years past their use-by date, but this is the Philippines where such things are happily ignored. Like the jeepney drivers, these buses also never refuse a fare. As more passengers climbed aboard, folding seats were pulled out offering seats in the aisle, which made it quite a performance when anyone at the back of the bus had to get off. So, over-loaded and over-worked, our tired old bus ploughed its sweaty way (no air-con, on this bus, no windows either, just open sides) back down through the rice fields in the baking sun. But the excitement wasn't over yet. In late afternoon the engine suddenly raced out of control and threatened to shake itself off its mountings - and gave us a good shaking too - and with these final death throes it expired in an impressive cloud of steam. Death due to overheating: our bus wasn't going any further.

So we all cheerily piled out and flagged down other overcrowded buses, snatching seats where we could get them. By the time we were getting near Manila these buses were pretty full, not just of people, but sacks of rice, vegetables, chickens, baskets, suitcases, babychairs and anything else that people wanted to transport. The only seat left for me was right at the rear of the bus. To get there I had a bit of scrambling to do as all these obstacles were packed in the aisle. Eleven hours after leaving Banaue, without breakfast, lunch, or dinner, I arrived back in Manila, having survived on bottled water and dried mangoes.

That's travelling in the Philippines for you!

Chapter 33

No Common Sense

Norman Kirkpatrick, formerly Principal Teacher of Art in Thurso High School, Scotland, was talking to my younger son, Euan, on the phone one night after reading of my encounter with a typhoon.

"You know, Euan, I have the greatest respect for your father, both as a friend and former colleague. He is an extremely intelligent man capable of a level of thought that I could never aspire to..." (but when Norman makes one of those pregnant pauses after such a build-up you just know he is going to deliver the knockout punch!) "...but he has absolutely no common sense!" Euan was in total agreement!

Maybe they are right.

Judge for yourself.

After an overnight stop in Manila, I planned on moving to Sabang Beach, near Puerto Galera, on the island of Mindoro. You get there from Manila by bus and boat, a journey of about 3 to 4 hours. I hailed a taxi at the hotel to take me to the bus station where I would put my life again in the hands of a maniacal Filipino bus driver in the hope that he would get me safely to the port of Batangas. When the taxi driver asked me where I was going, he told me, "You won't get there today. I've just heard on the radio that a typhoon warning has been issued for that area. Are you sure you want to go on to the bus station or should I take you back to the hotel?"

Well, I told you before, if the world can play dirty tricks on you this is one of the most likely places on earth for it to happen, and here it was at it again - or was it just bluffing? I had previously heard typhoon warnings that came to nothing, just some overnight heavy rain and a breeze. Maybe this would be the same. The track of a typhoon (known as a hurricane in the Atlantic or cyclone in the South Pacific and Indian Oceans) is notoriously difficult to predict. A warning is a statement of risk. It is not a cast iron certainty. Ever the eternal optimist I told him, "Och, just keep going. It may come to nothing."

"Oh, I don't think so. They said it was expected to be a category five typhoon. That's a big one, the most severe."

"Och, we get hurricane force winds regularly in the north of Scotland. We call it a 'bit of a breeze' where I live!"

Such bravado! Truth is, I actually like a good storm. My late wife once told me on seeing my excitement when hurricane force winds had been forecast, "You're mad. Look at you! You are never happier than when you see a deep depression coming. You can't wait to get out in it." I spent that January night in the north of Scotland on my boat in the harbour with two anchors out to keep her off the quay and six mooring lines, two of which had been 'sprung' with heavy weights to avoid snatching and breaking. Two of the unsprung lines broke, but the rest and the anchors kept the boat safe. Six other boats in the harbour were smashed or sunk that night. I worked, adjusting the lines constantly as the tide rose, battling all the time to counter what punches the storm may throw at me, and it worked. It's a great feeling to have encountered nature at her roughest and, by careful consideration of the risks involved, to have taken appropriate action and survived. And I had that feeling again.

As the bus left the city and the wide horizons of south Luzon opened up before us, I could read the signs clearly. A classic storm was imminent. Away to the southeast the sky had that pearly-grey look about it with the sun a ghostly glow behind a thin sheet of high cloud, while down low towards the horizon, the dark, storm clouds were gathering ominously; a leaden grey wall that promised rain, lots of rain, on an approaching warm front and then, with the following cold front, would come the wind….a lot of wind. A category 5 typhoon is also called a super typhoon, with sustained wind speeds of more than 138 miles per hour (222 km/h). Comparing that with 'gale force' winds of around 40 mph gives you an idea of the wind force to be expected. That could cause a lot of damage, build up enormous seas, cause extensive flooding. I felt a sense of foreboding, coupled with an undeniable build up of excitement. Och well, I thought, I'm in need of an adventure; it should be interesting.

At the port of Batangas, all sailings had been cancelled. Crowds of people milled around going nowhere; some looking worried, some confused, and the Filipinos among them sat around with that vacant look that said 'Que sera, sera,' whatever will be, will be. It's as good an attitude as any in such a situation. I checked at the booking office. All ferries had been cancelled until the typhoon warning would be cancelled. I too was going nowhere, for a day or two at least.

So, what next? I reckoned hotel rooms might be difficult to find in Batangas on such a day. My attitude was to turn this to some advantage. About 30 km along the coast lay Anilao, another place reputed to have good diving. With a typhoon imminent there would be no prospect of any diving, but I could at least check the place out and maybe come back sometime. I hired a motorcycle trike to get me there and booked a room at a small coastal resort near the village. I was their only customer. There were no hotels in the village.

My room was at the end of a row, at the end adjacent to the beach. Not ideal in a typhoon I thought, but there was a massive sea wall to break the force of the waves. The building was of concrete block construction, its thatch roof was well netted and the windows had heavy tarpaulin covers over them. I thought they might be suspect in a strong wind, and I was proved right, but otherwise it seemed capable of weathering a storm.

The annoying thing was that all this time there was little wind and the sea showed no more than a slight motion. Boats could easily have made the 75-minute trip across, but I know how quickly things can change at sea. Many ferries have foundered here in recent years with significant loss of life so it made sense not to take risks. There are times when you just have to sit tight and ride out the storm. I walked down to the village to see what Anilao was like. There was not much to see. A few fisherman's huts along the shore, a string of expensive dive resorts further round the bay and a main street of about two hundred metres with a small fruit market, maybe a dozen tiny shops all selling the same things, clothing, phone cards, cooked food (but when was it cooked? I remembered a recently upset stomach), and that is it. Everything shut by 6pm, so no swinging nightlife here, which was just as well, as by that time the storm was beginning to make its presence felt.

With nothing else to do I was in bed by 7pm, reading a book. By 8.30 I had to give that up when I was plunged into darkness. The electricity power lines had fallen casualty to the force of the wind or fallen trees, so I shut my eyes to the howling, banging and crashing that was going on outside as wind and waves thrashed the coast in fury. I slept through all this until 1.30am. When I woke then I could feel the gusts of wind build up with horrendous force, their terrifying shrieking forcing all desire for sleep out of the mind. This was something to live through. At least I hoped I would live through it!

All we need now, I remember thinking, is an earthquake to create a tsunami to coincide with the typhoon and then I really would be having a Philippines experience!

Two or three for the price of one is not uncommon here. This was another white-knuckle ride of a different sort. It had that peculiar mixture of fear, fascination and, I have to admit, sheer elation that I always get in a fierce storm, an overpowering desire to be part of it. I grabbed my torch and got out of bed. I was standing in water. The floor was already flooded with a tide of rain-water being forced under the door and coming in through the roof. I opened the door. Everywhere was in complete darkness. I shone my torch towards the sea wall.

Enormous, frothing, white-capped waves rose mightily out of the gloom, thumped against the sea wall and the earth shook, sending shudders right through the walls of my room. Spray flew skywards, mingled and fell with the torrential rain that had by now saturated the thatched roof. The wind was lifting it in places and it was now leaking badly and being battered by flying debris: tree branches, coconuts, and bits of driftwood hurled up by the waves and carried on the wind. Flying coconuts were hurtling maliciously through the air like canon balls: deadly missiles, thumping malevolently on the ground, into walls and roofs. Branches, ripped off trees, were flying like spears through the darkness. The ground was covered in debris: leaves, driftwood, nuts, branches, and water several inches deep. It was mayhem.

If you had a desire to get yourself killed, this was the night to fulfill it. I pondered on the mathematical probability that I could walk from my hut to the gate and still remain alive. No chance. It would be similar to walking into a hail of machine-gun fire, a life expectancy measured in seconds, not minutes, with so much stuff flying through the air with lethal force. Several trees were already down. I decided to keep my interest purely theoretical and not risk a practical test. This was not a night to be out in at all!

Having satisfied my curiosity, I went back to bed, but not before I had taken some additional precautions. I reckoned this must now be about the height of the typhoon's ferocity, but just in case it did exceed my expectations and lifted the roof and the sea came tumbling over the wall and tried to sweep me away in its surge, I packed my rucksack, sat it on the bed to keep it out of the rising tide of water that surged under the door and had everything ready for a quick getaway, just in case. If that were to happen, the odds of survival were not in my favour, but at least I felt I was keeping my options open. Like putting a lifejacket on when an aircraft is about to plunge into the sea, it probably won't save your life, but it will make it easier for search parties to find your body. It just feels better to have done something. I climbed into bed again, snug beside my rucksack, and closed my eyes.

A few minutes later I heard it: the rising wail of the wind and the shuddering of the building that tells you a big one is coming as it builds up in an enormous surge. I could feel the pressure build up in my ears. I remembered a similar sound and pressure wave years ago back home, seconds before a huge spruce tree snapped like a match stick about six feet above ground level and crashed into my house. This was another big one and more things - heavy, hard, lumpy things – were attacking my walls and roof. There were crashes and bangs all over the place as things broke loose and took off into the air, hitting other things as they went, and hitting my wee house too. How much more can it take? I wondered. And still the howling rose in a magnificently fearful, screaming crescendo, like an approaching high-speed train with its whistle blowing. It was awesome. I lay flat on my back and every muscle tensed. I trembled and sweated with anticipation, excitement – and fear!

With a crack like a gunshot, I sat bolt upright. As I did so, I heard the tinkling sound of broken glass crashing down behind me on the bed. The curtain rail above the window ripped itself off the wall and, with the curtain still attached, flew around for a bit in the vortex of air that spun around my room as the wind howled through the broken window. Then it draped itself over me. Was this to be my shroud? Looking on the bright side (why am I so eternally optimistic in the worst of conditions, yet can be so gloomy in the most minor mishaps?) I thought, well, at least the broken window helps to compensate for the failure of the electricity supply, which had rendered my ceiling fan inoperable. I now had plenty of air circulating. But where was the broken glass? I shone my torch on the pillow and there, sticking into the recess in the pillow just where my head had lain a split second before, was an arrowhead of glass about 18 inches long which would surely have skewered me well and truly in the eye, probably digging deep thorough the eye-socket into the brain and killing me had I not reacted instinctively, and so quickly, to the crack of the breaking glass. Looking on the bright side again, I mused, my speed of reaction had not diminished with age. That must have been the quickest sit-up I ever performed. It's comforting to know you can still do it when you have to. I felt the odds of survival were improving.

The situation now called for some re-assessment. By now the leak in the roof was worse and water was pouring on to the bed. I got up again and slid the bed to the opposite corner of the room so that it missed the stream pouring in from above and this also reduced the risk of personal injury should any more glass decide to fly around with intent to share a pillow with me. I also repositioned my rucksack on the bed, between me and the hole that was once a window as a further defence against glass and other flying objects, for who knows what else might now come zooming in through the hole. Having satisfied myself that my risk assessments were sound and all possible precautions had been taken and luck was on my side tonight, I fell asleep again surprisingly quickly and I slept very soundly, remaining blissfully unaware of anything else until 6.30am.

One of the staff of the resort came down to check that I was still alive and seemed relieved to find me so, and indeed in good spirits in spite of the events of the night. I had repositioned the bed and the arrowhead of glass so that she could see exactly how closely I had escaped death or disfigurement. The poor girl was horrified at the thought of what might have been, of her finding me lying there in a pool of blood with an 18 inch glass arrow sticking out of my eye socket. She promptly removed me to a room at the opposite end of the row, as far from the sea and prevailing wind direction as possible. Not that it mattered now. The worst was over.

The scene outside in the grey light of dawn was one of utter devastation. Palms hung their heads sadly, torn and forlorn, completely denuded, looking like giant matchsticks. Other trees lurched sickeningly, bearing scars where branches had been torn from them, some still clinging like broken limbs dangling limply in the breeze. Fallen trees, broken branches, twigs, leaves and palm fronds carpeted the place, covering every square inch of ground, obliterating completely the footpaths and even roadways. Coconuts lay around, dozens of them, like spent shells on a battlefield. It would indeed have been suicidal to go out in that at the height of the storm. The wind had now abated somewhat, but still blew quite hard with heavy squally showers. It looked.... well, it looked like a typhoon had struck the place!

But, looking on the bright side, I was happy to have lived through it without injury. Happy too were the frogs. So much rain had fallen and created new lakes where none had existed before and they celebrated joyously. The noise of their pleasurable croaking was deafening, like a crowd at a football match. I have never heard anything like it. It put a smile on my face. There is always something to be cheery about.

Typhoon 'Durian' had indeed been a category five storm, the highest rating given to typhoons. In the Philippines the number of fatalities was in the thousands with hundreds more reported missing. Many have never been found. Most of these were in the Bicol province where a huge landslide of volcanic ash, turned to slurry by the rains, had swept down the hillside and swallowed entire villages - and the people living in them.

Two days later I managed to get a boat to Sabang Beach. The village looked like the aftermath of an air raid; roofless buildings stood forlorn, smoke curled lazily upwards from dozens of fires burning the wreckage of homes, fallen branches and trees, and from all over the bay came the incessant sound of hammering as men worked, repairing damaged buildings. There was still no electricity supply when I left after more than two weeks there, but many places had generators allowing limited power supplies for part of the day. Many homes and guest houses had no water supply and along the hideously narrow streets young men pushed large barrows filled with water bottles and gas cylinders to supply homes and restaurants. With no power, cash machines at the banks and card readers in shops for credit cards could not operate. The local telecommunications mast was a useless metal stump, having had its top blown away.

The island's trees looked like someone had sprayed them with weed-killer. They were now defoliated and forlorn, with drooping, broken branches. It's amazing how sad-looking a typhoon-ravaged palm tree can look with its head of fronds shorn away, or left with only one two hanging limp and mournful. Their plight had changed the landscape. There were now clearings, allowing views of houses that were previously completely hidden; but the houses themselves were often just as sad and forlorn looking as the trees, many seriously damaged with windows and doors blown in, many with roofs missing or partly damaged. Yet just as in the bombed cities of Europe in the Second World War, the people were remarkably resilient and cheerful. As always, the Filipinos went about their business with great cheerfulness, always smiling. Life in Sabang went on as usual and, apart from the obvious signs like the power loss and water supply problems, it was easy to forget after only a few days that it had ever happened.

It was then early December, late in the year for typhoons, but yet another struck only 10 days later. The greying skies had all the tell-tale signs. The sea, slicked silkily smooth with that oily calm so characteristic of the period before the storm, flexed its muscle ominously in a restless swell, rising and falling slowly. The day was windless, the air still and quiet. Eerily quiet. Nature held her breath before another onslaught. The rain arrived at night, then came the howling wind. This time we were lucky and missed the worst of the wind as the centre of the storm tracked a good bit to the south of us. In the morning it was reported that Boracay had been devastated. Hundreds of trees had been blown down, several resorts were completely trashed, several boats had sunk, and at least a hundred people were missing.

We had torrential rain, floods and gales. The one road that leads into Sabang down a steep hill rapidly became a roaring river. I walked knee deep in muddy brown water. Here too my roof leaked. Water poured down the wall. I had another puddle on the floor, but this time no other problems. I slept well.

And well away from the window!

Chapter 34

Champagne and Sardines

It sounds impossible, but it is just another of life's challenges. As a novel way to bring in the New Year at Moalboal on Cebu Island, Savedra Dive Centre had organised a short night dive just before midnight so that we could celebrate the change of the year and toast the event by drinking champagne... underwater!

Yes, underwater!

Just eleven divers signed up for it.

And whose name was first on the list?

Well, have you ever heard of a Scotsman turning down the offer of a free drink - even if it was 30 feet below the surface of the sea?

Around 11.45pm we were all kitted up and given a briefing. We walked across the narrow street to the shore and entered the water. The rendezvous point was a sandy bottomed pool about 50 metres out from the shore at about 10 metres depth. Once there we sat on the sand in a circle with our torches lighting up the scene, waiting for the clock to tick its way to mid-night.

Our dive guide gave the signal as Jan 1 arrived and one of the divemasters opened the bottle of champagne. Now this is where it gets interesting. The way to do this underwater is to invert the bottle so that its bottom is up and its neck is down. When the cork pops out, the pressure of the sea, which at that depth is twice the surface air pressure, forces the champagne to stay inside the bottle, more or less. A thumb placed over the mouth of the bottle helps. The bottle opener passed the bottle to the man on his right,

You remove your regulator (breathing apparatus) from your mouth, raise the bottle to your lips and blow air into the bottle. The air rises to the top of the bottle (which is really the bottom of the bottle because it is upside down) from where it cannot escape. The air you blow in forces the champagne downwards, out of the bottle and into your mouth and you get a healthy swig of bubbly champagne. You then put your thumb over the opening of the bottle and pass it on to the diver next to you and so it circulates around the group. Swallow the champagne and put your breathing apparatus back in your mouth. This is important, otherwise you will breathe in seawater and spoil the taste of the champagne, not to mention the risk of death by drowning.

It is easy, in the euphoria associated with this unique experience, to forget that you are sitting on the floor on the ocean!

By the time you shake hands with those around you to wish them a happy new year, the bottle has come round to you again. So you have another swig. Now, it is well known that diving and alcohol do not mix well, so that was the limit. We then pottered along the house reef for a few minutes more before returning to join in the festivities ashore. It certainly provided an unforgettable way to start the year.

I enjoyed the diving there. One of my dive buddies was Annabelle, a lithe, sixty-three year-old woman who had been diving for about 40 years. Trained as a diver in the South African Navy, she had logged several thousand dives. She was a delight to watch as she glided along so effortlessly, even though she was a bit of a delinquent underwater. She got a bit frustrated by divemasters who tried to impose what she regarded as unnecessary restrictions. Extremely competent and very efficient in her air consumption, she discovered that I was the only other diver in the group who could come close to matching her in air consumption, so she told the dive manager that she wanted me, and no one else, as a dive buddy.

It was a nice compliment. It suited me too as I wanted to take my time and take photos and she was happy to explore for me, poking her head into holes to seek interesting subjects for me to photograph, without always driving on as many divers do.

That New Year's Day we were diving together and the rest of the group, as usual, pounded off into the blue and left us behind. Time passed and we glided slowly onwards towards the rendezvous point with the dive boat. We eventually surfaced after 71 minutes underwater. The others had surfaced after about 50 minutes. When I climbed back aboard the boat the divemaster smiled. "Good dive?"

"Very good," I smiled back, "a good way to start the New Year."

The others were not smiling. A weather front had arrived, bringing with it a cool wind and rain and a chilling drop temperature and there they were, dripping wet, with raindrops falling from their noses, looking cold and thoroughly miserable. They had been sitting there shivering for over 20 minutes waiting for us.

I smiled at them. "Sorry to keep you waiting." I wasn't really of course. I had enjoyed my dive very much, but I felt I had to say something placatory. Not one of them smiled back. I turned to Annabelle who was sitting with her back to them divesting herself of her dive gear.

She smiled at me mischievously. "I don't think we are very popular, John," she muttered, "but who cares? It was a wonderful dive to start the New Year with. I'd like to thank you for being my buddy."

Sardines. Hardly a word to get you excited, is it? Not like cries of, "Whale Shark!" or, "Manta!" Those giants of the deep are truly breathtaking sea monsters. But you can't imagine many divers hyperventilating about coming face to face with a sardine.

However, try to imagine you are a diver down in the depths, maybe 25 metres below the surface (around 80 feet or so) on a bright, sunny day with good visibility. You are cruising slowly along a sheer, undersea cliff festooned with brightly coloured soft corals. Large Gorgonian fan corals spread their lacy beauty out from the cliff face and vividly coloured butterflyfish and angelfish dart in and out of the labyrinthine holes and tunnels that perforate the coral. A dozy turtle lies resting on a sandy ledge, conserving air and energy after feeding, or maybe exhausted after a night's egg laying or other procreative activities, its drowsy eyes begging you to leave it in peace. A large moray eel's head protrudes from a dark hole, the jaws open, neck muscles pulsating, forcing water through its gills where it extracts life-giving oxygen. The occasional lone shark silently patrols below you, effortlessly gliding through the dark, blue depths.

All is normal. It is just another very pleasant morning dive; bright, colourful, relaxing in that filtered morning light that illuminates the scene with soft hues. It feels good to be down there. Suddenly it darkens. It is now gloomy, almost as though you had entered a tunnel. You look up to see if you had drifted under a large overhang, but no, it is not solid rock that stops the light getting to you.

It is sardines. Millions of them. Barely six inches long, but in such density that they block out the light like a dark storm cloud, they hover restlessly above you at around 18 metres. At least that is where the bottom of the school of fish is. The top of the school may be around 7 or 8 metres depth, but how far does it extend? 100 metres? 200 metres? More? It is impossible to tell for it disappears into the blue oblivion far beyond the range of visibility, about 30 metres on that fine morning.

The divers slowly advance from below. With startling rapidity the school of tiny fish reacts magically as though it were one, every one of those millions of fish instantaneously prompted by the possible threat of the approaching divers to dart and sway, the cloud they create forming surreal patterns in the ocean. How they all know we are getting near is a mystery as you cannot see more than an inch or two into the school, so densely packed are they. Yet the panic reaction of the fish around the periphery is enough to alert, in a split second, every one of the millions there, making them take evasive action - all at virtually the same time.

The school swings rapidly one way, then the other, flashing with light, the sunlight reflecting from their silver sides as they turn. A diver with a camera approaches the underbelly of the school and it suddenly opens, creating a vertical tunnel all the way to the surface through which the sunlight shafts down the tube. The diver moves to one side of the tube to get a closer picture and the school metamorphoses into a giant wave, like a tsunami about to break on a beach, its surface streaked with flashing silver as the fish propel themselves away in terror, tiny tails working so hard and fast it is almost impossible to discern the movement.

It is constantly on the move, any slight change in the environment causing it to swing and sway, tumbling like a breaking wave or opening wide like a huge mouth. It is fascinating, awesome, almost frightening in appearance; for although each fish is so tiny, the sheer scale of this dense school of fish is overpowering and it seems to develop a mind of its own, a group personality and dynamic that dominates each individual within it. It does not present the disciplined power of an army on the march; it is more like a crowd out of control, that has lost all reason, responding only in mass panic, dissipating its energies in flight. Yet its sheer immensity creates an illusion of power that simply dominates the environment.

Notwithstanding its awesome size, it is a timorous thing, having no more of a mind than that of each tiny individual. So despite its often surreal and sometimes threatening appearance, large, black, swaying, nightmarish thing that it is, it contains no more threat than that of any one small fish in it. It is all about appearance, not substance. Create an impression, an illusion of size and power, and potential predators may leave you alone. As the hairs on a dog or cat become erect when threatened to give a larger and more menacing aspect to their appearance, so too does this enormous school of small fish create an illusion of power.

However false that illusion may be, it is still mightily impressive. And to be down there in close proximity to it brought a new understanding of the lives of the fisherman in my home country, my own ancestors among them who, in the 19th century went to sea with their nets in small open boats in pursuit of the sardine's Scottish cousin, the herring. Often referred to as the silver darlings, they brought prosperity to so many coastal communities when they were caught in huge numbers. It is easy now to believe the stories that when a net surrounded the school of fish they were so densely packed they could be scooped up in baskets. Old fishermen's tales? No, definitely not. Not after seeing the density of that school of sardines.

It had arrived a few months previously off Moalboal, or more accurately Panagsama Beach, a small former fishing village, which is on a peninsula jutting out into the sea just to the west of the town of Moalboal on Cebu island. Having taken up residence there it had become a talking point for the boatloads of divers who make the daily trip to explore the walls of Pescador island, without doubt the star attraction in the area. Its sheer vertical sides drop down into the deeps and are a riot of colour and marine life, offering a superb dive.

But it was the sardines, in appearance a humble nonentity of a fish yet such nutritious food, that had become the main talking point. Where did they come from and why? When will they leave again? Will there be a command from the King Sardine, if there is one, unlikely as that may be, that all others will follow? How do they communicate with each other so that they can react so swiftly, as one, and never collide with each other, always maintaining only a few millimetres separation between neighbours. And when they do move on, how do they decide where to go next? Who knows? It was one of the most fascinating sights I have ever witnessed underwater and never tired of re-visiting daily.

Having been here once before for only a few days I was amazed at the number of people who recognised me. Being such a small place, Panagsama Beach and its one little dirt road that masquerades as a street, soon gets to know you. All the wee shopkeepers speak to you as you pass, ask your name and where you are from, how long you are staying. Dina, the lady who cleaned the rooms at the resort, chatted to me often and invited me to her granddaughter's fourth birthday party. She had a whole roasted pig to be eaten with a delicious fresh fruit salad dessert and plenty to drink. When I got to the party I discovered that I had the only white face there. The rest were all Filipinos. I felt honoured. That's what I like about small places; you really get to know people. But how can they remember me from among the thousands of visitors they see each year? Is it the Scottish accent?

Other than that, I am just a quiet, nondescript individual...

Like a sardine.

Chapter 35

Watch Those Bubbles!

Everyone knows that if you release air underwater the bubbles float up to the surface. Right? So when you are diving and you see your air bubbles doing the very opposite, descending into the depths of the ocean instead of rising upwards, it may cause a degree of disorientation. What is happening to the laws of nature? Why are your bubbles going down instead of up, doomed to be swallowed up in the depths - and you with them? You don't need a depth gauge to tell you you are going down; your ears hurt with searing pain as the pressure increases.

"Watch those bubbles!" That was a friendly bit of advice in the latest email from Josh, my dive guide on my first trip into Burmese waters. He had written of his latest adventure in Flores, Indonesia, a special, invitation-only expedition exploring places where the currents were extreme and no diver had dared to venture before. It was an expedition for experienced dive professionals only, the guides who operate in the turbulent waters around the myriad of islands on that southern volcanic chain that stretches from Java to Papua - and it was strictly for volunteers.

He described one of those washing machine dives where the current did everything to disorientate the diver, where the down current was so strong that even the air bubbles did not go floating up to the surface as they should, but were swept down into the depths and compressed, the errant forces of nature acting against the laws of nature. He and his co-divers survived the ordeal and, knowing that I have a wee bit of a thirst for adventure, offered that timely reminder: "If you are diving in strong currents, watch those bubbles." Just over a week later, his words were ringing in my ears.

We had crossed Sogod Bay from Padre Burgos in South Leyte to Panaon Island to dive around a headland called Napantao, proclaimed to be the number one dive site in South Leyte by our guide. He looked apprehensively at a small headland where some rocks protruded above the surface, each with a bow wave like a ship, as the current raged around them. Beyond that, the sea was whipped up in a tormented dance of erupting, irregular, conical waves. The current was swirling with whirlpools and eddies streaked with foam. I know the forces at play in such waters and how they can toss even a heavy boat around. What might they do to a handful of divers? I expected him to say, "No diving here today," but we had come about 10 miles for this dive. "This is the number one dive site in South Leyte," he said and then, with a look of concern on his face, he muttered, "It also has the number one current." His concern was justifiable. He paused for a moment.... "OK, we go diving. Current is going this way so we go with it, keeping the wall on our left."

Well, the current was going "this way" out there in the deep water, but the headland had caused an eddy in the small bay on the north side where the boat dropped us and in there it was flowing the opposite way. We plunged straight down to the reef to gather on the bottom, otherwise the current would have had us scattered before we even began. Grouping there, we then had to fight against the eddy towards the wall, a sheer cliff dropping down 50 metres to a narrow shelf from where it continued to drop to the sea floor 1500 metres (nearly 5000 feet) below.

After several minutes of very slow and tiring progress fighting the current by clawing across a steep slope, we reached a patch of slack water close to the cliff where we could rest for a moment. Ablaze with colour and populated with hundreds of fish, I gazed in wonder at one of the most impressive walls I have ever seen, but not for long. The sea wanted to play with us.

As we drifted close towards the headland, the current picked up again, this time sweeping us along with increasing velocity. I was in the lead at this point and noticed that the fish a few metres ahead were not lying horizontally as the others had been doing. They were standing on their tails, facing upwards towards the surface. That was a clear indication of a powerful down current dropping off the shelf above us and I heard Josh's words in my ears: "Watch those bubbles!"

Well, I did, Josh. And like you, I noticed when I exhaled, that my bubbles, instead of soaring upwards to the surface, were going downwards, being compressed in size from that of an apple, to that of a golf ball and then to a marble size by the increasing pressure of the deeper water. My ears were already feeling as though six-inch nails were being pushed into them as the pressure increased the pain to screaming point. One hand was already on the inflator button of my buoyancy vest, pumping more air in to compensate for the downward thrust, the other squeezing my nose as I blew heartily into it to equalise the pressure on my ears. The ears popped at last and I checked the depth reading on my dive computer. I had dropped about 15 metres in a few seconds and I was still descending. I pumped more air into my buoyancy vest and felt it tighten around me. At last, filled up with air, my balloon-like shape now arrested the descent.

My mind was already running ahead. Where you get strong down currents, you may also find a few moments later some strong upward currents - and that is potentially much more dangerous. And with my buoyancy vest filled with air, that would help accelerate me in a rapid ascent, a potentially life-threatening situation. The volume of air in your lungs doubles every 10 metres you ascend threatening to rupture your lungs if you do not get it out quickly enough. Micro bubbles of nitrogen can form in your blood stream in a rapid ascent and that can lead to decompression sickness, the bends, resulting in serious illness, paralysis, or death. So, after I had satisfied myself that I was not plummeting to the ocean floor thousands of feet below, I was immediately anticipating what might happen next - and it did.

Without any warning at all it felt like a big hand had lifted me upwards and was propelling me rapidly to the surface. Again the bubbles gave a clue. I was soaring upwards as fast as they were, not a good sign at all. The dive computer on my wrist was beeping a rapid ascent warning and flashing the word SLOW - SLOW - SLOW at me. The immediate imperative was to arrest this rapid ascent.

I was exhaling air from my lungs continuously and I grabbed the emergency release toggle on my right shoulder and jerked it down. This opens up a dump valve at the highest point of the buoyancy vest. The remaining air exploded outwards. Having dumped virtually all the air, gravity took control again and I began to descend once more to get back down to a similar depth to compress again and then ascend very slowly after that.

At this point the currents threw another joker in the pack and the wall, which had always been there about 2 or 3 metres in front of me, receded into the blue gloom and disappeared as another contrary current swept me out to sea. Five of us had entered the water. Now I could not see any of them. The currents had played cat and mouse with us, tossing us around, backward, forward, downward, upward and now outward and I had no idea where any of the others were. Events were happening so quickly, my reactions were instinctive, based on training and experience. It certainly focuses the mind. This was a time to stay cool, calm and concentrate.

Levelling off at about 18 metres, I had an image in mind of the vectors at play. The eddy turning back northwards from the south bay was deflected outwards by the headland. Angling my body to the direction of the current rather than swimming straight against it, I slowly forced my way across the current to where I guessed it would be less severe, out of the flow of the eddy. A few minutes later I could see the wall emerging from the gloom again. I found a ledge and slung out my reef hook. This was a time to simply hang on, resting and reflecting on the sheer rapidity and power of events, allowing my breathing to get back to normal again, wondering where the others were. I gazed around and above me. No one. Nothing but fish, loads of them, all working furiously, flicking their tails to keep them heading into the current.

The procedure when you get separated from the group is to wait for one minute and then ascend slowly, do a safety stop at five metres for three minutes, put up a surface marker buoy to let the boat crew see where you are, and then carry on up to the surface. I checked the time on my dive computer and looked around again before ascending. Two columns of bubbles rising in the gloom reflected some sunlight. Someone was out there in the deeps, pushing hard to get closer to the wall, but not yet visible. Slowly, the dark forms of two divers took shape. It was Larry from the USA and Philipp, my buddy from Germany. We re-grouped, exchanging OK signals and slowly made our way up the wall and on to a gentle slope. It seemed sensible to abort the dive at this stage, having already consumed a fair amount of air fighting the current, and we had lost the others. I slung my reef hook again and invited Philipp to hang on to the end of its line. Hooked on to the rocks, we lay side by side completing our decompression safety stop. After three minutes we slowly we made our way to the surface. The boat was hove to about 100 metres off and came over to pick us up.

Our guide and the other missing diver were already on board. They had been swept outwards and aborted the dive after only 19 minutes. We had logged 33 minutes, but it was one of the most exciting and challenging dives ever.

Larry who lives in the Philippines and had dived that site many times before shook his head in disbelief. "I have experienced strong currents there before, but never anything like that." Of course, it was just after the full moon and in full ebb, 3 hours between high and low water when the current is at its strongest. Then he giggled, "Anyone fancy another dive there?"

"You bet!" I retorted. "But in another couple of days when the moon has waned a bit and the current is less ferocious."

And we did do it again.

Twice.

Three days later it was almost impossible to believe it was the same place. This time the current was gentle, visibility clear and that wall... well, it had the wow factor right enough. A riot of colour, festooned with corals, sponges, anemones and algae of every colour imaginable, it was teeming with fish, big and small, adding yet more hues to the scene. It was a dream of a dive. The first one had been more of a nightmare!

I had some predictable responses when I emailed that story to my many correspondents around the world, suggesting (yet again!) that I am crazy with no commonsense for diving in such conditions. I know, I know, but och, it is stimulating to test yourself now and then in trying conditions. And if my mother did not get an "Oh, THAT boy!" kind of story every so often she would have withered away. She needed a bit of heart-thumping excitement to keep her alive. She finally expired in Sept 2010 aged 95, but not as a direct result of reading of the adventures of "THAT boy!" I think it kept her alive all these years just waiting for the chance to thump me with a rolled up magazine for all the worry I had caused her.

A large island on the eastern extremities of the Philippines, Leyte dangles down along the edge of the Pacific Ocean. It was here in 1944, under General McArthur, that the Americans set foot on the Philippines in the relentless push across the Pacific towards Japan. Having been ignominiously driven out in 1942 by the mighty Japanese offensive that swept over Malaysia, Singapore, Indonesia and the Philippines, McArthur had promised the Philippine people, "I shall return," as he retreated from his Philippines base. Two years later he did, in the biggest amphibious landing of the war in the Pacific, and the Philippines were eventually freed once more.

Most of the battle for Leyte took place in the northern parts. Southern Leyte then, as now, was wrapped in a more gentle way of life. It is a quiet backwater, seasoned with only a few sprinklings of modern technology, like the ubiquitous tiny karaoke bars that flourish throughout the Philippines where the locals go to enjoy the pleasures of listening to each other murdering popular songs every night. Nowhere is so much agonisingly bad singing enjoyed by so many as in the Philippines where karaoke (more usually called videoke here) ranks alongside texting each other on mobile phones and communicating on Facebook as the main leisure pursuits. No other nation in the world can match the Filipinos for texting messages. It is a national addiction.

A week spent in this quiet rural province made a pleasant change from the hurly-burly of life in the evening rush hour in Dumaguete where I had been based for a coupe of months. People grow rice, harvest coconuts, and go out fishing using the small outrigger canoes typical of these islands. Dug-out hulls, shaped from a single tree trunk, are still being made here although plywood is favoured by many now, being easier and quicker to fashion into a boat. Slim, only wide enough for one small man's hips to fit inside them, they gain stability by having bamboo outriggers lashed on to them using strong nylon fishing line. They are often powered by paddle, but single cylinder petrol engines such as those used on lawnmowers are commonplace now and give them a fair turn of speed.

Telephone lines only snaked their way in here four years ago and many settlements still only have diesel generated electricity rationed to a few hours in the evenings - to keep the karaoke machines running. More remote villages don't even have that. The pace of progress is slow.

The diving is all centred down in the south of Leyte, one of the less accessible parts of the Philippines. Getting there from Dumaguete took me twelve hours using a variety of modes of transport. A motorcycle trike took me to the small ferry port that links Negros with Cebu island. After the 20-minute ferry crossing and a three and a half hour bus ride, I arrived in Cebu city. A taxi took me from the bus terminal to the docks where Philipp, who had flown in from Frankfurt the previous night and was my dive buddy for this trip, was waiting for me. We had met diving at Palau and kept in touch, meeting each year for some diving. A three and a half hour voyage by ferry saw us land on Leyte at Hilongos at 5pm where a minibus was waiting to take us to the dive resort near Padre Burgos, another hour and a half by road.

The best dives from a photographic point of view were the night dive at Padre Burgos Pier and the house reef, just along the shore in front of the resort. The pier dive was the best night dive I have ever experienced. On certain nights of the week it is reserved for divers between 6 and 9pm and it was teeming with life. Living among the piles supporting the pier were at least two different kinds of seahorse, frogfish, various pipefish, ghost pipefish, stonefish, lionfish, sea scorpions, shrimps, brittle stars, crabs, sea slugs; almost buried in the sandy bottom by the side of the pier lay the patient jaws of the snake eels and stargazers, eyes and mouth both upward turning, just waiting for a tasty meal to swim past and be snapped up. It was a delightful 75 minutes of diving by torchlight and never more than about 50 metres from the shore.

Peter's Dive Resort on Leyte provided a very pleasant week's diving with three dives each day. The food was good too with porridge on the menu for breakfast, although I had to add the salt myself. Are the Scots the only ones in the world who add salt to their porridge at the cooking stage? How the rest of the world can eat it without salt beats me. Without salt it is like wallpaper paste, or so I would imagine, as I have never actually tried to eat wallpaper paste.

On our arrival at the resort, a Filipino boy took us to our beach bungalow, opened up, and with a flourish of his arm he indicated the large double bed. "Nice big bed. Good for honeymoon." He smiled knowingly, eyes flashing. I scowled back at him.

"Aye, maybe so," I growled, "but if I wanted a honeymoon I would have an attractive lady with me! While I enjoy my friend's company, a honeymoon with him was not part of the plan. I ordered a room with twin beds."

"Oh, I am so sorry," he apologised. "I thought it was a couple the room was booked for." The fact that we were two males did not matter. They are very tolerant of homosexuality here. Anyway, it was no problem to pull the bed apart for it was actually two single beds clipped together.

As the nice big bed split into two singles, I grunted at Philipp, "Huh. Just my luck to have you as my buddy. Why couldn't you have been an attractive young lady?"

Chapter 36

Do As The Filipinos Do

A 6am departure from Leyte and another long day's travelling took us back to
Dumaguete for the second week of Philipp's holiday. I had suggested that he
might consider staying at Mike's Beach Resort at Dauin, which was to be the
base for our diving operations.

Six dives over two days at Apo Island gave Philipp a glimpse of its
spectacular coral gardens. Home to 450 coral species and 2,500 fish species,
Apo offers a range of diving conditions; gentle meandering dives among lush
coral gardens and exhilarating drift dives, flying along on strong currents, but
nothing so tormented and unpredictable as those we had experienced the week
before at Napantao, Leyte.

After diving at Apo we switched to a different kind of dive, exploring the
shores of Negros around Dauin which again revealed the amazing diversity of
marine life among its patches of coral and sandy banks. I was sure he would
enjoy the change and after his first dive at Dauin Marine Sanctuary Philipp could
only say, " Wow....Wow.... Wow." It delivered a good show for us: seahorses,
ghost pipefish, leaf scorpions, several varieties of frogfish, dragonets, razorfish,
nudibranches, several varieties of shrimp including many of the completely
see-through commensal shrimps that live among the fronds of anemones. One
of the best places I have experienced to dive with a camera, it once again offered
me photo subjects hitherto unknown.

Unfortunately, on our final day's diving, my camera flooded. A tiny piece
of grit had found its way into the channel that the seal fits into. It worked fine at
3 metres, but under the greater pressure at 10 metres it flooded. Result, one
camera ruined. It was insured so I managed to get a replacement, but I felt like
a part of me was missing when diving without a camera, so until the new one
arrived I had to seek something else to absorb my attention. And that is not
difficult in a crazy country like the Philippines.

Some of my regular correspondents had heard on TV news that Mount
Mayon, one of the most active volcanoes in the Philippines, was on the verge of
a major eruption and immediately assumed that I would be there. I had to assure
them that I was not sitting on its slopes with my usual lack of commonsense
(What is happening to me? Am I growing up at last?), waiting for the lava or
pyroclastic flows characteristic of its recent eruptions to come sweeping down
and engulf me. I was at least 500 kilometres to the south. Mind you, I admit to
harbouring a desire to be there. If only there had been a direct flight! It did look
ominous and had been making many rumblings and dozens of earthquakes were
recorded around it daily. The crater was glowing brightly and tens of thousands
of tons of sulphur dioxide had been expelled into the atmosphere.

Ironically, while around thirty thousand people had been evacuated from its environs and were being accommodated in emergency shelters, thousands more were pouring into the area to see the fireworks and an enterprising local landowner arranged a special viewing area to accommodate them. Volcanic Tourism was booming and brought much more income to the area than would be spent by the government on relief for those evacuated, so it was not all gloom and doom.

There's something delightfully improper about that, but that's life in the Philippines for you. Nothing seems 'proper' here. How about teaching your girlfriend to drive a car on an airport runway, while a Cebu Pacific Airlines Boeing 737 with 120 passengers on board is making its final approach? It is true! On one of the islands a young man ignored all the rules about airport runways being only for aircraft to land and take off. Numerous warnings had been issued about encroaching on the runway, but this young man was the airport manager's son and, in a society infamous for corruption and nepotism, he decided that gave him the right to ignore such rules. He had the girl drive out of the jungle (the airport could not afford a perimeter fence!) and on to the runway just as the plane was on its final approach. The pilot immediately aborted the landing and the first indication the couple had that the plane was there was when it roared overhead with the throttles opened fully to give it the necessary lift. How does that rate on the "improper" scale? Anarchy reigns supreme here.

And nowhere is anarchy more evident than on the roads. Knowing that nobody bothers with the rules is a sort of liberating experience and driving a motor bike means you can dodge through dense traffic, drive on the wrong side of the road, ride up on the pavements, scattering pedestrians in a happy-go-lucky, swashbuckling manner. Anything goes. It makes driving fun when you get over the initial fear.

One way street? So what! If it gets you to your destination quicker to go the wrong way down one, so be it. Enjoy the friendly waves and shouts of the other bikers and the ubiquitous motorcycle tricycle cab drivers as they pass you - on both sides. At least I thought it was friendly waves and shouts I was getting (Well, I get accustomed to people recognising me and calling me in a friendly manner when I return to these islands!) until I reached an intersection and had to slow down to cross the path of the oncoming traffic and I then heard clearly the words "ONE WAY STREET!" being shouted at me by a friendly Filipino driver. It never even struck me as odd that the oncoming traffic should be passing me on both sides of the street as I cleaved my way through the middle of them. There is nothing unusual in that here. Mayhem is normal.

You drive on the right side of the road here. Well, sometimes. If it suits you better to drive on the left to let you pass a line of traffic, go ahead and do so. It is all delightfully improper, but that is what the Filipinos do. Don't worry about the long line of heavy traffic coming headlong towards you, a hundred wheels or more threatening to crush you into pulp on the dusty road. The aim of the game is to play it like fairground dodgem cars. Be courageous. Have faith. You just barge in and somehow you find a slot in the mass of wheels, assorted ironmongery and human bodies - up to five at a time perched on a motorbike - jostling for position on the road. Filipino drivers are an appreciative bunch and will heartily applaud your kamikasi courage and skilful roadcraft with long, celebratory toots on their horns. This is much more fun than doing the usual tourist things, like visiting ancient churches, museums and waterfalls.

With Filipinos being of relatively slight build, you can easily cram about 20 or more inside a jeepney, but the Filipinos are adaptable people. The bodywork is cleverly constructed with additional hand and footholds on the exterior and a ladder to allow access to the roof, so they can pile on even more, sitting on the roof and hanging from the sides. How many people can they carry? There is always room for one more. They never refuse a potential customer. Add up the passengers crammed inside and the cling-ons outside and you may find between 30 and 40 on board as the engine growls its smoky way along a dusty pot-holed road threatening to hurl people off with every lurch and bump. And if one or two roll off, well, Filipinos are light-weight, resilient people and bounce well and the bus will wait for them to climb back on to their suicidal position once more, laughing as they wipe the roadside dust from the grazes on arms and legs. Every customer on board means another fare for the driver, so who cares?

Health and safety regulations?

Ha Ha Ha...

Welders weld without using a face mask, grinders grind away smoothing welds without eye protection as the sparks fly up to their faces. They have long eyelashes and that does the job OK so why waste money on buying goggles? Protective footwear? Steel workers handling heavy bars of steel, builders handling concrete blocks, blacksmiths standing at the anvil knocking sparks off hot metal, stripped to the waist, in shorts, all are equipped with the standard industrial footwear here - bare feet in flip flops!

Such casual attitudes are so widespread yet, at the other extremity, bureaucracy in the Philippines stretches the meaning of frustration well beyond its limits. How can it take more than two months to allocate a registration number to a wee motorbike? Yes, more than two months! And that is after all the necessary paperwork has been completed and sent off. But what can you do? Shrug your shoulders and get on with life. Que sera sera.... Who cares? Go ahead and drive your unregistered motorbike around the streets with gay abandon. Like every other traffic rule here it is just one more rule to be ignored. Since riding around on my waiting-to-be registered bike I have noticed many more cars and bikes without registration plates doing the same. Why worry? As with the rules of the road, just do what suits you. Do as the Filipinos do.

Now why a simple motorbike registration application requires two months to process I do not know, except that it must keep a lot of Filipinos working for the government, passing that bit of paper around and letting it sit and mature for two months before deciding what registration number to offer. How difficult and time-consuming can that be? And no doubt when the number is finally designated, an office junior is called to carry it from that desk to the post clerk who records the details and passes the registration document to yet another one who puts it in the envelope, before passing it to yet another who puts on the postage stamp, measured exactly 10 millimetres from the top right hand corner. It has to be done right so the contents of the envelope have to be checked by another supervisor as well as the measurements for the position of the stamp, of course. Then someone else has to carry it to the post bag for dispatch and then someone else finally takes it away for posting..... And all this only takes two months? How's that for fast work? Or is my imagination running riot?

Och well, keeping all these paper pushers busy contributes to the welfare of their families and puts food in their mouths, so that makes me feel better. It's only a number plate to stick on the back of the bike after all, one that nobody bothers about anyway so it seems the whole exercise is utterly pointless. Easier just to buy a bike, stick a label on it saying Reg Applied For and go about your business, for nobody is interested enough to check.

Another example of bureaucratic nonsense arose when I applied for a visa extension. It is simple. Fill in a form, show your passport, provide a photocopy of it, pay a fee and get the passport stamped. Simple? Aye... right.

I had that simple experience once in Boracay, no problem, but a year later when I applied for an extension in Dumaguete I saw a classic example of bureaucratic lack of trust, or spinning out the work needlessly. Here the application form had to be read first by one clerk, the passport and the passport photocopy scrutinised and the money counted. She then passed it to another clerk who, in her own good time, counted the money again and also checked the passport and photocopy. She then signed the form and passed it back to the first clerk who also, in her own good time, (and heaven help you if 12 o'clock comes within that good time for then she will have to stop for her lunch break) picked it up and took it to where the big boss sat at his computer. In his own good time, he checked the form and the passport and the passport copy again and counted the money a third time and scanned the passport through the computer to see if I had been found guilty of anything nasty (like a crime of "moral turpitude", as it says on the immigration form you have to fill in if you ever fly to the USA.)

What on earth is moral turpitude? I had never even seen the word turpitude until I flew into the USA. What would a non-English speaker make of it? Same as me I suppose, just tick the No box and hope that the computer doesn't know too much about you. And who would confess to having been found guilty of a crime of moral turpitude on the flight path down to New York when the form says you will not be allowed into the country if you tick the Yes box? It is then a bit late to find that out! Madness in bureaucracy is not just confined to the Philippines, but let's get back to the Philippines again.

The computer did not find me guilty of any act of moral turpitude, or whatever it was looking for and churned out a letter, two copies, one for me, one for the boss man telling us in black and white that I was not a criminal and was not on any black list, at least as far as the Philippines authorities knew, and that I may be allowed to stay for another two months.

He then put that document with the form and the passport and the copy of the passport and the money back on the pile of papers waiting for the second clerk who, in her own good time, came into his office again and picked it up. She also read that I was morally non-turpitudinal and therefore acceptable as a guest in the Philippines for a while longer and passed it to the first clerk who, in her own good time (and you are now sweating, watching the hands on that clock ticking ever nearer 12 noon!), was enabled (at last!) to stamp your passport and the accompanying documents and put the money in the cash box. She passed me my passport with the visa extension inserted with only seconds to spare before the clock struck 12 and I walked past the next applicant with a smug look on my face as his shoulders sagged and he was told to come back at 2pm.

Of course, only one person could do the job in about two minutes: read form, scan passport, count money, stamp documents. Done. But hey, this keeps three Filipinos in a job. And it keeps the applicant waiting for at least an hour or so, unless the lunch break intervenes and then you have to come back in the afternoon. And after two months you have to go through it all again if you want to stay longer.

That is what living here in this crazy, but likeable, country is like. I am adapting to the way of life (does that mean I am going crazy too?), tolerating things that would make me explode back home, buying food locally, cooking it and living cheaply. I like living cheaply, and I can cook porridge for breakfast every day here and that is cheap. The low cost of living here does make you think. I now shriek in horror when my monthly food bill soars to less than the cost of a room for one night in a good dive resort - without food. It makes me ask myself if I can afford to go on diving.

You do look at things differently when you live here.

You do as the Filipinos do.

Chapter 37

Sometimes

Sometimes things go wrong, even in paradise. In the space of three weeks I had flooded my underwater camera at Dumaguete, taken my mobile phone diving with me (they don't like that very much, so it died too) and broken the fittings that held the strap on my new bi-focal facemask while diving at Siquijor, an island with strong traditions of sorcery and witchcraft. That left me wondering if I had offended someone and been cursed.

I flew back to Manila and on down to Mindoro, to Sabang, Puerto Galera, a mecca for divers. I went diving again, but not for long. After only one dive I was feeling cold and shivering, which is very unusual for me as the sea temperatures here are higher than the hottest air temperatures in summer in Lochcarron. I had also developed a headache during the dive. I had a hot shower, went to bed and slept till 4pm, woke up with a thumping head, high temperature, fever, body aching, feeling weak, all typical flu-like symptoms.

The next night the sweats started and the fever broke, and I slept and slept, day and night. Two days on I was feeling a bit better, but still weak and with no desire to engage in any activity. And that is unusual for me. Five minutes sitting on my backside doing nothing usually puts me under stress.

Being back there did have its pleasurable side though. I have dived there so often and know so many people that it was quite a welcome home I got. Before even getting off the boat, there were porters on the shore shouting, "Mr John! I carry your bag to Captain Gregg's, right?" I lost count of the number of welcomes I got in the two hundred metres from the boat to the dive shop. Even Louie, a gay waiter at one of my favourite restaurants rushed out and gave me a hug. This discomforted me somewhat and I shrugged him off roughly.

"Hey, steady on Louie, we don't go in much for hugging guys where I come from!" I growled at him. There are quite a few ladyboys around here and I didn't want any observant ones to get the idea that I was huggable material. It felt good to be back, but not for long.

I broke a tooth. The remaining stump proved to be difficult to remove, and after 50 minutes of pushing, pulling, wrenching, cutting part of the gum away and grinding bone away to get at the curled up root, the dentist finally heaved a sigh of relief. So did I! I leaned forward to wash out my mouth. Blood poured out of my nose. It was not an ordinary nose-bleed. The blood was coming from the tooth cavity, flowing up through the sinus channel into which the tooth root had been embedded. When the tooth was extracted it had left a hole in the wall of the sinus channel.

So I now had a hole in my sinus opening into the tooth cavity, and that created some interesting problems. When I was drinking a glass of beer and tried to swallow, the pressure forced the beer up into the sinus, from where it flowed into the nose, ran down the nose, over my lips and into the glass again. I was drinking constantly recycled beer. Now for a tight-fisted Scotsman, that is not a bad thing. It means you can make one glass of beer last all night and never get drunk. That was the bright side of things. The downside was that I was beached, no diving till it healed up.

This enforced break from underwater exploration encouraged me to do some exploring on land. I had never investigated the hinterland of Mindoro, a large, mountainous island with few large centres of population. The mountains drop steeply into the sea so there is little in the way of coastal plain settlements in the northern part of the island. Deep river gullies carve their way into the dense jungle-clad mountains. It is not an area traversed by roads. Apart from the coastal "highway", which in places was still a very rough, rocky track with precipitous drops, there were only a few rough, dirt roads entering some of the mountain valleys for a mile or two. I travelled up one of these roads. Soon there were no bridges, so the track became more of a footpath that forded rivers at various points. The only vehicles using it were buffalo carts.

You don't have to travel more than a few miles up into the mountain valleys from the coastal road to find yourself in a different world. The almost impenetrable mountains of Mindoro are home to the Mangyan people. Mangyan is the generic name for eight indigenous groups found on Mindoro island, each with its own tribal name, language, and customs. The total population has been estimated at around 100,000, but no official statistics are available because of the difficulties of counting remote and reclusive tribal groups, many of which have no contact with the outside world.

The Mangyan tribes are mainly subsistence agriculturalists, planting a variety of sweet potato, upland rice, and taro. They also trap small animals and wild pig and the forest provides fruits and coconuts in abundance. Those who live in close contact with lowland Filipinos sell cash crops such as bananas, ginger and wild honey. Their traditional religious view is animistic. Only around 10% have embraced Christianity, despite 400 years of Spanish and American colonisation.

Riding the motorbike up a rough rocky road for couple of miles or so is all it takes to lead you into a valley divided by a broad river. A hanging bridge suspended over the river connects a conventional Filipino village on one side with a Mangyan village on the other. The Mangyan people here have plenty of contact with the outside world, so are not as reclusive as those further up the valleys, and their way of life has been modified. Their village has been provided with rows of new concrete block houses, each measuring 5 metres by 4 metres, painted in bright colours, which stand out in contrast to the vernacular bamboo and thatch huts. These houses bring sanitation to people who previously only knew of the forest for disposing of body waste. They also have a fine elementary school.

Walking through the village you notice that there are few people to be seen, certainly none in close proximity. If they see you coming they drift into their homes until you have passed. Camera shy, they do not like to be photographed, but they are tolerant of photos being taken of the village. To all intents it looked pretty much like any other village. The people you do see at a distance here look pretty much the same as the lowland Filipinos, but in the wilder areas they wear only loincloths, the children nothing at all, and reputedly get very aggressive if they see someone pointing a camera at them. My guide refused to go beyond the more civilized village. When you look at the dense jungle and high mountains, it is not hard to understand how these tribes can live in seclusion without any contact with the outside world. They have all they need to survive, albeit in a manner that we may regard as inconceivable. Food is not a problem; the forest provides. Medical care is confined to bush medicine. Girls are often pregnant shortly after puberty and may have numerous offspring throughout their fertile years. There are no statistics regarding life expectancy, but it is probably pretty low. It is hard to conceive of such a way of life within only a handful of miles from TV, telephones, computers and motor vehicles. I wonder what they do when they have toothache.

Teeth are handy things to have, not just for eating but also to grip the mouthpiece of your diving regulator and that had become a bit of a problem. Being of a rather impatient nature, always wanting things done NOW, I have always been a gnasher of teeth when my frustrations with delayed events builds up. Well, maybe I gnashed those teeth too much for there are not all that many of them left now. I had a lower jaw denture which had cracked after only ten months of use due to my gnashing of teeth. It was repaired just before I left home, but it broke only ten days later. I had a good excuse. It was all Ray's fault - it always is. Mr Ray-From-The-USA, my occasional dive buddy and verbal sparring partner who drives me insane (well, maybe a bit more insane than I was before) gets the blame for everything, including gnashing my teeth. He usually deserves it. Besides, what is a good buddy for if not to shoulder the blame when things go wrong?

With my run of bad luck, was it any wonder that I was gnashing my teeth and broke my denture in the process? I could still wear it, but as one of the anchor points had broken right off, whenever I tried to eat, it jumped about a bit. It had a mind of its own and was all over the place, biting me viciously, necessitating a discreet withdrawal from my mouth, dripping with blood, and into my pocket, which was a bit of a nuisance at every mealtime. It was only of cosmetic value thereafter, allowing me a personable aspect when I smiled. OK, that may be debatable, but I try to maintain a positive outlook and smiling helps. Sometimes.

I was suspicious that another of my few remaining front teeth was teetering on the brink of collapse and sure enough it developed a raging abscess in the roots and had to come out. That left one solitary lower incisor to do all the biting from the bottom and most of the chewing too as it was the only tooth left on the bottom which matched up with a tooth on the top. Food was forever rattling around in my mouth futilely looking for a pair of matching teeth to grind it up. That meant meals took a long time to eat, so much so that I was almost hungry for the next meal by the time I had finished the one I was trying to eat. With all that extra work to do it was only a matter of time before that lonesome tooth fell victim to fatigue from stress and overwork, became wobbly and it had to come out as well. That left me with only my two bottom canine teeth remaining to greet people with a lovely, welcoming, Dracula smile.

It was strange at first when people started to back away from me. I sniffed my armpits, but there was no repulsive odour there. No, it was definitely only when I smiled that people backed off. Mothers chased their children off the streets. Babies began to cry. I only noticed it when sitting on the lavatory. A mirror on the wall allowed me to study myself and it was then that I noticed how hideously vampirish I could really look when smiling. As Mr Ray-From-The-USA would have said had he been there, in that vulgar American fashion of speaking, "That's enough to scare the shit outta me." Which was quite a handy thing actually. I never suffered from constipation. One smile was enough to scare the..... yes, you got it right! Anyway, something had to be done.

Dr Jonna de Chavez-Lopez, my charming Filipina dentist, had the answer. New dentures, top and bottom, and they were made and fitted within twelve days of the initial consultation. Back in the UK, it took several months for me to get my previous single denture made, and it only lasted ten months. It was a delight to do business with her. She is an excellent dentist and has customers coming all the way from Australia and the USA, as well as me from Scotland. An enterprising travel agent in Brisbane saw potential in marketing dental holidays to the Philippines. Flights, hotel, diving and dental treatment with Dr Jonna is cheaper than the price of dental treatment alone in Australia. Not a bad deal!

And when she fitted the new teeth and gave me a mirror to see the result, I had to smile and it did not scare her one little bit, for I was now, in her own words as she smiled back at me, "Guapo!" (Handsome!). And that made me smile some more. Well, OK, she would say that, wouldn't she?

Anyway, armed with my new teeth and guapo smile, as I flew onwards to dive at El Nido, Palawan Island, I reflected on my varying fortunes. Setbacks are temporary inconveniences, and bad luck events reputedly come in threes. Well, on the material side of things, I can confirm that old wives' tale as being apparently true: I flooded my camera, drowned my phone, dropped my bi-focal mask, breaking the fastener that fixes the strap onto the mask. So that's three events there!

Healthwise, I'd had my dose of flu and ruptured sinus, which had prevented me from diving. That was a running total of two, which left one more to come. Trust me, I used to be a teacher of mathematics! I therefore felt uneasy. Sometimes there are diseases that inflict themselves upon the traveller. Usually these are no more than a minor inconvenience; a mild dose of diarrhoea is quite common. With this risk in mind, I always travel with a first aid kit containing some supplies to cope with such an event; paracetamol, immodium, broad spectrum antibiotics and intestinal flora baccilus to replace the good bugs that get flushed out when diarrhoea strikes. Usually it is not too bad...

But this time was different!

I had a very unpleasant dose of food poisoning at El Nido. It drained me of all intestinal matter between 2am and mid-day, much of which time I spent seeing nothing more than the four walls of the lavatory. The dehydration was extreme and I was gulping water by the gallon. The interesting thing was that for several hours it was all passing through the intestine, not the urinary tract, which is probably a good thing as it flushed everything out. It was not until after mid-day that I finally had a pee. That gave me significant pleasure; it was a signal that the body was on the road to recovery and water could be directed through the usual channels again.

It wasn't just the diarrhoea that bothered me, it was the accompanying symptoms, a thumping headache, raging temperature, body aches, and a nausea so powerful I could hardly sit up in bed to drink water. It was a struggle to get to the toilet without fainting. I was crawling to stop the blood draining from my head. But it was that feeling of severe dehydration that was so worrying. After almost four days of starvation (the body just refused food), medication, a diet of water and very little else, I was well on the way to recovery.

El Nido and its diving was one of two attractions that lured me to Palawan. The other was the famous underground river at Sabang, a small village on the west coast with a spectacular beach, just under a two-hour bus ride from Puerto Princesa. This river winds its way through and, for over 8 kilometres, underneath the limestone hills of Palawan and is a world heritage site due to its unique biodiversity. Boats take you from the jetty at the village to the next bay where the river flows out of its cavern and into the sea. Here you transfer into small outrigger canoes equipped with large torches powered by car batteries and paddled by one man who acts as guide for exploration of the cavern. It is quite low and narrow at the beginning, but in the middle it opens out into a massive and extremely impressive chamber, likened to the dome of St Paul's Cathedral in London by one of the early English explorers here. It provided an interesting diversion from diving.

Another interesting feature here was a small restaurant that had "Fresh Woodworm" on the menu! No one was eating there. I wonder why? I had to go in. However, you have to order in advance to be able to taste this local delicacy, a large worm that eats wood and can be found in dead trees in the mangrove swamps. You place your order and someone goes hunting for your worm and brings it to you, still wriggling. Well, at least you know it is fresh. Filipinos will eat anything.

El Nido is a village hugging the shore of Bacuit Bay in northwest Palawan, an area with the most spectacular scenery in the Philippines. Towering limestone cliffs rise vertically from the sea. Islands, which at first glance appear to have no landing places, only sheer vertical walls, suddenly reveal small hidden bays and lagoons completely locked within the fortress-like cliffs. These cliffs have been eroded by rain into some grotesque shapes, some like cathedral spires. It is breathtaking scenery.

Over the last twenty years, as the area became more popular with divers and tourists, the nature of the village changed from a cluster of bamboo and thatch huts along the shore to a bustling village of concrete roads and tourist accommodation, from very cheap to very expensive. Yet it is still relatively primitive. It only has an electricity supply between 5pm and 2am.

Getting there can be a wee bit of a challenge. The choice is between a 30 hour ferry trip from Manila, which is not an attractive proposition given the safety record of Filipino ferries; a flight to El Nido from Manila, which is expensive because only small planes can land at its airstrip; or flying into Puerto Princesa, the island's capital, which unfortunately lies about 240 km to the south - and the road north from there is....well, let's say it is not not much of a road at all and is not the most comfortable of rides.

The choice is between a 7 hour journey by air-conditioned mini-bus packed with 10 people, so it is cramped, or even longer by bus which is probably just as cramped not only with people, but sometimes also with vegetables, pigs, goats, chickens, and the innumerable cardboard boxes that Filipinos always seem to carry with them when travelling. The bus has a sort of air-conditioning. It has no windows, so you do get a blast of air about you, but you are eating and breathing fine road dust for at least 4 hours when it bumps its way over the northern part of the road, which is just a dirt and rock road. Even in the minibus this was a very uncomfortable journey as the drivers seem to want to get the agony over as quickly as possible and drive flat out over the most rough and rocky parts of the road. It was a real boneshaker of a ride. I have never been bounced about so much.

Sometimes this may lead to mishaps. On the way north we had a puncture. The tyre was so worn, without any tread left on it, that it was completely chewed up by the sharp rocky road. On the way south the vehicle leapt around so much that the rope tying down the luggage on the roof rack worked its way loose and one rucksack was tossed overboard. It was only many miles further on that the driver became aware of this when he got a phone call telling him that a bag had been found on the road and they were checking all the drivers to see who had lost one. The bag contained a laptop computer, mobile phone and passport so you can imagine the look on the owner's face when he discovered his bag had jumped overboard several miles back. Travelling by road in the Philippines is always an adventure.

I debated for a time which method to use, bus or minibus. I asked the receptionist at the hotel in Puerto Princesa what time the buses left. She looked vague.

"Maybe 6am…or 7am…. or 8 am?"

"Maybe? Is there not a scheduled time of departure?"

"Well, sort of, but the bus waits till it fills up with enough people to make it worthwhile going, so sometimes the 6 o'clock bus may not go till about 7, if there are enough people on it by then, or sometimes maybe even 8 o'clock. You just have to wait till the driver decides when to go."   And she shrugged her shoulders. This is Palawan. This is the Philippines.

Then she told me it would be better if I let her book the minibus for me as it would pick me up at the door of the hotel in the morning. If I went by bus I would need to hire a motorcycle trike to take me to the bus terminal on the far side of the city to wait for who knows how long. I am not a good waiter. That was enough for me.

"OK. Book me a seat on the minibus. What time will it be here?"

"Maybe 6.30am, or 7 am or…." She shrugged her shoulders again.

"OK. I get the picture, but at least I will be sitting here comfortably waiting for it - and you are sure it will come?"

"Oh yes. It always comes…. sometimes."

Chapter 38

Worldwide Fellowship

I sat up front on the ferryboat at Batangas Pier. The crew appeared to be in no hurry to cast off. It was already 15 minutes behind the scheduled sailing time. They just stood around and waited. I waited. I had no option. It was their boat. And this is the Philippines after all, where nothing ever seems to leave on time. Eventually, one flustered young man appeared on the quayside and hurriedly made his way down the gangplank on to the boat. He sat opposite me and wiped the perspiration from his forehead. The crew hauled the gangplank aboard and cast off.

I looked across at the young man. Something familiar about that face, I thought. He looked at me. Was that a flicker of recognition? We looked at each other on and off for a few minutes and all the time I was becoming more certain that I had met him before, but when and where, and what was his name? He looked at me again and then his finger came up, his face brightened with recognition and he exclaimed triumphantly, "It's John!" The world is indeed a village. It was Conor McEntee, a young Irishman from Belfast, with whom I had dived in 2007 at Gili Trawangan in Indonesia.

"What brings you here?" I asked.

"You actually," he replied. "It was your stories of diving in the Philippines that inspired me to come back out to this part of the world. I am following the advice you gave me back then in Indonesia. I was diving at Coron last week, it will be Puerto Galera this week and Panglao the week after that, all places you recommended. Your advice was spot on. I love the Philippines. I am sorry I only booked for three weeks. I should have made it three months."

He was the second person I had dived with at Gili Trawangan to appear at Sabang. On my previous visit, it was an English girl who had also acted on my advice. So often, even in the most remote locations, I hear my name being called out. It comes from being a member of that informal worldwide fellowship of scuba divers.

I was heading this way to dive at Anilao with my Filipino friend, Rolly Baron, whom I had met the previous year on Oceanic Explorer, while diving the Coron wrecks. He was making a series of TV dive programmes at that time and filmed me diving, interviewed me, and used some of my photos on his TV shows. Rolly was keen to encourage people into diving and my enthusiasm and knowledge of many of the world's best dive spots he found inspirational, but was amazed that I had only started ten days before my sixty-first birthday.

"But most people here in the Philippines are dead at that age!" he exclaimed.

We had promised each other we would meet and dive together again so this was a planned re-union. He had phoned me to say that he was filming a conference of the Professional Scuba Divers Association at Sabang and asked if

I would join him there and we could cross to Anilao after it was over. That was OK by me as it is one of my favourite dive spots in the Philippines. No matter how often I dive at Sabang, I keep finding things I have never seen before.

Puerto Galera, the port of galleons, named when the Philippines was a Spanish colony, is the name of a small town and lovely peninsula at the north end of Mindoro, a large, mountainous island about three hours travelling time from Manila. It has a sizeable population of foreigners who have settled there, mostly Europeans, Americans, and Australians, many with Filipina wives or partners. Its main attraction is diving and the centre of the action is the tiny village of Sabang tucked into a cosy bay on its north coast.

Sabang reminds me of Mediterranean villages clinging to the slopes and shores of small bays, the buildings crowding right down to the waterfront with little space between them. The village is very compact and you can walk from one end to the other in ten minutes. There is only one street into the village and the rest is a maze of narrow alleyways where you often have to stand sideways to let someone else pass. It is a shambolic place that has never been blessed with the touch of the town planner. But this is the Philippines where planning seems to be an alien concept: they do things on impulse here.

Despite the frequent power cuts and poor drainage, I like the place. It has a certain character to it, but it is not to everyone's liking. If you like everything pretty, all nice and clean and tidy, this is not the place for you. However, the diving is very good. It has some good restaurants and bars and some nightlife. You can dance at the disco till around 3am. It is swarming with Koreans, Russians, Americans, Australians and Europeans: Germans, Swedes, Norwegians, Dutch, Swiss, Austrians, French, Italians and a few British. It offers some excellent dive sites and diving and accommodation can be found at affordable rates. Overall it offers excellent value for money. More than anywhere else, this is where I have formed and sustained so many lasting friendships.

My three regular American buddies, Mike Colibert, Tony Kirksey from Oklahoma and the irrepressible Mr Ray-From-The-USA Casavant from Connecticut, were first encountered there as they boarded MV Stella Maris on her way to Tubbataha Reef along with Mark Hawkins and Jason Shaw, both of whom I have met again, Mark in the Solomons and Jason at Palau. All great guys, we have since shared dive experiences in Borneo, Solomon Islands and Thailand as well as back at Sabang. Philipp Baumgartner, from Germany, another regular dive buddy who has been infected by the Sabang bug, I first met at Palau when he heard the Scottish accent. We buddied up then and have met regularly for dives at Sabang, South Leyte and Dumaguete in the Philippines, Lembeh Straits and Ambon in Indonesia and Sipadan in Borneo. It is great to have such fine friends to go diving with in various places. Each year they ask me for my itinerary and then select places they would like and join me. But that is not enough for the indefatigable Mr Ray-From-The-USA. Ever intent on haunting me and disrupting my peaceful existence, he came to Scotland to torment me and on his first day became involved in a Mayday call-out in a force 9 gale when we had to abandon lunch and went out in my boat to search for a dive boat on the rocks and two missing divers. We did locate them and all were recovered safely, but I told him. "See, wherever you go you create havoc!" I even introduced him to several of my friends - and amazingly they are still my friends! - and he enjoyed some interesting glimpses of life in the Highlands of Scotland.

"You mean you don't lock your door when you go out?" he asked in amazement.

"Why would I want to do that? People won't be able to put things in the house for me then."

"Oh Gee, that's a good one!" He mocked.

But his tune changed when we returned from a few days away sailing and there on the table was a bottle of The Glenlivet, a highly acclaimed Single Malt Scotch Whisky. It was a Thank You gift from the divers who had been in distress. His eyes opened wide in astonishment: "How did that get there?"

"I told you. That's why I don't lock the door. They would not have been able to put it there for me if I had locked up."

"Oh, the folks back home will never believe this!" he roared. (He does not know how to talk quietly) "We lock our homes to stop people taking things out of them. Here you leave the doors unlocked so people can put things in. Oh, I gotta tell them all about this!"

One of the significant encounters for me at Sabang was to be paired up for an afternoon dive with Paul Allen, an Englishman, a serious underwater photographer who now lives for much of the year in the Philippines. Underwater photography, like all wildlife photography, demands a lot of patience, often staying in the environment of a particular subject until the fish will accept the photographer's presence. Then they are more likely to relax and offer themselves to the lens for good clear images. The problem in a normal dive is that the other divers don't want to hang about. They want to get on and cover ground. To them, a photographer is just a nuisance. As a serious photographer who has dived extensively throughout the world, Paul generally doesn't like having other people around hounding him on or disturbing the fish and he was not too keen on the idea of having to buddy with me and hoped that I wouldn't crowd him or run out of air forcing him to come up early. I feel the same way. Other divers can be a nuisance.

So I prowled around taking pictures and left him to do his. We simply maintained visual contact, occasionally inviting each other to have a look at some interesting subject and it worked out well for both of us. I was pleased when he requested that we surface before I did, and my underwater behaviour as a photographer seemed to satisfy him. We had developed a respect for each other and at the end of the dive we got together to talk and look at images. He even invited me to join him a few days later for a shore dive, a rare compliment, just the two of us walking in from the dive shop, and we spent a glorious 90 minutes underwater in Sabang Bay and were never more than about 200 metres from the dive shop.

He then invited me to his apartment to dine with him and look at more of his work. His girlfriend, Rey-an, cooked a delicious dinner while we talked and watched slide shows of his work from different parts of the world. His photography exemplified the standards of achievement I must aspire to.

Studying his work and listening to him talk, I learned more about underwater photography from him than from any other source.

I enjoy the company of men of action and Paul is not only an experienced cave diver, wreck diver and underwater photographer, he is also a serious rock climber. As we talked, our respect for each other grew and a lasting bond developed. My lifestyle of travelling the world and sailing he found inspirational and he Rey-an joined me for some sailing on the west coast of Scotland the following summer. Paul and Rey-an now live near Dumaguete where he is now exploring the Negros coastline and discovering many interesting specimens.

The words 'Daddy Bob' will achieve instant recognition from just about everybody who lives in Sabang, and a good many other places in the world where you may meet divers. Bob Kieran, veteran diver and old man of the sea from California, was a bit of an institution in Sabang, for many years instructing and guiding at Captain Gregg's, one of the earliest dive shops to set up business there. Bob married a Filipina a few years back. A veteran of a four divorces, (well, he is from California! - and is maybe a slow learner too!) he knows his way up the aisle blindfold by now, but told me that if this had been the first wife there would have been no others. A likeable and generous man, he seems to have found happiness with his adorable wife, Hannah. Now in his 70s and resident at Dumaguete, Negros, Bob is still working with Adventure Dive based at Mike's Beach Resort at Dauin, just a few miles along the coast from Dumaguete.

On my first dive at Sabang with Bob as guide, he paired me up as a buddy with a Canadian respiratory therapist from Calgary, David Schaffland, who then worked in a hospital in Saudi Arabia and took time off for diving three or four times per year. This was a fortuitous meeting. David and I quickly developed an understanding underwater as a buddy team and also forged a strong bond of friendship on land. It is not a bad idea to be good friends with people upon whom your life may depend! For several years now we have dived together and developed such an uncanny understanding that we can almost read each other's minds. Either of us may suddenly articulate a thought that the other has in mind and was just about to speak about. This understanding and my complete trust in his competence should anything go wrong creates a great feeling of comfort when diving. I know if I get engrossed in taking photos, David will be keeping his eye on me, and vice versa.

After supporting me as a buddy for a few years, always keeping a watch on me while I was taking photos and the rest of the group disappeared and guiding me back to the group, he eventually got hooked on the photography aspect too. Having been an accomplished landscape photographer for many years, he is now an underwater photography enthusiast. We often just ignore the rest of the group now and do our own thing. The divemasters know our competence, experience and knowledge of the area, so it suits us fine and allows them to concentrate on guiding the others who are usually much less experienced and may not know the dive sites.

Despite the age gap of a generation - I am older than his parents and he is younger than my younger son - the age difference is irrelevant, and although it may look like a father /son relationship, it is not. At times it seems the roles are reversed and he treats me like his kid brother, often showing the pained look of the elder sibling longing for the day when I will at last grow up - but that won't be for a while yet! We know each other's minds and have no problem speaking openly and honestly to each other as we both engage in what I call Schaffland-style diplomacy. Some observers might call our exchanges frankly brutal, yet they are without the tension that often appears in family relationships.

When out dining and we engage in the usual bit of banter with the waitresses, he likes to seek advantage by putting me in my chronological place, telling them that I am his Dad, a cheap, foul stroke to try to gain an edge in competition for their attentions. It could be argued that he is handsome, despite the considerably extended forehead - his hairline only starts in line with his ears – and his sharp wit and undoubted charm always raises a laugh among the girls. As the waitresses chatted away to each other in Tagalog he chipped in, "Be careful what you are saying now! We both know quite a bit of Tagalog, and I know when you say kalbo, (the Tagalog for bald) you are talking about me." The girls giggled.

And I chipped in, "And I know when you say, guapo, (handsome) you are talking about me!" His eyes rolled heavenwards.

"I apologise for my Dad, modesty has never been one of his endearing characteristics."

New friendships form almost every year and old friends are revisited. That's what I like about Sabang, and the international fellowship of scuba divers. When you go diving you accept that there is always the small risk of something going wrong underwater. That is when you depend on your dive buddy, someone who is paired up with you to help you out in a crisis. Diving is therefore an activity that encourages the establishment of an ethos of support. Divers interests vary and some like to cruise around taking in the big picture, while others like to take things slowly and search for interesting specimens. Having a good buddy whose dive style is similar to your own, and whose competence matches, or is superior your own is therefore an advantage. The relationship established underwater can be a good basis for strong friendships on land too as you know that your life may depend on the support of your buddy. It is therefore a powerful bonding activity. I cherish the bonds I have formed with these friends, and many others with whom I have dived, sometimes in fairly hazardous conditions when it offers a sense of comfort to share a difficult situation with someone you know and trust.

Ask any world traveller to name their favourite place and the answers all have one common denominator. It is not so much the physical nature of the country that brings it to the top of most people's list, but the nature of the interactions with the people they have encountered. Throughout my travels around the Pacific Ring of Fire I have been blessed with hospitality. Name a place and immediately I see in my mind the people I met there, people with smiling faces, welcoming me into their society. I see those faces against a backcloth of location, which may be one of beauty, or grim, grinding poverty. Yet they always smile. However remarkable the scenery, and there are many beautiful locations worth seeing mentioned in this book, it is the human element, the nature of the interactions with indigenous people and other travellers, that makes each place distinctively memorable.

The people who inhabit those countries around the Ring of Fire live with the constant uncertainty that they occupy a land that may suddenly and dramatically change its nature within moments due to an earthquake, which could bring death on a large scale. They may fall victim to a resurgence of volcanic activity from a mountain that has lain dormant and benign for hundreds of years. They may be swept to their deaths by landslides or floods. Or they may look in horror as the sea that has been their livelihood, the provider of food for generations, suddenly turns malevolent as a dreaded tsunami thunders down on flimsy coastal villages and pushes far inland, sweeping all before it; cars, buses, houses, and the people in them. They are no strangers to catastrophe. Many know grief and horror on a scale most of us can never conceive.

Yet they smile and say to you, "Welcome to Jakarta," as they stand in soaked clothing watching the floods sweep their ramshackle homes away, or welcome you to their tsunami-smashed fishing villages, or earthquake-shaken homes. These are the simple acts that touch the heart and imprint images indelibly in the mind.

Although I have experienced many earth shaking moments in this part of the world, most had only mild effects, yet as I mentioned in my introduction, when you see the refrigerator behaving in an incongruous manner, dancing across the floor, it does have a rather disturbing effect, especially at around 2.30am when your mind is fuddled by sleep. We become disoriented by events peculiar to what we perceive as normal. To the people who live with these events daily, this is normality. Catastrophic events are soon shrugged off and life goes on. While writing the final chapters of this book on the island of Mindoro in the Philippines, there have been several earthquakes. My apartment has trembled, and sometimes I have too wondering how big this one is going to be, but they have all been mild here. However, a bit further south on Negros, near Dumaguete, many people lost their lives when an earthquake measuring 6.9 on the Richter scale struck. Only six weeks prior to that in the same area, more lives were lost in dramatic floods and landslides when more than a month's rainfall fell in two hours. I had been diving there a week before the floods and also again a week after the earthquake. I seem to have been lucky in my timing of these visits.

So many people I have met have remarked enviously, "You are so lucky to have such an interesting lifestyle."

But their sentiment begs the question: is lifestyle a matter of luck?

To that I give a resounding, "No!"

It is a matter of *choice*.

I did not feel lucky when my wife suffered an horrific illness and died of cancer at the age of forty-nine. I did not feel lucky to have to manage alone, when suffering ill health, the pressures of maintaining a house and garden, a demanding job and involvement in community activities. However, my reaction to that unenviable situation was to get up and go, see the world, carve out a new existence... *live*.

"Are you not afraid, going to all these strange places?" they ask.

Well, I cannot deny that there has been the odd twinge of fear, but that has been countered by my thirst for knowledge, adventure and exploration, not only of alien environments, but also of different cultures.

Shortly before she died my wife counselled me: "Make the most of every day. There is nothing to fear, except fear itself."

Those words ring in my ears each time I feel that stomach-knotting sensation of fear. Even after eighteen years since her death, she is still there - guiding me, nagging me to get things done. And her advice has been good. I feel privileged to have had fun, interest, excitement, adventure and made some wonderful friends of many nationalities in those countries around the Ring Of Fire, both among the indigenous people I have met and that informal worldwide fellowship of divers.

In an ageist society it is a privilege to be able, during my late sixties and into my seventies, to enjoy a lifestyle more often assumed to be the prerogative of younger people. In most physical activities, performance declines with age. However, diving is not quite like that. Once in the water, there is no stress on the joints. Having neutralised your buoyancy, you are weightless. You can then raise your entire body weight, plus the weights of your air tank and the lead weights you have to add to get you down there, by merely breathing in - no muscular effort required. By going slowly you can stay underwater longer. Your technique and superior performance often earns the respect and admiration of those of a younger generation who may rush about expending energy wastefully. That is good for morale.

It also seems to be a good antidote to the ageing process. As my doctor said at a recent health check, "Whatever you are doing, keep on doing it!"

And that... is precisely what I intend to do!

The End

Boarding House Reach

Five strangers come to spend the weekend in a guest house on the Norfolk coast. The Reach offers sanctuary for guests Hacker, Phoebe, Audrey, Philip and the landlady, Stella – all of them drawn together by the secrets of their past.

As the strands of their individual stories are woven together, each guest will confront the painful truths of their personal lives and, as the hours tick away, confess their sins. In a story which encompasses blackmail, rejection, infidelity, redemption and love, the characters of *Boarding House Reach* know they can run, but will they ever escape the stark reality of their tangled lives?

Published by Matador May 2014
ISBN 9781783063390 (pb)
ISBN 9781783065646 (eBook)

Mazzeri

Love and Death in Light and Shadow
A novel of Corsica

It is the last summer of the twentieth century in Calvi, Northern Corsica, and an old man sits watching the kites fly. The festival of the wind is a lively and colourful celebration, but the old man's heart is heavy, he has heard the Mazzeri whisper his name. He accepts that people prefer to believe the dream hunters belong to the past and yet he knows only too well that at night they still roam the maquis in search of the faces of those whose time has come.

Ten years later in the high citadel of Bonifacio, in the southern tip of the island, Richard Ross, armed with only the faded photograph of a Legionnaire standing beneath a stone gateway, finds the locals curiously unwilling to help him uncover his family's roots. He rents a villa on the coast and meets the singularly beautiful Manou Pietri, who enchants him with tales of the megalithic isle, its folklore and the Mazzeri – the dream hunters.

For a while Ric's life beneath the Corsican sun is as close to perfect as he could wish. Then a chance encounter with a feral boy turns Ric's life upside down, and he is drawn deep into a tangled web of lies and deceit. On an island where truth and legend meet, where murder is commonplace and most crimes go unsolved, only the Mazzeri know who will live...

Published by Matador June 2013
ISBN 9781780885384 (pb)
ISBN 9781780885814 (eBook)